*Excel*erate

The New Economy is the registered trademark of Nuala Beck & Associates Inc.

First edition

Canadian Cataloguing in Publication Data

Beck, Nuala, 1951-
Excelerate : growing in the new economy

ISBN 0-00-255425-9

1. Canada – Economic conditions – 1991-   *.   I. Title.

HC115.B43 1995   330.971'0647   C94-932373-X

95 96 97 98 99 ❖ HC 10 9 8 7 6 5 4 3 2 1

Printed and bound in the United States

Exce/erate

GROWING IN
THE NEW
ECONOMY

Nuala Beck

HarperCollins*PublishersLtd*

To the millions of Canadians who, like myself, care passionately about the future of our country, and to one very special Canadian, my dearest husband, Frank.

CONTENTS

TABLES AND CHARTS

ACKNOWLEDGMENTS

So many people and experiences touch our lives in so many different ways, changing and enriching us in the process. Although I was born in Canada, I had the opportunity to grow up in many different countries abroad. It was a wonderful experience, and I will always be so grateful to my mom and dad for the chance to learn and live among different cultures, languages and beliefs. As I got a little older, I came to understand my parents' great love for Canada and to appreciate this nation's diversity. Since my first book, *Shifting Gears*, was published just over two years ago, I have had the great good fortune to travel more extensively in my own country, meeting Canadians from all walks of life and listening to their stories, questions, concerns and opinions. Mom and Dad, you were so right—there are many wonderful and exciting places in this world, but there is no place like *home*.

Now that *Excelerate* is finished, I am looking forward to more free time at home on evenings and weekends. The best decision I ever made in my life was to marry Frank, and the second best decision was to become an economist. Frank and I are going to take some time out to enjoy long dinners together and go to the movies on Saturday nights. And I'm going to get Liam to clean up his closet when he's not writing some of the most interesting papers on political economy that I have had the pleasure to read. I'm looking forward to pleasant phone calls with my parents and Frank's parents, and my very dearest Aunt Frances. It's been so long since they have heard from me regularly, they probably think I have expired. I thank them for their patience. I have been blessed with a family to love and be loved by.

Liam, Chris, Ellen, Carrie, Tim, Lisa and Jamie have a very special place in my heart, and *Excelerate* begins where *Shifting Gears* left off—with a chapter dedicated especially to their hopes and dreams.

My deepest appreciation goes to my partner, Anne-Marie Richter, who runs the firm, the research and me. In the ten years that we have worked together as different sides of the same coin, it has never ceased to amaze me how well we collaborate. In her exceedingly organized manner, she cast her trained eye on every number and percentage change and trend in this book. But our relationship extends far beyond business efficiencies. She is one of the nicest, most decent and caring people I have known in my lifetime, and I love her dearly.

Derrick Reisky and Joseph Connolly are two extraordinarily talented, hardworking and perceptive economists. They're my "A" team, and they're also my dear friends. Life is good when you enjoy the people you work with, and I'm grateful every day for Derrick and Joseph's competence, dedication and good cheer.

Teamwork is a hallmark of the New Economy, and Tim Kuepfer and Steve Carpenter epitomize some of its finest qualities. They give new meaning to the adjectives *smart* and *nice*, which make an unbeatable combination in any economy, old or new. Tim constantly impresses me with his computer savvy, his professionalism and his ability to handle extraordinary volumes of data and analysis with ease. What's more, he is as accomplished on the guitar as he is in economics.

Melanie Patterson is always smiling and she always stays until the job is done. She's a pleasure to work with. How she keeps track of where I am, what I'm doing and what needs attention next is one of life's great mysteries.

My final thanks go to HarperCollins; Tom Best, Deborah Bjorgan, Susan Broadhurst, Judy Brunsek, Jill Lambert, Jane Rowland and Iris Tupholme make the business of book writing a pleasure. But without Rebecca Vogan's special talents, my manuscript could not have become the book you are about to read.

Nuala Beck
Toronto, Canada
April 1995

*Excel*erate

begins to break down. And as some CEOs begin to lose their jobs, many more upgrade their skills. You can see the fear in their eyes, too, "Can I *survive* these changes?"

Old, slow and costly structures are being replaced with new ways of doing business. New machines, new processes and new ideas are replacing old technology, old methods and old concepts, but the key difference is that these innovations allow more to be produced from less: less time, less effort, less waste, less cost, lower prices. And these changes are creating bigger markets than anyone had ever dreamed possible. The prize is *wealth creation*—a bigger pie can offer everyone a larger slice.

Industries that were once the great employers and creators of wealth in our country are no longer at center stage. Some are a mere shadow of their former selves, and many others don't even live here anymore. In a normal process called economic evolution, new industries have replaced these old engines. More people today are employed in the software business than in mining companies.

As "new" replaces "old," a thousand questions ring in our ears: *What is produced? By whom? Where? For how much? Using which technologies? Whose work force? In what alliances? Where should we invest? On whose advice? Using which instruments? In which markets? In which currencies? Under whose leadership? Based on which ideology? In a trade bloc? For how long? With whose help? Subject to which regulations? According to whose rules? Answerable to whom?*

As we craft a new conventional wisdom and write a "new" rule book for the New Economy, nothing is etched in stone.

Some political parties have already been swept savagely aside. God help the next elected representative at any level of government in this country who fails in creating a vision of where we're heading and precisely how we're going to get there. Ideologies mean very little when honesty, decency, integrity and vision matter more. We're paying for leadership, and in the New Economy the consumer gets what he or she pays for. It's the law of the land.

INTRODUCTION

The old established and predictable world order of "us" versus "them" is gone. After the Berlin Wall came tumbling down in 1989, we peered across the chasm and saw faces that bore a striking resemblance to our own. The people on the other side of the wall felt the same fears, cherished the same hopes and dreams as we do. Suddenly, our different pasts began melding into a common future.

The same process has been happening, slowly but surely, across every economic, social, cultural, financial, political and institutional landscape. A bold new era is sweeping away old and established orders. The deep divides of "us" versus "them," with all the attendant neat and tidy boxes and envelopes that were so useful for so long, are being opened, some faster than others, and we're re-examining what we do—and what others do. And it's dawning on a lot of people that we can do more if we work together as a team. We look across the barriers that divided us, and we see our fears, our hopes and our dreams in "their" eyes, too.

In environments as rigidly structured as our workplaces, old economy "bosses" are being replaced by New Economy work teams. Nobody needs a "middle" manager when the hierarchy

The great restructuring of the 1990s is under way. But there's nothing really new about this upheaval because the economy has always changed. The Industrial Revolution, the Great Depression—now we call it something else.

But people who suggest that change is easy either have no idea what they're talking about or are lying through their teeth. The only folks who welcome a change are wet babies—for the rest of us, it's a darn uncomfortable feeling. It's human nature to fear the unknown, especially if we're asked to fly blind. We need road maps for that very reason—so we can *see* where we're going.

I have always loved research. It makes my pulse race. Like travel, it provides an unparalleled thrill of discovery and adventure because you never know what might be around the next corner. Research is exciting, but *applying* what we have learned and sharing the information makes the process most satisfying and worthwhile for me. What our research on the New Economy shows so clearly is that the future is now more predictable than many people realize. If we can avoid making a few utterly stupid mistakes along the way, the prize for Canada will be a world of prosperity for ourselves and for our children, the likes of which few people in Canada have even dared to imagine.

As a nation, we have been *shifting gears*, but it is time now to put our foot on the gas and get moving into the new world that's unfolding, not only in Canada, but everywhere. In this book, I have attempted to provide a series of road maps that can be used for planning our journey into the New Economy. It is my sincere hope that they will be helpful to as many of my fellow Canadians as possible. When people have access to facts, hard numbers and some new ideas, it's amazing what the results can be. All of a sudden, we can make up our own minds about which path we feel is right for each of us, and then *excelerate.*

My colleagues and I are steps away from completing identical research on New Economy road maps and on jobs with a future for the United States, and I hope to publish a U.S. edition of *Excelerate* to accompany the recently published U.S. edition of *Shifting Gears*. Americans are just as bewildered by the changes as Canadians are. And besides, I think it would be the right, neighborly thing to do. As we look across the border that divides us, we see our fears and our hopes and dreams in their eyes, too.

1

WHAT DO WE TELL THE KIDS?

One day last January, I was invited to talk to students at a down-town high school, one of those cavernous old buildings constructed in the heyday of the old economy, when it seemed as though prosperity and stability would march together into the future, inseparable and indestructible. We've all seen them—imposing buildings full of corbels and columns, their façades mimicking the Ivy League colleges, which in turn mimic Oxford and Cambridge, those centuries-old repositories of august scholarship.

I love the idea of going to schools. They're so much at the intersection of the old and new economies—old buildings and old ways of doing things intersecting with the raw intellectual material of the New Economy, the kids themselves.

I remember that day for several reasons. It was an appallingly cold day, one of those days that freeze the breath and hurt the lungs, and it seemed as though spring would never come. As I followed my guide into the echoing hall, my heels clattering on the stone floor, I was looking forward to my visit because it would be a chance to see how schools were dealing with the challenges of change. I was looking forward to talking with the students and getting a feel for what moves them.

As I plowed gamely down the hall, past the chattering crowds of teenagers in their uniforms of patched jeans and Gap sweatshirts, I felt increasingly out of place. How strange I must look through their eyes. . . . I suddenly remembered my own teenage years and how I saw some of my mother's friends, nice ladies, elderly ladies in their early forties, wearing skirts eighteen inches longer than ours, beehives perched on top of their heads. They wore girdles to lunch. "What planet are they from?" I used to wonder. Of course, those "nice elderly ladies" were the same age I am now. I could feel my confidence fading.

How could I possibly speak to these young adults in a way they would understand? What I had to say was relevant to them, important to them—essential to them. How could I make them see that this New Economy was filled with promise and opportunity for them? But the moment I was introduced to Carl, I knew I had to try.

Carl is the kind of seventeen-year-old you hope to God your fourteen-year-old never grows up to be. Carl had a pleasant, round face with a fashionable blond crew cut, but what I really noticed about him was the emptiness in his eyes. Cold eyes, cynical eyes, wary eyes. I found myself staring into Generation X eyes.

A chill ran through me as I thought to myself, we've lost him.

But is it any wonder that young people look at us the way they do? Teachers tell them every day, over and over, the same stories they hear from their parents and their parents' friends. They hear about the huge national debt, about the grotesque deficits they played no part in creating. Every day they're warned, Work till you drop, kid. Pay off the burden we've laid on you, the debt created by our generation—it's your debt now.

But whose debt is it, really? Kids *know* that at least our generation got to spend the money we borrowed. And we spent it on ourselves, on programs we created especially for us, on luxuries like the Registered Home Ownership Savings Program of the 1970s, on the liberal student loans we allowed ourselves, the kind of forgivable loans these kids will never see in their wildest dreams. All

through the '60s and '70s we spent, getting ourselves established
and our careers going. We set ourselves up, with help from our
steadily employed parents and our government's wildly expansion-
ary fiscal policy, so we could get into a labor market in which we
had the luxury of choosing from dozens of jobs. And if by chance
there weren't enough jobs to go around? Why, the government just
cranked the economy into higher gear. Ah, you could just hear
them thinking, a little more inflation won't hurt us!

And then, just when our parents started getting on in years, what
did our generation provide for them? Double-digit interest rates,
enabling them to accumulate more capital than they had ever
expected. We wouldn't have to worry about them in their old age—
they were fine, could even leave us something when they went.

We were all right, Jack.

Then we turned to the kids and said, You'd better work hard and
get yourself a great education, the best you can afford. But understand that even then you might never get a decent job, might never
pay off the debt we racked up. You'll have to pay for our pensions
somehow. And what about your old age? You'll have to look out
for yourself!

Is it any wonder that young people are cynical and that they
look at us the way they do? That chilling emptiness in Carl's eyes
motivated me to give the speech of my life that afternoon. I put
aside my notes and I spoke to those kids from my heart. About
their future in this New Economy. And I told the kids the truth.

Let's Tell the Kids the Truth

Their parents aren't telling them about the future because their parents are too scared. They know things have been changing, and
that the changes are substantial, possibly even cataclysmic. But
they don't really have a grip on what these changes mean.

All their parents see is trouble. They see the economy that

treated them so well for so many years crumbling around them. They see only disintegration, debt and chaos. They're deathly afraid, and the panic is only too apparent. Every teenager has seen the fear in a parent's eyes—Will I be next?

At school, kids talk to guidance counselors, but they get no help there. The counselors, by and large, direct them into the very industries their parents have told them are in trouble, the industries from which their parents and their parents' friends have been laid off. Is it any wonder that young people are cynical and that they ask, What is *our* future?

When I talk to parents and educators, they all ask me the same question in many different ways: What do we tell the kids? I've visited dozens of schools now. Although the locations change and the buildings change and the teachers change and the mood changes, in one way everything remains the same. In the well-intentioned eyes of the educators, you can see a look of desperation: We have no idea what's going on out there. How can we tell kids about the things we can't put a finger on ourselves?

What the kids don't see is that our generation has been blinded by our own worry. Their parents haven't seen the new industries taking shape among the old. Or, if they have seen them, they don't understand them well enough to be able to say, It's all right, it's all there. Don't worry, everything is changing, but change is normal. We're in transition from an old economy into a New Economy. That's the simple truth.

Transitions are hard, and this one was brutally hard on everyone. A lot of decent and hardworking people lost their jobs, and it wasn't their fault. They got caught in a transition that was much bigger than they were. The only crime they committed was showing up in the wrong industry at the wrong point in history. The truth is that good people have had their lives turned inside out by changes that they didn't cause and that they didn't see coming.

But things have always changed, and economies have always evolved. Let's not kid ourselves—we haven't invented change in the 1990s. Industries always grow, industries always decline, and only the smart ones and the lucky ones get on with the business of growth. Kids need to know that we're living through a process of change that is perfectly natural and evolutionary in nature. Things will continue to change well past our lifetime and theirs. Young people need to be told what the changes mean for them, that the world is not spinning out of control. There will be a world in the future with a secure place in it for them. We need to reassure them because it is a common perception that the change is accelerating—and I'm not at all convinced, from my firm's research, that that perception is in any way true.

We're in a transition. That's all. That's the truth of it. *And the hard truth is that it's not over yet.*

I remember so clearly a telephone call I received at my office one day from a young woman. She had a pleasant telephone manner, but beneath her polite and friendly voice was the tremor of desperation. I recognize that tremor now the minute I hear it because I have heard it so often, too often, in the voices of young people or in the voices of their parents. It's the sound of despair.

Susan told me that she had graduated from university eight months earlier and had sent out several hundred résumés. She hadn't received so much as one reply. I asked her about the industries that she had targeted in her job search, and my heart sank. She had graduated near the top of her class with a business degree in marketing. But no company seemed interested. Could I help her find her way, she asked timidly. We talked for a while about the things that interested her, about her hobbies and her hopes and dreams. I suggested that she might find a good future in the pharmaceutical industry; it was an area that appealed to her, and I told her that there were many companies, large and small, in Mississauga where she lived. I told her about the research my firm had done on the industry, how it was growing 2.3 times faster than our economy as a whole, and that, despite all the pressure from generic drugs and the imminent expiry of some prized patents, this was an industry with a future. In fact, with all the new drugs coming on to the market and all the competition in the industry, pharmaceutical companies needed to get their message to consumers. Marketing was vital to their success. I suggested that she should get right on it and not waste time seeking to build a future in the industries that were fast fading off the economic landscape—the ones to which she had applied.

Two months went by before I heard from Susan again. Her call came on a Monday at lunchtime, and from the tone of her voice I instantly knew that she had some good news to share. She was calling to let me know that she had started her first job that morning with a pharmaceutical company, one of the giants in the industry. Her pride and restored self-esteem were audible in her voice as she told me about her responsibilities as a junior assistant to one of the managers in the marketing department. I wished her all the very best, and told her that, if she worked hard and showed initiative, her life could unfold in the ways and directions of her choosing. I just wish all stories had such a happy ending.

Snakes and Ladders

This transition from old to new is like a perilous game of snakes and ladders—except that it isn't a game in these turbulent times. The economy is going through a paradigm shift, and the ladder we were all comfortable on, the old economy of mass manufacturing, has vanished before our eyes.

Before these changes, the economy was on a clear track. The rules of the game were understood. Everybody "knew" that a young man's future lay in the auto industry or in aluminum siding—industries in which the processes were well defined and customer needs were well understood. Everyone had a role in the process, a place in the world. Young people understood that, if they received the right training, they'd get a good job, almost without trying. Any company would jump at the chance to employ them, and they, too, could buy a cottage, have four weeks of holidays every year and retire on a decent pension. Everyone understood how it worked.

Sure, companies sometimes failed and jobs were sometimes lost—there are incompetent managers in any economy, old or new. But, as a whole, the economy was stable and secure. The people who worked in it could make plans and predictions, and be reasonably sure that their future would unfold as they expected.

Then, abruptly, everything changed. A new set of technologies was invented, new trade patterns were established and globalization became a reality. All those developments had been happening out of sight and out of mind, but suddenly they converged, and that nice, stable, secure ladder was pulled out from under us. Down the slippery slope we plunged.

It would be such a comfort to find someone to pin the crime on. Let's blame George Bush or Brian Mulroney or the CIA: last Tuesday after lunch, we *saw* them do it, we saw them bring on this global technological revolution. We have witnesses. . . . It would be so much more simple and comforting—to blame this world of change on someone or something: a government, a party, a union, a corporation, a person.

But as we grieve the loss of the old, familiar economy, we may miss the fact that there's a new ladder to climb.

The New Economy Is Larger Than You Think

The biggest mistake we can make is to believe that these turbulent changes will take place faster and faster, utterly out of control. In fact, our research indicates that once a new economy gets on track, stability returns. The (new) rules become understood. (New) customer needs become defined. The (new) industries where everyone "knows" you have a future become clear to everyone. The (new) educational standards are established. And two things happen: we understand where we're going and we calm down about the changes. A new conventional wisdom emerges. Stability reigns.

You would never know it from the daily newspapers, or from that cranky crowd at the U.S. Federal Reserve Board, who raise our interest rates for no good reason. They still accord the venerable industries of the old economy a center-stage significance that is no longer warranted by their size. The old economy only accounts for 12.9 percent of Canada's gross domestic product. After over a decade of downsizing, many of these old economy industries are actually rather small. Why, many of them don't even live here any-more, and they're not coming back.

Yet old people running out-of-date institutions still base their economic assumptions, and *our* interest rates, on the behavior of the old economy. They still measure the economy by the way obsolete industries perform, as though those industries are still sig-nificant indicators. We have to remember that those assumptions weren't wrong, that the world they depict did exist. But notice the verb tense in that phrase—*weren't* and *did*, not *aren't* and *does*.

Things have changed fundamentally. A New Economy has already emerged, and it's larger than you think.

In Canada, the New Economy already accounts for 58.9 percent of our gross domestic product. It's not an emerging economy; it's already here. But the turbulence is not over yet. The balance of the GDP—the industries that are neither old economy nor new—is made up by the Watch List. These are the industries that are devel-oping many of the characteristics of the old economy, but they could go either way.

WHAT IS...

The New Economy consists of industries that have not peaked structurally. While they ride the normal ups and downs of a business cycle, they are underpinned by long-term structural growth. Recession years are followed by strong and lengthy recoveries to new industry production records. Examples include semiconductors, instrumentation and pharmaceuticals.

Turnarounds are industries that have peaked structurally, but have begun to turn around and have started to display many of the characteristics of industries that are underpinned by long-term structural growth. Their future could be far better than their past, and they warrant close attention. Examples include rubber products and stamped, pressed and coated metals.

The old economy is past its peak in terms of contributing to gross domestic product. As industries peak, their free-fall is more severe than could reasonably be associated with a recession. Subsequent business cycle recoveries do not bring the industry back to its past glory. Examples of old economy industries include breweries and beverages, oil refining, textiles and steel mills.

The Watch List refers to industries in Canada that have not peaked structurally, but have either peaked in the United States or are displaying many of the economic characteristics of industries that are about to peak. They could go either way. Industries and sectors on Canada's Watch List today include government, autos and parts, housing, banking, trust companies, insurance and gold mining.

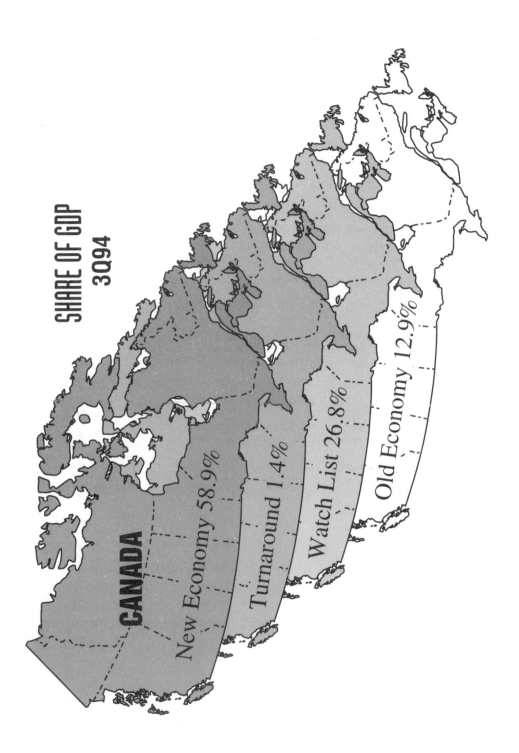

SHARE OF GDP
3Q94

CANADA

New Economy 58.9%

Turnaround 1.4%

Watch List 26.8%

Old Economy 12.9%

Life beyond Transition

When will we shift from the period of turbulence and transition into the stability of the New Economy? If we're lucky and smart, we could be through it in two more years; if not, we may have to ride it out for five years or even longer. Many factors could affect the timing, and we have three big hurdles to climb over before we reach the safer shores of this New Economy.

Hurdle No. 1: The political scene is the biggest wild card of all. Tell me our political will is strong enough to reduce the waste and inefficiencies that built up in the heyday of the old economy, and I'll tell you that the first major hurdle is behind us.

Hurdle No. 2: Tell me that special interest groups won't run whining and sniveling to their politicians, that instead they will take the "high road" and acknowledge that the cupboard is bare, and I'll tell you that the second major hurdle is behind us.

Hurdle No. 3: The Watch List is the third hurdle, because these industries could go either way. If they pull up their socks, get on with it and become suppliers to the New Economy, they will pull back from the brink. If they stand firm in their belief that "the world can change, but not my industry," then I can guarantee you that they will go tumbling into the old economy. And that will amount to a second wave of painful layoffs and restructuring as we move through the 1990s.

There's a Future for Generation X

So, in the end, what did I tell Carl and his classmates? I told them that the turmoil of this transition is not the whole picture. There are industries, big industries, mighty new engines that have already emerged, and those industries are creating jobs and growth and a future.

Don't waste your time, I told them, thinking about a world that wasn't your world. Don't wait for the world to return to what it used to be for your parents, because something better, something

15

much better, is unfolding for you. And you won't have to get a PhD just to get a job in a fast-food joint. This New Economy is big, and there are huge opportunities in it for *you*; so don't settle for just any job. Make sure that you fall in love with what you do for a living. Have the courage to live your dreams.

The message Carl and his classmates need to hear is that, in this new high-knowledge economy, it is more important than ever to stay in school and get the education and training that will give them a head start. But it doesn't matter what you study, I told them; you can choose marketing, marine biology, English, sociology, engineering . . . as long as you apply what you've learned in an industry that has a real future in the New Economy. And I showed Carl and the students who came to hear me speak that day the chart on the following page.

- If you have an interest in English—get a job editing software manuals. Anyone who has ever read a software manual *knows* that the folks who write them *need* the help!
- If you're studying marine biology—build your career in the booming ecotourism field, or in the entertainment industry, where, in the near-future, five hundred new TV channels along the superhighway will create a huge demand for nature films.
- Urban geography can open up exciting career opportunities in environmental consulting, or in water and soil testing.
- If you have an interest in social work, think about elder care in communities such as White Rock, B.C., or in the Niagara Peninsula, which are attracting huge retirement populations.
- For the thinkers with a burning interest in philosophy, one of the hottest fields emerging is medical ethics.
- If you have an interest in chemistry, get a job as a lab technician with a biochemical company.
- Everyone jokes about the students who take "bird courses." But the students today who study our feathered friends will find themselves at the forefront of the fastest growing leisure activity

16

EDUCATION FOR THE NEW ECONOMY

WHAT TO STUDY	WHERE TO APPLY WHAT YOU LEARN
ENGLISH	Software Industry, editing manuals; Communications Equipment Manufacturing, editing new product literature
MARINE BIOLOGY	Motion Pictures & Video Industry, Ecotourism
URBAN GEOGRAPHY	Waste Management Industry, Environmental Consulting
SOCIAL WORK	Community Social Services, Eldercare
PHILOSOPHY	Medical Ethics
CHEMISTRY	Biochemical, Agricultural Chemicals & Fertilizer Industry, Plastics & Synthetic Resins Industry
PHOTOGRAPHY	Taking photographs for medical journals and pharmacology journals
ELECTRONICS TECHNOLOGY	Electrical & Electronics Equipment Wholesalers
HEALTH SCIENCES	Registered Nurse Practitioners, Chiropractors
BUSINESS ADMINISTRATION	Software Industry, Waste Management, Pipeline Transportation Industry
PAYROLL ADMINISTRATION	Universities, Casinos, Recreational Facilities
COMPUTER STUDIES	Libraries, Museums, Elementary & Secondary Schools
MANUFACTURING TECHNOLOGY	Steel Pipe & Tube Manufacturing, Plastics & Synthetic Resins Manufacturing, Agricultural Chemicals & Fertilizers Manufacturing
BOOKKEEPING	Accounting Firms & Bookkeeping Services, Waste Management Industry, Community Colleges
OFFICE ADMINISTRATION	Natural Gas Distribution Systems, Sports Arenas

in North America today. That's right, *birdwatching* is set to become the most popular sport of the '90s! And the demographics of the baby boom will make this business positively fly as old boomers lay down their squash rackets and jogging shoes, and buy a pair of field glasses, instead. There will be books to write about birdwatching, clubs to run, courses to teach, bird feeders to manufacture, and birding stores to open and operate.

It's not *what* you study, it's *where* you apply what you've learned—that is the key. And you'll be further ahead if you apply your special talents in an industry that has a future, rather than in one that doesn't.

Not everyone has the interest, or opportunity, or ability to go on to university. If that's the case, I said to these kids, think about becoming a bookkeeper for a waste management company, a driver for a medical lab, a receptionist for an environmental consulting company. New Economy industries need a wide range of skills. They need manufacturing teams, and production and distribution operations, and a vast array of support services.

And I told Carl and the other students, who by now were listening intently, that Canada's software industry represented just one of so many good examples of the wide range of opportunities within a New Economy industry. Software companies need people who can sell software and write software; people who can package software and deliver software; people who can manage accounts payable, draft legal contracts and work in distribution. This is a *big* New Economy, and there's lots of room in it for everyone.

Does the Deficit Matter?

Some of the students that day wanted to know what could be done about the deficit. "Don't for a second think that the deficit isn't real or that it doesn't matter," I said. Those are big numbers, and they should frighten all of us—to our senses, I hope. In my firm's research, I explained, we had asked a brutally simple question: *What are deficits financing?* Everyone talks about deficit financing, but few people seem to ask this most basic of questions.

We found that, in the real world, there are two very different types of deficits: there are bad deficits and there are good deficits.

The bad deficits are easy to spot. They're the deficits of waste and inefficiency, the layers upon layers of government all duplicating each other's programs. These deficits aren't caused by bad people, but by a system that once upon a time was great, in a world that has moved on to other needs and wants. In these bad deficits, billions of dollars are being poured into industries and policies that will never produce another job as long as we all live. Billions of dollars are being borrowed every year to pay for programs that meet the needs of a world that no longer exists. Our tax dollars can't afford it anymore. Let's not pretend that we're creating wealth and prosperity when we're not.

Then I told the students about the good deficits, which are necessary and humane. The transition from the old economy into the New Economy has been costly. Millions of Canadians lost their jobs and had their lives turned upside down by change that they didn't cause and that no one, rich or poor, saw coming. The "good" portion of the deficit helped to ease the pain of transition. Few people have the stomach or the desire to go back to the times when social safety nets didn't exist, to the Dirty Thirties when millions of Canadians roamed the country in search of food and shelter.

But if good deficits are necessary and humane, they should also be *temporary*. The role of government now is to get people out of those safety nets so that they can integrate themselves into the New Economy. Our governments will be doing a terrible deed if they fail us in this task; if, by their inactivity, they create a whole culture of dependency in this country. Anyone who has ever suffered a serious physical disability knows that taking the first step is always the hardest. But we all have to take the first step on any

19

road to recovery, however frightening or agonizing that first step may be. We need government to take our crutches away.

But getting people integrated into the New Economy is easier said than done, with so many myths and half-truths circulating about what this New Economy is and isn't.

The Seven Deadly Myths about the New Economy

Myth No. 1: The New Economy is "just" a service economy. The mother of all myths is that we're becoming "just" a service economy, and people worry that we're going to spend the rest of our lives taking in each other's laundry. A nation built around donuts and coffee shops would be enough to convince anybody that our country's prosperity is behind us. The reality, however, is something very different. The New Economy is made up of goods and services, just as the old economy was. The only difference is that New Economy goods and services have a far higher knowledge content. Are we *just* a service economy? Hardly. After all, what are cellular phones and computers, if not manufactured goods?

Myth No. 2: The New Economy is "only" small business. Young people today wonder if they will ever have the choice of working in a large or international company. The truth is that the New Economy comes in all shapes and sizes. One size doesn't have to fit all. What are Microsoft, Motorola, Spar Aerospace and Corel Corporation, to say nothing of the telecommunications and entertainment conglomerates, if not very large businesses?

Myth No. 3: The New Economy is "just" high-tech. Wrong! While the engines that are driving the New Economy are sky-high-tech, the New Economy itself includes hundreds of vital supplier industries, such as natural gas, pipelines, packaging, trucking, computer paper, waste management and many, many more.

Myth No. 4: The New Economy is "only" an emerging economy, so it's too small to really count. Guess what! The New Economy already accounts for 58.9 percent of Canada's gross domestic product. Anything that accounts for almost 60 percent of an economy isn't just emerging—it has already emerged.

Myth No. 5: The New Economy is a "jobless" economy. I hear this one all the time. But the hard facts are very different: the New Economy already accounts for over 59 percent of Canada's total employment. Since 1984, the New Economy has already created over 800,000 net new jobs. A jobless economy? Hardly.

Myth No. 6: There's no job security in this New Economy. Many people actually fear that job security is a thing of the past. But lay-off rates in the New Economy are on average incredibly low. During the worst of the recession years, only 5.7 percent of the people employed in the New Economy lost their jobs. And over the last ten years, the New Economy's lay-off rate was only 2.4 percent.

Myth No. 7: The world of high growth is behind us. It's surprising the number of people who actually believe that our economy in North America will never, ever enjoy strong and rapid growth again. Wrong. Take a hard look at the underlying growth rate of this New Economy. As the chart on the next page shows, it's the old economy that's growing slowly—the New Economy has been on a strong growth track for years. Once the transition is over, just you wait and see. In our country, real growth rates of 4 percent or more will become the norm.

If you want to be a part of the New Economy, read on, because I am going to show you how to find a job, build your company, invest your money, get your community growing and make political sense of the world around us.

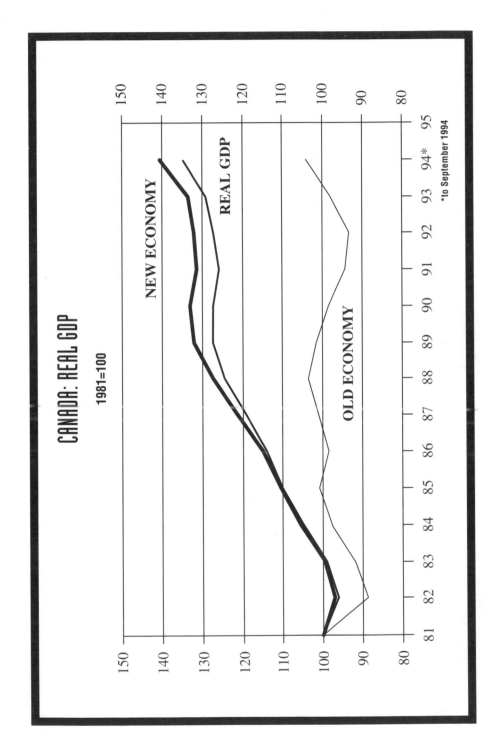

CANADA: REAL GDP

1981=100

NEW ECONOMY

REAL GDP

OLD ECONOMY

81 82 83 84 85 86 87 88 89 90 91 92 93 94* 95

*to September 1994

2

A ROAD MAP FOR YOU AND ME

There was a time when we would look to government to tell us what to do and where to go, what the jobs were and where opportunity lay. Lord knows, we pay our taxes and we have a right to expect our representatives to give us the help we need. We elected them to lead us, after all. They should be guiding us, telling us how the future that they are shaping for us will unfold.

But, unfortunately, governments are no further ahead than we are when it comes to knowing how to cope with the future. Like everyone else, they are still groping around, trying to understand what the changes are and what they mean. And even if governments had the answers, they couldn't afford to help us out. We're on our own.

There was a time when we would look to our schools and colleges and universities to give us the guidance we needed. "What should I study?" we would ask, and they would tell us, "Take this course and pass it, get the diploma or the degree, and you will get a job that will keep you for the rest of your life." But educational institutions are now turning their attention inward and asking themselves how they can become relevant again. They can't make our choices for us.

What about the media? They used to interpret the world for us. But we don't trust the media anymore. We question their approach, their special knowledge. Our own interpretations often make more sense than theirs do.

Do trade unions have the answers we're looking for? No, they don't. For the most part, unions are too busy trying to repair the damage and the devastating losses in their memberships brought on by the collapse of the old economy. The better organizations are trying to rebuild their ranks with New Economy members, and have little time and energy to spare for individual questions, even if they knew the answers—which they don't.

Will salvation come from the companies that employ us, or used to? It is tempting to look at "the company" in the old paternalistic way. After all, corporate leaders and managers have always been credited with knowing what was best. The unwritten promise was part of the old economy. If you show up on time and are competent and loyal, you will be looked after, has given way to pink slips and confusion and corporate strategies replacing corporate strategies that didn't work. Companies are in trouble. Managers are uncertain. How can they help us when far too many corporations can't even get it right for themselves these days?

So, if you can't turn to your government, and you can't turn to your bosses, and you can't turn to your union, and you can't turn to your academics and thinkers and educational institutions, and you don't trust the media—who are you going to call? Who can you rely on to show you the way?

Waiting for the Bus That Never Comes

Maybe reliance on others is precisely the problem. Instead of standing around forlornly at the bus stop, waiting for a bus that is never going to come, we should start making our own way home. If we wait for governments to find the answers, we'll be old and gray and still waiting. If we wait for companies to get on with the business of growth, we may be waiting well past our retirement years. If we wait for the unions, we'll be obsolete. And too many academics are still trying to protect their tenure while they figure out how many angels can dance on the head of a pin.

People know that the traditional oracles aren't answering any longer. That's why there is so much skepticism and cynicism, and so much worry and confusion and concern. There are so many of us wandering aimlessly around the economic landscape, when we could be finding the answers for ourselves.

Instead of packing the best years of our life with our creativity and our zest for living, developing the best ideas and producing the best work that we're capable of, we spend our time peering anxiously down the economic highway, waiting for that phantom bus. But waiting desperately for the world to return to what it used to be isn't working for any government or company or school board, and it certainly won't work for you and me. The traditional knowledge and power brokers are giving way to something new, something different and exciting: an ethic of personal responsibility in the New Economy.

Knowledge: The New Natural Resource

In a world that has become infinitely more dependent on knowledge, the traditional filters of government, management, unions, education and the media—the mediators and agents that came between the individual and the economy, and acted as our go-betweens—are being swept away. Knowledge workers don't want or need intervenors. They're more comfortable making up their own minds and making their own decisions. There's a new credo in the New Economy: "Give me the facts and I'll make up my own mind." This is not to say that the institutions of the past are irrelevant and have no place whatsoever today. They're just out of date.

And, as we move increasingly into a knowledge-based economy, our independence is a normal and natural evolution. Knowledge workers don't wait for buses that never come. They draw up their own road maps. They empower themselves.

I know, I know: if I hear the word *empowerment* one more time, I swear I'll jump out of the nearest window. But there's no escaping the fact that more and more people are taking control of their own lives.

I see it every Monday night when I drive by my local high school on the way home from work. There's a traffic jam in the parking lot caused by all the people who have signed up for courses, trying to succeed in a more knowledge-based economy. And it's not just in my community that people are pulling themselves up by their bootstraps by the hundreds, and spending their own money to equip themselves with the skills they need to survive and thrive in the New Economy. Every semester, thousands of Canadians are enrolling in high school adult education courses, and they're signing up at community colleges in droves. It's not that these people have nothing better to do on a Monday night. What they're doing is taking control of their lives. They're not waiting for Big Brother, Big Sister or Big Anybody to do it for them.

Four Vital Skills in the New Economy and How to Get Them

If you look at the basic skills that people need to function well in the New Economy, adult education can be the best thing anyone can do. But it can also be the biggest waste of time, especially if you unknowingly fall prey to two of the most common traps.

The first trap is setting yourself up to learn out-of-date material. You would be amazed by the number of people who sign up for courses, committing three months, six months or longer, and never think to ask, What exactly will I learn? It's a depressing fact that many well-meaning institutions are still teaching people how to use software programs that no one in the real world has used in several years—and a year is a century in computer time.

I remember interviewing candidates for an executive assistant position last year, and after meeting with eight bright and eager people, I almost threw my hands up in despair. We decided to screen applicants more closely ourselves because I didn't want to end up like Murphy Brown, with a different assistant from a temp agency answering my phone every week. We developed a simple test that would help us determine whether a candidate had the *basic* skills that were needed for the job. It was devastating to interview one person after another who had never worked in Windows, the no-longer-new Microsoft operating system for computers. Why hadn't they? The local community college hadn't upgraded its computers or its curriculum to reflect this new and very basic business standard.

The situation's the same in engineering programs, science labs and hairstyling schools. So, instead of signing up blindly for a course, call half a dozen businesses where you might like to work, and ask them what the standards are in their organization. Then take the courses that will get you the job you're after.

The second trap is learning a smattering of something in the mistaken belief that you can learn the rest and fill in the gaps on the job. Too many people are already running around with just a smattering of something, and they're condemning themselves to the long lines of the unemployed. It also saddens me when I see educators still assuming that, if they give students just enough information to get out the door, the students will find a job and learn the rest someplace else. But in the New Economy, companies are only hiring people who can hit the ground running. It's no longer good enough to know just a little about a lot. Either you know it or you don't, and if you don't, you're just wasting the company's time. Knowledge is the prized asset for most companies in the New Economy, and too many managers are spending more time and effort than they can afford training their workers and teaching the most basic of skills. You are automatically further ahead if you really do know what you're doing.

Here are the skills that all of us need to get ahead in these challenging times.

Skill No. 1: The Ability to Work as Part of a Team

It sounds so basic, doesn't it? But working as part of a team is really a lot tougher than most people are inclined to admit. After all, from the time we made it out of diapers, we were brought up to believe that we should only speak when we were spoken to; talking back might be something you could get away with only if your mother was just too tired to yell at the kids one more time. Is it any wonder that, when we got our first jobs, we knew enough to take orders from the supervisor—just do it, don't question it. But the old hierarchies are disappearing and are being replaced by working teams with no clear "boss." One of the major challenges confronting every working team is the ability to solve problems by recognizing and using the dynamics of group work. And it's difficult for many people to switch into teamwork mode, to think of themselves as people who provide solutions instead of people who carry out instructions. In the old style of management, workers were obliged to let the boss decide, to wait for a memo to come down from head office, or to follow a directive explaining how "they" wanted a particular job done.

But all of a sudden, there's no more "they"—there's just "us." We are now responsible for executing plans—and, in most cases, for thinking up the plans in the first place. You swing your car into the parking lot, grab your newspaper and head for your old familiar desk, only to find that your whole world has been turned upside down. The place looks the same, but it isn't. The old rules don't apply anymore, and there's no new rule book to show us how the game is played and what's expected of us in the New Economy. It can be terrifying to discover that we need to change the entire pattern of our life. Anyone who says change is easy has probably never been married. "Don't squeeze the toothpaste from the middle, honey—leave the toilet seat down, the way you found it, goddammit!" Anyone who says that old habits are easy to break doesn't know what they're talking about.

Problem-solving skills often come into play even before you get to work. Before you can become part of a problem-solving team— the typical module for the New Economy workplace—you have to get your personal problems straightened away. We have all seen people go through a tumultuous time as the old and familiar give way to the new and unexpected. Some people cope; others don't. Periods of great change and turmoil can often bring to the forefront personal insecurities and debilitating self-doubt.

The trouble is, if you can't solve your own problems, how on earth are you going to solve the company's problems? And if you can't solve the company's problems, how are you going to get hired—or, once hired, keep your job?

In the midst of so much economic confusion, and in the aftermath of this transition, there is bound to be a great demand for skilled counselors (a growth industry if ever there was one!). A good piece of advice is to keep your life in order and to remember that simple is far better than complex. Everyone in business has worked with someone, sometime, who has had a tough time functioning on the job, even in the good times. What becomes of these people in the bad times?

I remember one man I worked with many years ago before I started my own company. Every time the telephone rang, he almost had a heart attack. You could see this poor guy go pale before your eyes, because he didn't know whether it was his first ex-wife, his second ex-wife, his fourth mistress or his current girlfriend on the phone. In the heyday of the old economy, when there was enough room for everybody and almost every eccentricity was tolerated, companies were less conscious of performance. Today, however, you can almost hear what's going through the supervisor's mind: Can this person *contribute*? Is he with us, or is he off on another planet?

In addition to professional counseling, there is an endless supply of self-help available—books to read, community resources to tap into, a whole network of places to go and people to see who can help lighten a personal load and help you build a stable and secure future. Many of these useful resources teach the skills that allow people to solve their own problems, before they move into a company and attempt to solve the broader problems of business. If you can't work with yourself, how on earth will you be able to work with others?

Skill No. 2: The Ability to Communicate

This one is obvious enough—without the necessary writing and speaking skills, knowledge work is virtually impossible. Knowledge work depends on team-based problem-solving, which depends on lucid communications.

It still astounds me the number of people who enter the work force with a university degree, or who have had six or seven years of work experience, and still can't construct a simple business letter, the most basic communication tool there is. These are people who can't string two sentences together to make a sensible paragraph. Despite years of schooling, they just didn't get it. They were allowed to progress blithely through the system, unimpeded by instruction or correction, unencumbered by grammar, entirely innocent of syntax. But language skills are absolutely vital. As more and more people move off the production line and try to find their way in a knowledge-based economy, clear communication becomes more crucial than ever.

Knowing how to use the tools of this communications age is equally vital. Do you know how to send a fax, use a modem and navigate your way through e-mail? Don't ask me how many times I've received a fax and it's been a blank page. Why? Because the person sending the fax put the page in wrong-side up!

I addressed a marketing conference in the United States recently. The conference theme was "Meeting Your Customers' Needs in the 1990s." Speaker after endless speaker droned on about TQM (total quality management) and how the marketplace was changing rapidly. Over lunch, I asked the group at my table a question. "You're in the business of direct marketing," I said, "but what would you do if a potential customer called you up and asked you to give them a marketing presentation? After giving you the details of what they are looking for and why, the voice at the end of the line drops the bombshell: 'Oh, and by the way, we'd like to schedule your presentation to our management committee for two o'clock tomorrow, but you don't need to be present at the meeting and we don't want a conference call. Do it on our e-mail. Here's our Internet address.'"

I looked around the table at the direct marketers, at the blank stares. They all sat very still, looking uncomfortable and embarrassed, obviously far outside their comfort zones. And these people were the cream of the marketing crop—communication is integral to their business! To do a spiffy presentation, all they would have needed was a CompuServe account at about $8.95 a month, a $99 modem and some basic off-the-shelf software. To really dazzle the crowd, the latest version of Powerpoint would have produced a multicolored, multimedia showstopper—all in less time than it would have taken for the taxi ride to the airport during rush hour.

More and more high-knowledge customers are demanding that presentations and information of all kinds be delivered to them in the ways they use to communicate among themselves. It's going to get tougher to do business with people who are operating on a different knowledge base than you are. And if you have a serious interest in staying in business, you had better bring yourself up to scratch, or don't even bother going through the pretense of trying to compete.

These skills are simple to learn, and they're becoming easier to learn all the time. Remember that communications and software have progressed far beyond the point where you have to be a computer nerd or technology buff to understand them. That's the good news. Adult education courses and community colleges are packed full of good courses. Sign up and have fun learning (but remember to find out first exactly what you're going to learn), and within a few short weeks or months you will be able to hit the ground running when you join a new company. Or, who knows, you might even get to keep the job you have.

Skill No. 3: The Ability to Use a Computer

It is obvious by now that to make it this far you have to be computer literate. But don't just rush out and take the first computer course you see advertised. You will be miles ahead if you shop around first. Don't be afraid of asking, "What exactly are you going to teach me?" Too many institutions are still teaching people to use old clunkers, like 286 machines, that are already generations out of date. Unless a school can show you a room full of 486 computers or, better still, can brag about its Pentium processors, you're wasting your time and money. And run, don't walk, to the nearest exit if anyone suggests you start with a keyboarding course. Unless you want to break speed records, you're not there to take a high-tech typing course. (I swear, all the old typing teachers have gotten together and formed a dark plot, a conspiracy of the deepest order, to teach us how to type, once and for all!) The simple truth today is that you'll use a mouse as much as you'll use a keyboard.

But if you don't know much about computers, how can you ask the right questions and evaluate the answers? Here's a functional, but by no means complete, shortcut: you won't be too far off the mark if you concentrate on learning a Microsoft Office package. This is not a plug for Microsoft Corporation; Bill Gates is already a very rich man and doesn't need my help to sell his software. Their standard package will give you all the skills you'll need to become functionally computer literate and ready to fit comfortably into any New Economy office setting.

First, there is the word-processing package, Microsoft Word. New versions are being released with better bells and whistles all the time, so a telephone call to a local computer store will tell you what the latest version of the program is. At last count, they were up to release 6.0, and if an instructor tries to talk you into anything but the latest version, say, "Thanks, but no thanks. I'm not interested in a computer *history* course." Once you have learned how to use the program (and remember, a smattering of anything won't get you very far), you can easily learn to use WordPerfect or almost any other word-processing package that may be on the market.

Second, there is the spreadsheet program, called Excel. If you know how to use Excel, you can automatically pick up any spreadsheet that comes your way, such as Lotus 1-2-3. Whether you work with simple numbers keeping track of attendance at the local day care, or whether you need to wow the boss with your plant's performance numbers for the month, a spreadsheet program is a New Economy necessity.

Third, there's Powerpoint, a basic presentation package. If you learn this program, it's easy to pick up similar packages, such as Harvard Graphics. You'll find an incredible range of uses for Powerpoint, whether you want to bring your proposals up to date so that they look as professional as you are, or whether you want to remind your boss at raise time of your hard work. Powerpoint is a powerful communications tool that none of us can afford to be without.

Finally, there's Publisher. This is a basic publishing package that's versatile enough to produce a very professional newsletter for your group or your department. It can also generate everything from a three-sided brochure to a wide selection of business forms and letterheads. It can even make a terrific-looking paper airplane!

Skill No. 4: The Ability to Do Basic Math

Teachers aren't telling you that you need math just to torture you and make your adult life a misery. There are two very important reasons why basic math skills are vital in this New Economy. First, you have to be able to measure a world that is changing rapidly, and measuring that change is absolutely crucial. By what percentage did sales rise or fall last month? How many widgets made it through quality control in the past thirty days, and how does your ratio compare to your competitors'? Are your prices competitive in yen? How about deutsche marks? No matter what you do or will be doing, you're probably going to use analysis and calculations in the course of your work.

The second reason is that, whether the organization you work for is large or small, you will need a broader range of skills to function in the New Economy than you ever did in the old one. This fact is true for large companies that have been re-engineered and flattened out into fewer layers, with fewer divisions and fewer job functions; and it is also true for small companies that have been flat from day one. There is no sense asking who is in charge of the costing department when you're working in an organization of three people!

Upping the Educational Ante

If our public educational system will not or cannot meet the needs of the New Economy, it might as well declare itself out of business, because the private sector, made up of companies large and small, will take over and provide the service faster and cheaper in the process. Educators today would be wrong to assume that they have a monopoly on education. Private companies delivering public education are already flourishing in the United States. Distance learning is alive and well and thriving in this New Economy.

If you look back through history, each New Economy has upped the educational ante. By the end of this century, only a few short years from now, the country with the most knowledge workers will win. For a country such as Canada, this high-knowledge economy gives rise to some challenges, but it opens up even more opportunities.

The biggest opportunity for countries such as Canada is that our resource base can change rapidly from rocks and trees to knowledge. Knowledge is the most *natural* of all resources, and it can be developed by any province, by any community, in a very short space of time. Knowledge is the ultimate renewable resource.

In provinces such as Newfoundland, someone with a Grade Ten education can graduate, in six short years, with a university degree, a knowledge worker armed with the skills of the New Economy. In the old economy, developing our natural resources took far longer than it does today. You couldn't grow a tree in six years! You couldn't develop an oil field in six short years. And you certainly couldn't develop an entire mine site from start to finish in six years. Simply getting a proposal through the environmental assessment process could take that long.

If you think that this high-knowledge economy is a thing of the future, take a second look. As the chart on the following page shows, Canada's high-knowledge economy has been the major source of job creation for almost ten years now.

The prospect of getting left behind terrifies most people: Can I make it in this New Economy? Armed with the basic skills, however, you can set out to pick the right job in the right industry in the right community. Of course, having even the best skills provides no guarantee that you'll live a long and happy life. But it sure beats flying blind as you enter a New Economy in which the old rules no longer apply.

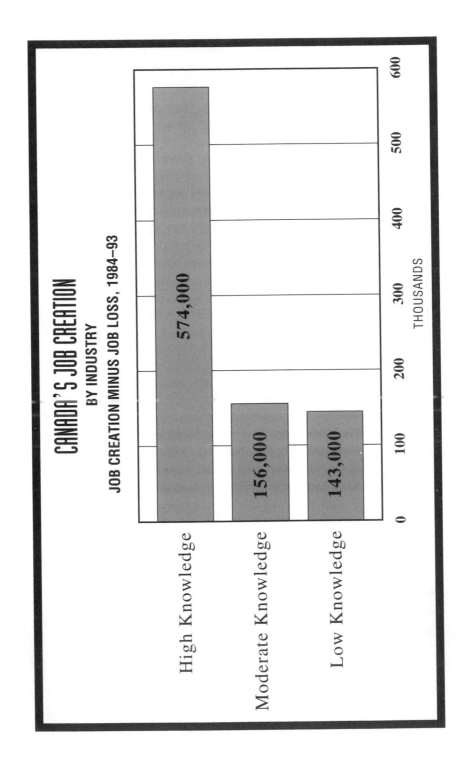

CANADA'S JOB CREATION

BY INDUSTRY

JOB CREATION MINUS JOB LOSS, 1984–93

High Knowledge — 574,000

Moderate Knowledge — 156,000

Low Knowledge — 143,000

THOUSANDS

3

FIVE-STAR JOBS IN THE NEW ECONOMY

When Chevy Chase starred in the movie *European Vacation*, the slapstick comedy about the American family that headed off on the quintessential disaster holiday, most people could relate to some of the hilariously unexpected scenes. Any family setting off on vacation knows these last minute fears: What if the promised resort with palm trees waving in the breeze turns out to be a dump, and the lavish buffets shown in the glossy travel brochure are the congealed leftovers from last season's tourist rush? What if the food is still moving when it reaches my plate?

In these modern times, holiday disasters can still happen, but few families or couples would set off for a precious holiday in the sun without thumbing through the travel brochure and checking out the rating of the resort. Is it a five-star luxury hotel (which we probably can't afford anyway), or is it a no-star motel that might, if we're very lucky, have hot and cold running water on the same day? Thankfully, tour operators rate the holiday packages they offer, and travel-rating guides are available for virtually any destination in the world. When it comes to our cherished holidays, no sir, we're not about to take any chances!

Rating guides are even available for restaurants in almost every city and burg on this planet. Who in their right mind would select a restaurant for a special family occasion or a special anniversary by letting their "fingers do the walking" through the Yellow Pages? Now, I'm all for preserving the spirit of adventure, but I'd still be a mite peeved if I'd gotten all dressed up for a special evening of romance, only to find myself sitting at the counter of the greasy spoon across from the bus station. Fortunately, rating guides take the mystery and peril out of these momentous life decisions, and it's not unreasonable for any of us to want to know what we're getting into.

For some reason, however, no one seems to have developed a rating system for jobs in the New Economy. No wonder Generation X is cynical. "You roll the dice and you take your chance," we tell them. "If lady luck is with you, who knows, you might end up in the job equivalent of a luxury resort." But we all know that there are far more dead-end jobs than dream jobs, and, if you're really unlucky, you could find yourself checking into the job equivalent of the Bates Motel, with Norman and his mother just waiting. . . .

Too many people are being sent out to apply for jobs that either already don't exist or soon won't, jobs that have a zero future, jobs that pay so little that your first thought on payday is, "Will my mommy take me back?"

And why? For no good reason. Probably because counselors stick to what they know, the old industries where their contacts may still count for something. It's human nature to stay with the familiar, even after common sense whispers, "It's time to move on."

In the old economy, of course, it was easy. There was a whole shopping list of secure jobs with a future. A worker at the local pulp mill had a future. Get into the office or onto the assembly line in any one of the thousands of factories that dotted our industrial landscape, and you were settled for your career, you could get on with your life. Who needed a job rating system? If you felt like finishing high school, if you had an interest in doing a couple of years of college, or getting a PhD, you knew what your options were.

But the world has changed. The traditional industries are either struggling for survival or no longer exist. In some cases, the companies have folded, or packed up and moved on, or downsized into a broom closet. In many cases, the technology that once gave an industry the edge has become obsolete, or the demand for the product has disappeared, or the jobs simply aren't necessary anymore—machines do the work ten times faster than people can.

For ten miserable years, we have watched our lives turn upside down. It has been like watching an economic tornado touching down in one industry after another, wiping out the hopes and dreams of so many. And night after night, through what has seemed the longest decade of our lives, we have watched the wreckage reported on the nightly news.

What saddens me most is to see the young people, middle-aged people and all the folks in the final years of their working lives—everybody, that is—frightened into believing that they had better hang on to *any* job they can get, and that somehow they should feel so grateful to have a job at all.

Have the Courage to Live Your Dreams

People have a right to build their hopes and dreams around a job that they actually enjoy doing. Life can be good if you are doing what you enjoy, in an industry that complements your own interests, with products or services you like and approve of. An industry where the people and the sounds and the smells just feel right.

Back in the 1950s and 1960s, there were thousands of contented people working in industry, in the offices or on the production lines of the GMs of this world. People who joined GM, more often than not, were people who actually liked cars—men (usually), who got their first hot rod when they were in their teens, and who spent the best summer months of their lives lovingly restoring every inch of shiny chrome, while they looked forward to Saturday night with their friends, cruising round town listening to rock 'n' roll. Nothing wrong with that. There's absolutely nothing wrong with doing what you like in an industry you can relate to.

People in the New Economy can and should have the same opportunity. "Fall in love with what you do for a living" is not bad advice for any job seeker, young or old. When you stop to think about it, you probably have a fairly wide range of interests. Most people do. Some jobs fit like a glove, while others never will. There are environments we like, behaviors we like, corporate cultures we like, activities and tasks that we like, and others that, inexplicably, we just don't. In any economy, old or new, it is important not to lose sight of what makes you an individual. Only *you* can or should decide what feels right for you. I can't help you there. But I can help you with a lot of other things.

Numbers Are My Life

I had spent an idyllic weekend puttering in the garden, the kind of lazy weekend in the suburbs where the most pressing decision is, "Should we turn the barbecue on now, or should we wait half an hour and then turn it on?" I had also found the time to indulge in one of my favorite pastimes—the Saturday trip to our travel agent's office at the shopping center across the road from where we live. Debbie, our agent, keeps me in a steady supply of travel brochures for Sunquest, Air Canada Vacations, you name it—she has it. I know, some people may prefer to spend their precious leisure time reading Plato's *Republic* or debating the ontological premise of a particular political philosophy. I readily confess to enjoying an hour in the shade daydreaming about warm, sunny, exotic places to visit.

I was particularly engrossed in comparing the merits of two resorts and turned to the front of the brochure for guidance. There

40

it was: the little box with the legend that explained to me, in very straightforward terms, why a five-star hotel deserved five stars, and why some vacation properties were accorded a two-star rating and no more. I admire simplicity. And I have little time for the seers who would attempt to make our world and all the things in it complex, obtuse and indecipherable to anyone beyond their cozy club. It smacks of elitism, and I don't like it. Yes, those people in the travel biz had the right idea.

The idea kept coming back to me; it just wouldn't go away. What if my colleagues and I could apply our research skills and the vast data at our disposal to sift out the jobs that have a real future and identify the ones that (sadly enough) don't? I had been bitten by the research bug (again), and I knew what I had to do.

There are many things I love to do—cooking, gardening, having friends over on a winter's Sunday for an impromptu dinner and evening of pleasant conversation—but what makes my pulse race is research. The thrill of discovery is without parallel, which is probably why I also love to travel. After months of thinking, probing, analyzing and literally running thousands of numbers through our computer programs, there it was—so clear, so stunningly simple, so relevant: a road map for this New Economy.

What my firm's hard research pinpointed, with a stunning and surprising degree of accuracy, is where people today can go to find a good job with a future. The path is clear, it is well marked, and no one needs to get lost along the way.

What's a Good Job?

Most people would agree with me that a good job is one that you stand a good chance of keeping. We've all seen or experienced for ourselves the turmoil of losing a job. It's not surprising that most people rate job security fairly high on their list. Low lay-off rates across dozens of industries in the New Economy can let you sleep well at night, secure in the knowledge that there's only a slim chance you'll lose your job.

And remember the days when jobs used to lead to something? When, if you were reasonably good at what you did, you might actually get a promotion and become someone's boss? There is no mystery why some people get ahead and other equally competent people don't. Jobs with a future that are stable and secure are readily available in the New Economy. In New Economy industries, where the work force is increasing by thousands of people each year, you stand a very good chance of getting a promotion, of being asked to help train and supervise the newcomers.

But there can and should be more on our wish list. Most people would also agree with me that a good job pays better than the national average. It feels downright good to get paid well for what you do. It bolsters the spirit and lets you indulge in some of life's little luxuries along the way.

It's a real boost to your self-esteem to know that, if you work hard and do the right things, you might actually get a raise. What a concept! Remember when raises were routine? But in so many industries, there's a better chance that your unborn grandchildren will graduate from the college of their choice than that your paycheck will rise! In industries of the New Economy, a growing pie allows you a bigger slice.

Many people long for a workplace in which their ideas will count for something. They'd like to hear their colleagues or their boss say, "That's a good idea, let's try that," or, "Let's put our heads together and think about new and better ways to do what we are doing." In old economy industries, the ones with a low or (heaven forbid) a declining knowledge base, you're more likely to hear, instead, "We're not paying you to think—you're being paid to do, so just finish your coffee and get back to work before the whistle blows." Industries with high or rising knowledge ratios are more apt to welcome your ideas. Why? Because the knowledge base *is* the asset base of the company, and these high-knowledge industries know that innovation is the lifeblood of their very existence.

And while we're at it, wouldn't it be nice to have a job that you could plan your life around? Many young people today long for the day when they will be able to say, "Let's buy that house," secure in the knowledge that they won't be living their life on a perennial roller-coaster ride of feast or famine, boom or bust.

Low lay-off rates, good promotion prospects, better-than-average pay, a raise every so often, a job where your ideas will count for something, a stable future—if any of these interest you, read on.

Rating Jobs from Best to Worst

Whether you're a company president on the lookout for a brighter future, a middle manager who has recently been downsized onto the long lines of the unemployed, a bookkeeper with a keen interest in getting ahead, a receptionist with two years of experience, or a forty-five-year-old steel worker who has just lost his job at the only company he has ever worked for, *you need to pick your industry with great care in these times of turmoil.* Not the job, not the occupation, not the company: *the industry*, that's what matters the most.

Jobs will be engineered and re-engineered many times over in the New Economy, but if you're in an industry that's growing, your chances of being offered a new job, and perhaps even a better one within the same company, are relatively good.

Occupations will come and go; some will be changed radically by technological advances, by new ways of doing things. Some occupations will become obsolete. But if you're in an industry that's growing, that has a future in the New Economy, you will have a far easier time retraining for a new occupation in an industry you know a great deal about.

Companies can also come and go. The well-managed company today could be bought or sold, and a new management, with precious little to offer, could be parachuted in from Cleveland. The owner's idiot son could show up one day in the corner office, and, in between squash games, merrily proceed to run the company right into the ground. There are many reasons why a once-good company can fail, and sometimes it isn't even the company's fault. But if you're in an industry that has a future, there will be other similar companies to which you can apply, where your skills and contacts and product knowledge will count for something.

But if you pick the wrong industry—well, that's a different story. The commercial refrigeration equipment industry is a cold example of the peril of showing up in the wrong industry at the wrong point in history.

Once upon a time, the commercial refrigeration equipment industry was growing, populated by a wide range of companies in a long list of locations. But in 1984, that industry went tumbling into the old economy, and, over the next ten miserable years, industry production tumbled 40 percent. Job security? A raise? With those kinds of industry odds working against you? No one's sense of humor could possibly stretch that far. It didn't much matter whether you were the president, the sales manager or the foreman. The industry's lay-off rate topped 74 percent, meaning that 2,534 people in the industry lost their jobs.

Companies went bankrupt, and where do you go if you have built your whole life in the commercial refrigeration equipment industry? It would be a complete waste of time and energy even trying to get a job down the street with the competition. Everybody was in the same boat, from the executive office to the shop floor. Would it make sense to apply for a job at one of the company's suppliers? Probably not. If their biggest customers are downsizing by more than 50 percent, there's a good chance the suppliers are feeling the big chill as well. And what about sending your résumé to the customers? You must be joking! They're probably the reason why your company's sales plunged—after all, if the customers were buying, your industry's sales would probably continue to grow and you wouldn't be out of a job.

If you pick the right industry with a future in the New Economy, the job can change, the management can change, the technology can change and even the company can change or go out of business—but you'll have someplace to go.

Let's take a closer look at those qualities we look for in a good job.

Job Security

Some industries are notorious when it comes to providing even a modicum of job security. Lay-off rates are high in some industries no matter how much the economy seems to improve. In Ontario, through the boom years of most of the 1980s, the *average* lay-off rate for old economy industries topped the 26 percent mark, 6.8 times higher than the average lay-off rate for New Economy industries in the province. When things turned ugly during the recession years of 1989 to 1993, the *average* lay-off rate in those old economy industries in Ontario soared to more than 30 percent.

For Canada as a whole, the story was a little better, thanks to the lower-than-national-average lay-off rates in industries in provinces such as British Columbia. Canada's *average* lay-off rate in old economy industries topped 15 percent between 1984 and 1993 and surged to 21.8 percent during the recession years of 1989 to 1993.

Want to know where to go to lose a job fast? Take a look through the following list of the Top 10 old economy industries in Canada with the highest lay-off rates. If you're looking for job security—look elsewhere.

TOP 10 OLD ECONOMY INDUSTRIES WITH THE HIGHEST LAY-OFF RATES

	Lay-off Rate
1. Cement Manufacturing	95.1%
2. Household Furniture Manufacturing	80.8%
3. Commercial Refrigeration & Air Conditioning Manufacturing	74.8%
4. Concrete Products Manufacturing	62.9%
5. Leather Products Manufacturing	62.1%
6. Steel Plate & Fabricated Metal Products Manufacturing	58.1%
7. Petroleum Refining	52.5%
8. Construction, Mining, Sawmills & Materials Handling Equipment Manufacturing, Power Transmission Equipment & Compressors	52.1%
9. Office Furniture Manufacturing	48.2%
10. Steel Manufacturing	43.5%

JOB ADVANCEMENT

If your company and industry are downsizing, as so many have and are doing with gruesome regularity these days, there's still a chance that you'll get a promotion, but it could be a fast track to nowhere. In an industry that is merrily shrinking itself into a broom closet, the owners (if any are left) or the trustees will always need someone to close the closet door and turn off the lights on the way out. But it can be pretty lonely at the top when there is no one left at the bottom. And there are better ways to scale the corporate ladder.

How can you tell if you're on a fast track to nowhere?

- When the cleaning staff at night outnumber the people who work there during the day.
- When the president talks about "stranded assets" on a first-name basis.
- When the company redefines "group benefits" to include a communal "in-basket."
- When you look at your career ladder, it has only one rung and you're on it.
- When the company song extols the virtues of Prozac.

In the real world, it is much easier to get a promotion that actually means something in an industry that's growing by leaps and bounds. If the industry you're in is taking on several hundred new-comers each month, you can bet that there will be big opportunities for the people already there. New openings and responsibilities will materialize rapidly as team leaders are required to show the new folks the ropes. Departments will be created, new needs will have to be met. In short, there is a real chance that you're going to be promoted and that you'll have a chance to grow with the company. And who knows—a competitor, supplier or customer that's expanding even faster than the company you're with might call you up with a job offer in the hope of luring you away.

If you're looking for a fast track to job advancement, the next list is a must-read. Here are the Top 10 New Economy industries in Canada that are hiring as fast as they can process new applicants— where you can find a future, in more ways than one.

TOP 10 NEW ECONOMY JOB CREATORS

	Net Number of Jobs Created: 1989-93
1. Elementary & Secondary Schools	46,934
2. Community-Based Social Services	19,137
3. Pharmacies & Drug Stores	18,224
4. Wooden Prefab Buildings, Cabinets, Door & Window Manufacturing	15,656
5. Universities	11,382
6. Medical & Dental Offices	11,077
7. Community Colleges	10,806
8. Hospitals	10,082
9. Restaurants & Catering	9,342
10. Electrical & Electronic Equipment Wholesalers	6,817

Good Pay

Everyone knows someone these days who has taken it in the neck with a substantial wage cut of 5, 10 . . . or 100 percent. And very few of those people deserved to lose the money, or their livelihoods. It's just that they were unlucky enough to find themselves working in an industry that couldn't afford to pay them anymore.

If you have already taken a salary cut, or are about to, please don't make the mistake of assuming that you've done something wrong or are somehow less worthy than you used to be. It's just that your particular pie isn't growing any more. And if you're working in the old economy, the pie's shrinking, which means that

TOP 10 NEW ECONOMY INDUSTRIES WITH THE BEST SALARIES & INCREASES

	Average Salary 1993	Average Increase 1993
1. Pipeline Transportation	$1,014/week	5.6%
2. Electric Power	$947/week	2.5%
3. Non-Ferrous Smelting & Refining	$887/week	1.8%
4. Natural Gas Distribution	$811/week	0.4%
5. Communications Equipment	$796/week	14.2%
6. Pharmaceutical Manufacturing	$774/week	10.7%
7. Engineering, Architecture & Technical & Scientific Services	$771/week	1.1%
8. Software & Computer Services	$757/week	8.2%
9. Electrical & Electronic Equipment Wholesalers	$757/week	5.6%
10. Electric Wire & Cable	$754/week	5.5%

people often have to take a smaller slice. It's time to take stock and decide for yourself which pastry shop you want to be in.

In industries that are growing and thriving, common sense tells you that there will be more to go around. And our research confirms that, on balance, New Economy industries pay better than the old economy ones.

People in these high-flying New Economy industries don't work any harder than people anywhere else. You might even argue that the stress of being in a dead-end job, in a company that has no future and in an industry that's in decline, is ten times worse than the stress and job pressure that often come from being where the action is. All that opportunity, with a better paycheck than most, is so *s-t-r-e-s-s-f-u-l*.

The list on page 49 identifies the Top 10 New Economy industries that pay the most and have the highest wage gains. The moral of the story is simple enough: some pastry shops smell a whole lot sweeter than others!

Smart Industries

How can you tell if an industry is likely to show an interest in new ideas? Maybe even your ideas? It's not as hard as it sounds to figure out which industries are dependent on knowledge and which ones are less so. If the knowledge ratio of an industry is rising, that's even better, because it indicates that the knowledge base of the industry is expanding, which means that it is more apt to be open to new approaches, new technologies, new ideas, new products.

A Knowledge Ratio™ is simply the number of knowledge workers as a percentage of the people who are employed. A Knowledge Ratio of 6 percent means that only six out of every hundred people are knowledge workers; a Knowledge Ratio of 66 percent means that sixty-six out of a hundred are knowledge workers.

Knowledge workers fall into three employment groups. The first group is the people with professional designations such as doctors, engineers, lawyers, accountants and actuaries—people with a lot of specialized knowledge. (One look at their fees, and you're left hoping that their brains are as big as their bills.) The second category is senior management, the people running the show (who had better be as smart as they look). Finally, there's the largest group of knowledge workers, the technical, engineering and scientific staff (the folks wearing the pocket protectors, who are often a darn sight smarter than they look).

In this high-knowledge New Economy, it is little wonder that the large companies in mature industries, whose silent credo was "we're custodians, not innovators," have suffocated beneath their own bureaucracy. But in the 1970s, most companies didn't really have to be open to such a wide range of new ideas—they "knew" what had worked for the last twenty years, so why change it? Then, in the 1980s, the world changed as the old economy gave way to a new one. Suddenly, we had to become a nation of "entrepreneurs," and many people, in many companies across a broad range of industries, got ground to dust in the transition.

But some industries are heading the right way. Let me tell you a funny story about liquor stores, and how they're adjusting to this new high-knowledge economy.

Liquor stores found themselves in deep trouble on two counts in Canada. The actual production and consumption of most alcoholic beverages have been on the decline, for many reasons. "If you drink, don't drive" campaigns have (thankfully) been very successful, lifestyles have changed (the two-martini lunch is a corporate no-no) and older baby boomers don't consume nearly as many buckets of suds as they did in their misspent youth. If market forces weren't enough to drive a liquor store to drink, government cutbacks and privatization certainly would!

But liquor retailing is slowly responding to the challenge of change one location at a time by raising their Knowledge Ratios.

I remember as a university student going into a liquor store in Ottawa (the one downtown in the Byward Market area) to buy a bottle of Baby Duck, all the rage among the first-year cognoscenti. I stood patiently in a long line waiting to pencil in the code on that little form (in those days it was probably against the law in Ontario to call a bottle of wine by its name). I then stood in an even longer line to hand that little slip of paper silently across the counter to the Liquor Control Board clerk, who invariably seemed to be the alumnus of some particularly hostile temperance movement. The only words that might be exchanged were, "Do you want it in a brown paper bag?" This ritual was old economy bureaucracy at its finest! If customers had suggested a wine-tasting, or suppliers had

TOP 10 NEW ECONOMY HIGH & RISING KNOWLEDGE INDUSTRIES

	Knowledge Base	Increase
1. Agricultural Chemicals & Fertilizers	High	60.4%
2. Museums & Archives	High	26.8%
3. Associations, Unions & Religious Organizations	High	11.7%
4. Sports, Gambling & Recreational Facilities	High	10.6%
5. Management Consulting	High	8.8%
6. Offices of Optometrists, Physiotherapists, Chiropractors and Other Health Practitioners	High	8.7%
7. Software & Computer Services	High	8.2%
8. Industrial Chemicals	High	7.9%
9. Business Services	High	7.2%
10. Medical & Dental Offices	High	6.4%

suggested offering recipes or brochures along with the product, they would have been told brusquely, "We don't do that here."

What a contrast to my recent trip to a liquor retailer in Alberta. I went into a small store to find wine for a dinner party that night and was offered small crêpes Suzettes to taste. Here was retailing for the '90s—including that mysterious substance called customer service.

The above list shows the industries with the largest increases in Knowledge Ratio. Some were smart to begin with and they're expanding their knowledge base by the month, while others are making a run for it, playing catch-up to the world that's changing all around them. If you're looking for the movers and shakers, you'll find them among these Top 10 high-knowledge New Economy industries with the big gains in knowledge workers—the folks who are *paid* to think.

A Secure Future

I don't think it's asking too much, I really don't. A job in an industry that's stable in its growth is not asking for the earth, moon and stars. Only a small percentage of people really thrill to wild adventure. Most of us will never take up skydiving, we'll never get the deep urge to run with the bulls at Pamplona, and, if offered the chance to climb into a formula race car and drive wildly along the corniche at Monte Carlo, most of us would probably wimp out, preferring instead the thrill of watching the race from the grandstand. Let's be honest.

Some industries are forever riding the wild roller coaster. You'll hear management say, "Things are looking up! Hang on to your hats, we're going to grow like mad." And sure enough, the following year, sales soar 60 percent. But, oops, the following year they're headed in the opposite direction, as sales plunge 40 percent. If you happen to like the taste of Maalox or you were born with a cast-iron stomach, you'll enjoy the constant chaos.

If, instead, you would prefer a slightly less frenetic pace, you'll pay close heed to the volatility of the industry's business cycle. Volatility is nothing more than the measure of the rate of change of the industry's growth cycle. It's a simple statistical task to calculate the standard deviation of an industry's business cycle behavior. Some industries are more volatile; other industries are less volatile. And it's up to you to decide how big a thrill you really want.

Before you let Harrison Ford in reruns of *Raiders of the Lost Ark* sway your judgment, think about what the boom–bust routine will do to your life. How, for example, can you consider taking out

TOP 10 LEAST VOLATILE NEW ECONOMY INDUSTRIES

	Standard Deviation
1. Universities	1.6
2. Museums & Archives	1.7
3. Elementary & Secondary Schools	1.8
4. Hospitals	2.4
5. Offices of Optometrists, Physiotherapists, Chiropractors & Other Health Practitioners	2.7
6. Medical & Dental Offices	2.7
7. Nursing Homes & Homes for People with Disabilities	2.7
8. Community-Based Social Services	2.7
9. Community Colleges	3.1
10. Recreational Sports & Clubs	3.7

a mortgage if you don't know from one year to the next whether you'll requalify at the end of the term? Will the industry be in one of those manic phases? Or will you find the head of human resources wandering stark naked along executive row with that strange and glassy look in his eyes . . . again?

If you would prefer the kind of growth that comes without huge volatility, refer to the list of the Top 10 New Economy industries with the lowest standard deviations above.

On the other hand, Harrison, if the bulls at Pamplona are no match for your bravado, here's a handful of industries that will have instant appeal.

TOP 5 MOST VOLATILE NEW ECONOMY INDUSTRIES

	Standard Deviation
1. Motion Picture, Video & Sound Recording	28.8
2. Clothing & Shoe Wholesalers	27.0
3. Steel Pipe & Tube Manufacturing	22.7
4. Management Consulting	21.8
5. Employment Agencies & Professional Search Firms	21.6

The New Economy Rating System for Jobs

If you have a strong desire to *excelerate* your career, this rating system for New Economy jobs will be a useful tool. By all means, read the list of five-star jobs to your children—they need your help and your guidance now. Whether you're the executive vice president in search of a better life or you're one of the many thousands of discouraged workers, who, at the first glimmer of a better economy, are flooding back into the labor force and need a road map, knowing which industries are the superhighways to success, and which ones are the unpaved sideroads leading nowhere, is a first and important step.

How to Interpret the Ratings

⭐ ONE-STAR JOBS—If you're looking for what could very likely be a temporary job, with no particular opportunities for advancement, and you have no interest in building a career.

★★ TWO-STAR JOBS—If modest pay and advancement are acceptable, you can live with some uncertainty about job security, and building a career is not a priority.

★★★ THREE-STAR JOBS—If you're in the market for average pay and average advancement opportunities and can live with some degree of job insecurity.

★★★★ FOUR-STAR JOBS—If you're interested in a secure future and enjoy an interesting learning environment with better-than-average job security and advancement prospects.

★★★★★ FIVE-STAR JOBS—If you're interested in a future and are looking for top prospects and excellent job security in a challenging industry where new ideas are welcomed with open arms.

Turn to Appendix A at page 171 and see for yourself how 157 industries in Canada compare. Each industry is on a separate page, starting with the best ones that the New Economy has to offer. When two or more industries are equally attractive, they have been placed in alphabetical order. Turnaround industries begin on page 259, Watch List industries begin on page 263 and ratings for old economy jobs begin on page 285.

4
A ROAD MAP FOR COMPANIES

Few companies have a mission to downsize themselves into a broom closet. Cost-cutting has become a sacred crusade when the real mission should be one of growth. Corporate executives today could learn useful lessons from the hundreds of industries in the past that faced change, read the wrong signposts and believed that downsizing would save them. Instead, they ended up in a vicious circle, cutting costs every few years in a loser's game of catch-up to the long-term structural decline that gripped their industry.

LIFE IN THE BROOM CLOSET

Just picture this scene in the boardroom. The board of directors waits breathlessly for the corporate announcement of a lifetime. Today, their hand-picked CEO will announce that he has achieved the ultimate corporate goal. This bold visionary hasn't just dreamed the impossible dream—he's achieved it! He hasn't just *cut* costs—he's *eliminated* them.

Gone are all those labor expenses that threatened to put the organization out of business—*the company no longer employs anybody*. Ever-escalating raw material costs and just-in-time inventories are now a thing of the past as well—*the company no longer purchases materials or supplies*. And to heck with Total Quality Management and grasping customers who never seemed satisfied, no matter how low the price—*the company no longer sells anything to anybody*. Finally, those contemptible corporate taxes have also been abolished—*the company no longer has any revenues*.

But show me a company that has no costs, and I'll show you a company that has just gone out of business. Sooner or later, companies have to get back to *growth*.

Rightsizing and Wrongsizing

In the real world, there is rightsizing and there is wrongsizing, and companies of any size and in any line of business must distinguish between the two. Far too many companies—and whole industries, in fact—fall into the trap of downsizing themselves into broom closets. Rightsizing occurs when organizations cut costs because new technologies or processes allow them to introduce efficiencies into a market that is growing structurally. Wrongsizing occurs when companies cut their costs in the mistaken belief that higher margins—on products that no one wants to buy anymore—will return the business to profitability. They won't. And wrongsizing can often do more damage to the business than management ever imagined possible. The oil and gas industry is a vivid example of a sector that wrongsized and paid a high price for its mistake.

When the price of oil collapsed to $12.25 in 1986, many large oil companies responded to the intense pressure on their margins by cutting their costs and laying off 1,366 people between 1986 and 1987. They shrank themselves, and did what everyone else had been blindly doing for years: they assumed that higher margins on structurally declining demand would be their corporate elixir, and that lower costs would tide them over until the world (and their demand curves) returned to "normal." But they weren't just wrong, *they were dead wrong.*

Guess what happens when a company cuts loose several thousand vigorous and talented knowledge workers? Many start their own companies. And those junior oil and gas companies jumped eagerly into natural gas, the fuel of choice for the New Economy. They ran rings around any integrated oil company that sat still, stodgily waiting for its demand curve to rise back up to its former glory. Oil was out, but gas was in.

The Fantasy of the Flesh Wound

Many industries have enormous difficulty confronting the lamentable fact that the demand for a product that has been near and dear to their hearts is slowly dying. There can be many reasons for this sad truth, although they are rarely the reasons that are discussed around the boardroom table or at management meetings. Usually, the demand dies because the world has moved on to other needs and wants, and consumers won't buy as much of what the industries are producing, or won't pay the prices that they once paid. With monotonous regularity, however, management kids itself that its company is only suffering a flesh wound—one that will heal once the recession is over, or the unfair Japanese or Korean competitors (or whomever) have been brought to heel, or the dollar falls to forty cents, or interest rates fall to 3 percent, or regulations are tightened or loosened. . . . Then the world will return to normal. But it never does.

Six little horror stories about six worthy industries should put the *fantasy of the flesh wound* to rest, once and for all. All have lived through savage declines, but none of them had to. Instead, they could have opted to get on with the business of growth.

Horror Story No. 1

In 1977, the meat products industry peaked structurally, and, over the next sixteen miserable years, production of meat products tumbled 23.7 percent in Canada. Of course, the decline in demand didn't happen all at once . . . these things rarely do. Lifestyle changes brought on this structural change: people were choosing different protein sources; an affluent work force was opting for a salad at the food court instead of bologna sandwiches from home. And as immigration and travel changed consumer preferences, the meat products industry suffered slowly, until it finally recognized that it had been roasted alive.

To counter a 23.7 percent collapse in the industry's output, a 5 percent cut in costs is farcical, and trimming the fat by a further 5 or 10 percent is irrelevant. Downsizing alone could never—and hasn't—restore these companies to their former glory. The meat products industry would have been far better served if it had focused on its top line and decided to get back to growth—by asking people what meat products they were interested in and responding to these ideas by using new technologies in its processes; and by finding new markets for its products. Instead, the industry allowed sweeping trends to take control, and cut costs ruthlessly.

But it could have been worse. They could have been in floor tiles.

Horror Story No. 2

The floor tile, linoleum and coating industry slid down the slope of structural change from its peak in 1974. For nineteen nightmarish years, output dropped with a vengeance, declining 37.1 percent between 1974 and September 1994. To have provided even a momentary respite for this industry, the Canadian dollar would have had to have fallen off the face of the earth. There was no point blaming free trade, because the decline was underway before the Canada–U.S. Free Trade Agreement was signed. And don't even think of blaming NAFTA, because Mexico was still primarily a tourist destination when this industry tumbled into the abyss. But instead of doing some serious top line thinking that would have stirred the demand, the industry downsized, wondering what had hit it. The moral of the story is that industries of all shapes and sizes can fit into a broom closet.

Horror Story No. 3

The machinery industry used to be a large and impressive business that generated $4.3 billion of real gross domestic product in this country. But that was in 1980; the industry is 14 percent smaller now. It doesn't buy as much, it doesn't employ as many people and it doesn't pay as much in property taxes anymore—property taxes on broom closets are quite reasonable, even in expensive cities such as Toronto. Instead of pulling itself up by its bootstraps, the machinery industry downsized. It should have been embracing new technologies and making brilliant new inroads into the burgeoning business of instrumentation, robotics and computer-assisted manufacturing, but instead the industry concentrated on moving backward. It could and should have moved forward into the New Economy.

Horror Story No. 4

In 1984, joggers were still content to plod along in their self-inflicted pain, racquetball was still the rage and Trivial Pursuit was still a fun game to play (until you realized that the people you played with had memorized all the answers). Structural change can creep up on any industry and in the most unexpected ways. After the sporting goods and toy industry peaked ten years ago, wave after wave of structural change swept over it, and by late 1994 the industry was a pale reflection of its former self, smaller by over 20 percent. An aging population can be both friend and foe: it shuts down some product lines but opens vast new opportunities in other sports, such as birdwatching and fishing. But when was the last time you came across a birding store at the local mall, or flipped through *People* magazine and saw an advertisement for fishing gear? Instead of becoming top line thinkers in this growing New Economy, the sporting goods and toy industry focused on its bottom line and watched it shrink, slowly but surely. But it didn't have to be that way.

Horror Story No. 5

Despite every environmental reason in its favor—as well as the fact that it's cheaper and sometimes faster than our offending automobiles—Canada's urban transit system peaked structurally in 1981, and the industry, measured by its real gross domestic product, downsized by 47.5 percent over the next twelve years. Many of the mounting transit deficits have strained the public purse strings mightily, and we should be grateful that the manufacturers of women's white gloves never had access to tax money the way many transit systems have. Instead of recognizing the new needs of a changing population (the lack of a decent transit system to York University, with its population of over 50,000, is incredulous in this day and age), the industry has idled in the slow lane, and has paid a high and unnecessary price.

Horror Story No. 6

The beverage industry in Canada is the ultimate good news/bad news example of how some segments of an industry can drown, while others can catch the next wave. Distillery products peaked in

1977, and by late 1994 had contracted by 54 percent. The brewing industry's decline, in contrast, has been rather gentle, at 17.5 percent from its peak in 1979—thanks, in part, to the temerity of micro breweries who, like the junior players in the natural gas industry, found new markets and cooked up popular new products. But the big splash in the beverage industry has been created by soft drinks. Together, the bottled water winners in the marketplace and the private label market for soft drinks have helped the industry catch the next wave of growth. The soft drink segment exemplifies how any industry can seize opportunities and change with the times.

Don't Unplug Your Knowledge Assets

In far too many industries, wrongsizing isn't just sort of the wrong thing to do—it's the *worst* thing to do. When restructuring begins to bite at the bone—*at the knowledge base and knowledge capital of the organization*—these companies end up creating their next wave of competitors, as the oil industry learned the hard way in the 1980s. Their erstwhile employees build new organizations that in many cases are unencumbered by the old corporate infrastructure they left behind.

In the old economy, few companies would have seriously considered unplugging their equipment or selling off their machinery when tough times hit. In the New Economy, knowledge assets have replaced physical assets as the basis for a company's growth and future prosperity. No company can afford to make the mistake of laying off its assets base because it will need those knowledge assets when it begins to grow again.

The essential lesson that corporate Canada needs to learn is that there is a world of difference between rightsizing and wrongsizing. And the most useful tool that I have discovered to distinguish between the two is the Knowledge Ratio. When a company rightsizes, its Knowledge Ratio will either hold steady or even rise

63

briskly as new cost-saving technologies or processes are introduced or re-engineered. But it's a different story when a company wrong-sizes—the number of employees drops, the payroll costs drop . . . and the Knowledge Ratio drops, draining the company of the intellectual capital vital to its future success. I have often wondered how much growth companies could have financed for themselves and their stakeholders if, instead of doling out generous severance packages, they had used those hundreds of millions of dollars to finance new growth.

Top Line Thinking in the New Economy

Rigorous financial stewardship that keeps a company's costs to a minimum should be a given in any economy, old or new. Cost control is never out of style. But there is a huge difference between a bottom line that *looks* good because costs have fallen faster than the company's revenues—and a bottom line that *is* good because the company's top line is growing rapidly. A handsome bottom line can be a mirage or a reality, and some companies, strange as it may seem, opt for the mirage, believing that their top line is growing when it isn't and won't.

Back in the heyday of the old economy, the simple solution for a company intent on growth was either to buy a competitor or, when those became scarce, to buy into a related industry, and integrate vertically or horizontally. Companies employed this strategy, secure in the belief that their industry was growing and that related industries would also enjoy long-term structural growth. Timing mistakes were made—buying high, just before a recession hit, for example—but a year or two later the industry would return to normal and begin to grow once again.

Many a CEO has spent a sleepless night pondering how a large company can get even larger in today's economy. The inevitable answer is usually some kind of acquisition, especially if the company has some cash on the balance sheet (although a lack of cash has never deterred some). What far too many old economy companies have yet to realize is that, in this New Economy, they can't *buy* the future— but they can *create* it.

Here are three good reasons why an old economy strategy of buying growth can be a recipe for New Economy disaster.

1. Buying a larger share of a declining industry creates only the illusion of growth. If companies actually stopped to think about it, few would choose to become a bigger fish in a pond that's evaporating. Becoming the largest producer of goods or services that no one wants to buy anymore does a real disservice to the company's shareholders.

2. If your current product lines have no real future, chances are that your main suppliers or buyers probably have little potential for growth. Contiguous industries aren't always in the same boat, but they often can be.

3. Buying into a New Economy industry that you know little about can doom you to disaster from the start, because there will be little or no synergy in the knowledge base. It may be tempting for a fish products manufacturer to buy into a semi-conductor manufacturer, but believe me, they'd be better off if they diversified into aquaculture.

The best answer is to look deep into your industry—the one you know the most about—and position yourself as a supplier to the New Economy. You can often find important growth segments right beneath your nose. They will allow you to develop the new products that people want to buy, to introduce new technologies that could revitalize your company and to find a secure place in new and growing markets.

We've Got to Get Back to Growth

I remember vividly a meeting in my office with the CEO of a U.S. paper and forest products company. The usual practice at meetings of this nature is to shake hands, exchange a few polite pleasantries in the boardroom over coffee or tea (which is served in the good china cups and saucers), and then warmly present everyone at the meeting with a business card.

This meeting was different from the start. The very first thing the CEO said as he shook my hand was, "Get me out of my industry—I can't stand it anymore." An odd way for a meeting to begin, admittedly. I asked if he would like some coffee and suggested that he tell me if he had any ideas, at this stage, of what he might like to get into when he got out of the industry he was in. "Yes, yes," he said, "get me into semiconductors. That's an engine, and I want to be an engine." He had obviously read my first book, *Shifting Gears*. A question raced through my mind: *Could I honestly see this company going nose-to-nose and toe-to-toe with Intel?*

As we talked at great length about his forest products company, about the product lines and market pressures and competitive forces in the industry, not just in the North American market, but globally, I zeroed in, deliberately, on the segments of his industry that were particularly well positioned in the New Economy. We considered the new grades of paper that had a future in today's markets, the voracious demand for computer paper in the workplace (they lied when they promised us a paperless society), and in the burgeoning home computer market. Why, every week a household shopping list would now include bathroom tissue, paper towels and computer paper. We discussed the opportunities for *new* products in an old industry, and how the horizon for recycled paper products was expanding before our eyes. Never mind the old economy and the long term decline in newsprint.

Before our first meeting had drawn to a close we had agreed that it would make far better sense for him to keep his company in an industry where its knowledge base could really count for something, and reposition the company, instead, into the segments of the paper industry that were either in the New Economy or highly leveraged to it. We agreed that our next step would be to lay out a strategy in which his company would become a premier supplier of paper products to some of the mightiest engines driving the New Economy. As the meeting drew to a close, we did exchange business cards—with *genuine* warmth.

It is essential for company managers to get a fix on whether or not their companies have a real future in the New Economy, at least to know where they stand. If you find that you're in the old economy, don't go jumping off the nearest bridge—or into semiconductors! There are very practical ways to reposition your firm into New Economy segments of old economy industries, or to restructure your company with some merger and acquisition work at the division level or to market your way into the New Economy, simply but effectively.

If your company has a genuine desire to grow and adapt, to become a creator of wealth in this country and to position itself for a world of global growth, it is worth spending the time to create a New Economy business plan for your organization. You don't need to take a leave of absence or cancel meetings and appointments for the next three weeks—just work quickly and quietly through the following four New Economy workbooks, using numbers that every company, large or small, has at its fingertips, and if you have any questions, call me.

DOES YOUR COMPANY HAVE A FUTURE IN THE NEW ECONOMY?

*Excel*erate Mini-Workbook No.1

Does Your Company Have a Future in the New Economy?

To determine whether your company is in the New Economy, the old economy, on the Watch List or in a Turnaround industry that is quickly catching the next wave of long-term growth, follow these steps and then fill in the mini-workbook that follows.

Step 1: Check off the industries that you are in. You're doing *nothing more complicated* here than listing what industries your company is in. If you are in one industry only, check off the one you're in. If you are in six different businesses, check off the six you're in. (This has nothing to do with the industries that you are selling to—that will come later.)

Step 2: Beside each industry you have checked off, write in the company revenues that you derived from that industry last year.

Step 3: Add up the total revenues that appear on the New Economy page, and quickly calculate the percentage of your company revenues that the New Economy represents for your firm. Then do the same for the old economy, the Watch List and Turnarounds. You now have a rough idea of where you stand. You know four very meaningful ratios that tell you what percentage of your company is in the New Economy, the old economy, on the Watch List or in Turnaround industries.

NEW ECONOMY ENGINES & SUPPLIERS

The following industries have not peaked structurally. While they ride the normal ups and downs of a business cycle, they are underpinned by long-term structural growth. Recession years are followed by strong and lengthy recoveries to new industry production records.

NAME OF INDUSTRY	YOUR REVENUES
___Software & Computer Services	$_____
___Natural Gas Distribution Systems	_____
___Pharmaceutical Manufacturing	_____
___Electric Power Industry	_____
___Elementary & Secondary Schools	_____
___Plastics & Synthetic Resins Manufacturing	_____
___Electrical & Electronic Equipment Wholesalers	_____
___Waste Management	_____
___Communications Equipment	_____
___Community Colleges	_____
___Museums & Archives	_____
___Offices of Optometrists, Physiotherapists, Chiropractors & Other Health Practitioners	_____
___Universities	_____
___Hospitals	_____
___Medical & Dental Offices	_____
___Pipeline Transportation	_____
___Spectator Sports, Gambling & Recreational Facilities	_____
___Agricultural Chemicals & Fertilizer Manufacturing	_____

NAME OF INDUSTRY	YOUR REVENUES
___Engineering, Architecture & Technical & Scientific Services	$_____
___Motion Picture, Video & Sound Recording Industry	_____
___Recreational Sports & Clubs	_____
___Accounting Firms & Bookkeeping Services	_____
___Community Based Social Services	_____
___Consumer & Business Financing	_____
___Telephone Companies & Telecommunications Carriers	_____
___Water Transportation Services	_____
___Business Services	_____
___Hairdressing Businesses	_____
___Logging & Forestry	_____
___Non-metal Mining	_____
___Commercial Printing	_____
___Heavy Engineering & Industrial Construction	_____
___Lawyers & Notaries Offices	_____
___Libraries	_____
___Metal & Metal Products Wholesalers	_____
___Newspaper & Magazine Publishing & Printing	_____
___Non-ferrous Smelting & Refining	_____
___Paint & Varnish Manufacturing	_____
___Associations, Unions & Religious Organizations	_____
___Machine Shops	_____
___Pharmacies & Drug Stores	_____
___Computer Manufacturing	_____
___Heating Equipment Manufacturing	_____
___Restaurants & Catering	_____

NAME OF INDUSTRY	YOUR REVENUES
___Aircraft & Parts Manufacturing	$_____
___Nursing Homes & Homes for People with Disabilities	_____
___Water Transportation, Shipping & Ferries	_____
___Advertising Agencies	_____
___Management Consulting	_____
___Fruit & Vegetable Processing	_____
___Investment Dealers & Investment Management	_____
___Sawmills, Planing & Shingle Mills	_____
___Coal Mining	_____
___Hardware, Tools & Cutlery Manufacturing	_____
___Publishing	_____
___Trucking & Transport	_____
___Food Wholesalers	_____
___Food Stores & Supermarkets	_____
___Hardware, Plumbing, Heating & Air Conditioning Equipment Wholesalers	_____
___Bus, Truck & Van Manufacturing	_____
___Department Stores	_____
___Commercial & Industrial Builders & Developers	_____
___Employment Agencies & Professional Search Firms	_____
___Highway & Heavy Construction	_____
___Hotels & Motels	_____
___Men's Clothing Stores	_____
___Ornamental & Architectural Metal Products Manufacturing	_____
___Plastic Products Manufacturing	_____

| | YOUR |
NAME OF INDUSTRY	REVENUES
___Wooden Prefab Buildings, Cabinets, Door & Window Manufacturing	$_____
___Children's Clothing Stores & Miscellaneous Clothing Retailers	_____
___Women's Clothing Stores	_____
___Bedding, Hotel & Restaurant Furniture Manufacturing	_____
___Clothing & Shoe Wholesalers	_____
___Electric Wire & Cable Manufacturing	_____
___Industrial Chemicals Manufacturing	_____
___Movie Theaters	_____
___Platemaking, Typesetting & Bindery	_____
___Recreational Vehicle Dealers	_____
___Steel Pipe & Tube Manufacturing	_____

Your company's leverage to
New Economy Engines and Suppliers $_____

What percentage of your
total company revenues
does this figure account for?   _____%

TURNAROUND INDUSTRIES

The following industries have peaked structurally, but have begun to turn around and have started to display many of the characteristics of industries that are underpinned by growth. Their future could be far better than their past, and they warrant close attention.

NAME OF INDUSTRY	YOUR REVENUES
___Rubber Products & Tire Manufacturing	$_____
___Cosmetics, Perfumes & Personal Care Products Manufacturing	_____
___Stamped, Pressed & Coated Metal Manufacturing	_____
Your company's leverage to Turnaround industries	$_____
What percentage of your total company revenues does this figure account for?	_____%

WATCH LIST INDUSTRIES

The following industries have not peaked structurally, but have clearly peaked in the United States or are displaying many of the characteristics of industries that are about to peak. They could go either way.

NAME OF INDUSTRY	YOUR REVENUES
___Federal Government	$_____
___Municipal & Local Governments	_____
___Insurance Companies	_____
___Provincial Governments	_____
___Banks	_____
___Motor Vehicle Manufacturing	_____
___Car Dealerships	_____
___Railroads	_____
___Credit Unions	_____
___Auto Parts Manufacturing	_____
___Airlines	_____
___Auto Parts & Accessories Stores	_____
___Insurance & Real Estate Agencies	_____
___Real Estate Operators	_____
___Motor Vehicle & Parts Wholesalers	_____
___Motor Vehicle Repair Shops	_____
___Trust Companies	_____
___Airport & Aircraft Servicing	_____
___Gas Stations	_____
___Homebuilders	_____

Your company's leverage
to Watch List industries $_____

What percentage of your
total company revenues
does this figure account for?   _____%

75

OLD ECONOMY INDUSTRIES

The following industries are past their peak in terms of contributing to gross domestic product. As industries peak, their free-fall is more severe than could reasonably be associated with a recession. Subsequent business cycle recoveries do not bring the industry back to its past glory.

However, old economy industries can become integrated into the growing New Economy by producing new goods, using new technologies to revitalize the industry, and by finding new markets, either domestically or abroad.

NAME OF INDUSTRY	YOUR REVENUES
___Broadcasting	$_____
___Dairy Products Manufacturing	_____
___Public Transit	_____
___Railcar and Locomotive Manufacturing	_____
___Machinery & Equipment Wholesalers for Construction, Forestry & Mining	_____
___Tobacco Products	_____
___Petroleum & Natural Gas Exploration	_____
___Petroleum Products Wholesalers	_____
___Paper Box, Carton & Bag Manufacturing	_____
___Petroleum Refining	_____
___Plumbing Fixtures, Valves, Pipes, & Other Fabricated Metal Products	_____
___Printing Ink, Adhesives & Additives Manufacturing	_____
___Ready-Mix Concrete Manufacturing & Delivery	_____
___Agricultural Implements	_____

NAME OF INDUSTRY	YOUR REVENUES
___Beverage Manufacturing	$_____
___Dry Cleaners & Laundries	_____
___Feed, Flour & Cereal Manufacturing	_____
___Detergent & Cleaning Products Manufacturing	_____
___Pulp & Paper Manufacturing	_____
___Bakery Products Manufacturing	_____
___Cement Manufacturing	_____
___Household Appliance & Furniture Wholesalers	_____
___Primary Textile Manufacturing	_____
___Shipbuilding & Repair	_____
___Steel Manufacturing	_____
___General Food Products Manufacturing	_____
___Meat & Poultry Products Manufacturing	_____
___Veneer & Plywood Manufacturing	_____
___Metal Mining	_____
___Major Appliance Manufacturing	_____
___Office Furniture Manufacturing	_____
___Construction, Mining, Sawmill & Materials Handling Equipment Manufacturing, Power Transmission Equipment & Compressors	_____
___Industrial Machinery, Equipment & Supply Wholesalers	_____
___Lumber & Building Material Wholesalers	_____
___Textile Products Manufacturing	_____
___Wire & Wire Products Manufacturing	_____
___Concrete Products Manufacturing	_____

NAME OF INDUSTRY	YOUR REVENUES
___Retail Fabric & Yarn Stores	$_____
___Steel Plate & Fabricated Metal Products Manufacturing	_____
___Iron Foundries	_____
___Shoe Stores	_____
___Glass & Glass Products Manufacturing	_____
___Household Furniture, Appliance & Furnishings Stores	_____
___Household Furniture Manufacturing	_____
___Leather Products Manufacturing	_____
___Bars, Night Clubs & Taverns	_____
___Coated & Treated Paper Products Manufacturing	_____
___Commercial Refrigeration & Air Conditioning Manufacturing	_____
___Drilling Contractors	_____
___Farm Machinery, Equipment & Supply Wholesalers	_____
___Fish Products	_____
___Office & Store Equipment & Supplies Wholesalers	_____
___Snowmobile & All-Terrain Vehicle Manufacturing	_____
___Storage & Warehousing	_____
___Sugar & Candy Manufacturing	_____

Your company's leverage
to old economy industries $_____

What percentage of your
total company revenues
does this figure account for?   _____%

*   *   *

Were you surprised by some of the sectors that are in the New Economy? Most people are. It's tempting to assume that only high-tech industries are growing structurally, or that only "new" industries have a future worth talking about.

One of my favorite industries is agriculture. It's a mouth-watering example of an industry that has demonstrated remarkable resilience and adaptability to change through the ages. Tractors have replaced the horse-drawn plow, new crops have replaced old crops, and agriculture is at the forefront of the New Economy as a big user of (New Economy) information beamed down by (New Economy) satellites. While the whole sector faces enormous challenges as marketing boards fall by the wayside, as the GATT changes world trade and as governments lose their ability to subsidize the hardy folks who feed us, I'm very hopeful that agriculture will continue to adapt, and that it will seize the huge opportunities that are sure to come about as the result of breathtaking advances in biotechnology.

Another of my pet examples is ornamental and architectural metal products, an industry that's been around since the days of Robin Hood, when the Sheriff of Nottingham would lower the iron gate at the castle while his men searched the keep in vain. The demand for castle gates has been in long-term structural decline for a couple of centuries (we hear that Robert Campeau tried to revive demand a few years back, but without success), but the good news is that the industry has adapted well: the hot product today is wrought-iron patio furniture. As long as the industry continues to introduce new products people want to buy, it will remain a player in any new economy that comes our way.

Food stores may not leap to your mind as thriving businesses in the New Economy either, but rest assured that the industry is alive and well in this world of change. When Loblaws introduced its President's Choice line, it single-handedly globalized our shopping carts each week with "Memories of Singapore" and dozens of

NEW ECONOMY HALL OF FAME

BC Telecom Inc.

BCE Inc.

BCE Mobile Communications Inc.

Bracknell Corporation

C-Mac Industries Inc.

CAE Inc.

Canadian General Investments Limited

Canadian Tire Corporation, Limited

Cara Operations Limited

Central Fund of Canada Limited

Chai-Na-Ta Corp.

Cinram Ltd.

Cognos Incorporated

Cominco Fertilizers Ltd.

Corel Corporation

EMCO Limited

G.T.C. Transcontinental Group Ltd.

Gandalf Technologies Inc.

International Verifact Inc.

Interprovincial Pipe Line System Inc.

IPSCO Inc.

ISG Technologies, Inc.

ISM Information Systems Management Corporation

Kaufel Group Ltd.

Mackenzie Financial Corporation

Maritime Telegraph & Telephone Company, Limited

MDS Health Group Limited

Métro-Richelieu Inc.

Mitel Corporation

Moore Corporation Limited

Newbridge Networks Corporation

Newtel Enterprises Limited

Northern Telecom

Nova Corporation

Nova Scotia Power Inc.

Philip Environmental Inc.

Premdor Inc.

Provigo Inc.

Québec-Téléphone

Quebecor Printing Inc.

Scott's Hospitality Inc.

Sears Canada Inc.

SHL Systemhouse Inc.

Softkey Software Products Inc.

SR Telecom Inc.

Teleglobe Inc.

Telus Corporation

The North West Company Inc.

The Toronto Sun Publishing Corporation

Torstar Corporation

Transalta Corporation

United Corporations Limited

other taste treats that only a global village could offer. Long gone (and sadly missed) are the Meatloaf Mondays of our childhood.

New Economy Hall of Fame

The simple fact is that if an industry continues to introduce new products that people want to buy; if it uses New Economy technologies to revitalize its industry; and if it finds new markets, it will remain a part of every New Economy that comes along. So what if an industry isn't an engine? Suppliers succeed as well, as our friend in forest products discovered to his sheer delight.

But you can always find companies that are going the wrong way. They either have a wretched sense of direction, or, at the very least, they're getting bad advice. And you need to ensure that your company isn't one of them. That's why we track the trend in these ratios for our clients. It may be a huge relief to discover that you're deriving 60 percent of your revenues from New Economy businesses, but relief can quickly turn to desperation if you find that this figure is way down from what it was a few years ago, when your company was deriving 70 percent of its revenues from New Economy sectors! Obviously, you're going the wrong way.

When we calculated these ratios for publicly traded companies, we found plenty of good news and plenty of bad news. Many companies had rapidly rising New Economy ratios, and I am sure that sharing this news with the readers of their annual reports would do their stock prices a world of good in today's market.

Fifty-two companies on the TSE 300 have New Economy ratios of 100 percent—meaning that 100 percent of their revenues were derived last year from selling into the New Economy. Opposite is the New Economy Hall of Fame: the companies that deserve recognition for how well they are positioned to achieve long-term structural growth. Investors looking for TSE 300 companies that are

Good Customers, Bad Customers

If the New Economy ratio that you have just finished calculating isn't quite as high as you would like it to be; or, if you find yourself stuck in the old economy; or, if you're in the New Economy, but have the uneasy feeling that your customers aren't, the next three mini-workbooks will help you to set your course, for two reasons:

- Old economy companies can market their way into the New Economy by attaching themselves to a New Economy customer base.
- Corporate history books are littered with examples of New Economy companies that had good products and bad customers.

In the real world, there are good customers and there are bad customers—and your company's future depends on your managers being able to tell the difference between the two.

What's a bad customer? Invariably, it's an old economy customer that can't even afford to pay its rent anymore—*so how on earth can you expect it to help you pay yours?* Old economy customers are nice people, but are you willing to risk the future of your company and the livelihoods of your employees for a customer who has not changed, or will not get on with the business of growth? I'm all for nurturing a prospective client, and there are lots of companies worth waiting for, but you need to draw the line. I do so whenever I see a company sitting down and waiting for the (not-so-inevitable) end to happen.

The insurance industry is a particular favorite of mine because I admire the vitality of most of the people in it, and it tends to be populated by those who really enjoy dealing with others. That's why I was so surprised when an agent who had attended a seminar I had given in the United States faxed me a letter filled with frustration and disappointment. He had made a mid-life career change and joined a highly respected insurance company, a household name in the southern states. But after a few years in the business, he was far behind the high hopes he had set for himself. He asked me for some marketing advice. As he described the potential clients he had been visiting and revisiting with no obvious success, I was quite sure that he had been stocking his appointment book with old economy leads. I was right. This poor man had spent *years*—not days, or weeks, or even months—*years* trying to sign up people and companies who were wedded to the old economy. "Come back next month (or year), when the business picks up, and then we'll do something" was a phrase he had heard over and over again.

But it's not just insurance agents, it's lawyers, accountants, engineers, consultants, stockbrokers and a long list of other professionals who unwittingly stock their electronic Rolodex with old economy prospects. And there are many New Economy companies that now wish that they had hitched their wagon to a New Economy client base, instead of to the old economy customers who went out of business—and took their New Economy suppliers with them.

This mini-workbook will guide you through the task of classifying your customers. Are you selling to the New Economy, the old economy, the Watch List or to Turnaround industries? First, follow these steps.

Step 1: Take a printout of the list that breaks down your company revenues by client.

Step 2: Beside each customer's name, write in "New Economy," "old economy," "Watch List" or "Turnaround," depending on the industry each one is in.

Step 3: Now, add up your company's revenues coming from your customers that are in each group—New Economy, old economy, Watch List, and Turnaround industries. Mark the total for each category on the worksheet.

Step 4: Calculate what percentage of your total revenues are coming from customers in each category.

GOOD CUSTOMERS, BAD CUSTOMERS

List your customers and the revenues you receive from each. Then, beside each name, write **New Economy**, **Turnaround**, **Watch List** or **old economy**, according to the industry each customer is in. See Mini-Workbook No.1 for industry classifications.

NEW ECONOMY = N
TURNAROUND = T
WATCH LIST = W

YOUR CUSTOMERS	REVENUES	OLD ECONOMY = O
_____	$_____	_____
_____	$_____	_____
_____	$_____	_____
_____	$_____	_____
_____	$_____	_____
_____	$_____	_____
_____	$_____	_____
_____	$_____	_____
_____	$_____	_____
_____	$_____	_____
_____	$_____	_____
_____	$_____	_____
_____	$_____	_____
_____	$_____	_____
_____	$_____	_____
_____	$_____	_____
_____	$_____	_____
_____	$_____	_____
_____	$_____	_____
_____	$_____	_____
_____	$_____	_____
_____	$_____	_____
_____	$_____	_____
_____	$_____	_____
_____	$_____	_____
_____	$_____	_____

		NEW ECONOMY = N
		TURNAROUND = T
		WATCH LIST = W
YOUR CUSTOMERS	REVENUES	OLD ECONOMY = O

YOUR CUSTOMERS	REVENUES	
_____	$_____	_____
_____	$_____	_____
_____	$_____	_____
_____	$_____	_____
_____	$_____	_____
_____	$_____	_____
_____	$_____	_____
_____	$_____	_____
_____	$_____	_____
_____	$_____	_____
_____	$_____	_____
_____	$_____	_____
_____	$_____	_____
_____	$_____	_____
_____	$_____	_____
_____	$_____	_____
_____	$_____	_____
_____	$_____	_____
_____	$_____	_____
_____	$_____	_____
_____	$_____	_____
_____	$_____	_____
_____	$_____	_____
_____	$_____	_____
_____	$_____	_____
_____	$_____	_____
_____	$_____	_____

Your company's total revenues: $_____ % of total **100%**

Total revenues from New Economy customers: $_____ % of total _____

Total revenues from Turnaround customers: $_____ % of total _____

Total revenues from Watch List customers: $_____ % of total _____

Total revenues from old economy customers: $_____ % of total _____

*   *   *

By now, you're either jumping for joy or reaching for the nearest bottle of Excedrin. If your company is in the New Economy and is selling to the New Economy, that's a doubleheader. If your company is in the old economy, but you're selling to the New Economy, you'll be okay. Believe me, you'll probably do just fine because you're already positioned as a supplier to the New Economy.

But heaven help you if you're in the old economy and you're selling to the old economy. Or, if your company is in the New Economy, but your customers aren't. And you have some real business planning to do if your company is in the New Economy, but your revenues are from the Watch List.

MARKETING TO THE NEW ECONOMY

***Excele*rate** Mini-Workbook No. 3

MARKETING TO THE NEW ECONOMY

In this third mini-workbook, you'll get the chance to examine your company's marketing plan for next year from a New Economy perspective. Take the time to fill this mini-workbook out if you're in the New Economy and want to stay there, or if your company isn't quite what you hoped it would be. Because, when all else fails, you can market your way into the New Economy. And I'm going to show you how.

Step 1: Get your marketing list for the next year—the names of the companies that you will be targeting for sales in your company's next fiscal year.

Step 2: Beside each potential customer's name, write "New Economy," "old economy," "Watch List" or "Turnaround," depending on the industry each one is in.

Step 3: Now, add up your company's expected revenues from your potential customers that are in each group—New Economy, old economy, Watch List and Turnaround industries. Mark the total for each category on the worksheet.

Step 4: Calculate what percentage of your total expected revenues are forecast to come from potential customers in each category.

MARKETING TO THE NEW ECONOMY

List your marketing prospects and the revenues you are forecasting from each potential customer. Then, beside each name, write **New Economy**, **Turnaround**, **Watch List** or **old economy**, according to the industry each customer is in. See Mini-Workbook No.1 for industry classifications.

YOUR PROSPECTS	EXPECTED REVENUES	NEW ECONOMY =N TURNAROUND =T WATCH LIST =W OLD ECONOMY =O
_____	$_____	_____
_____	$_____	_____
_____	$_____	_____
_____	$_____	_____
_____	$_____	_____
_____	$_____	_____
_____	$_____	_____
_____	$_____	_____
_____	$_____	_____
_____	$_____	_____
_____	$_____	_____
_____	$_____	_____
_____	$_____	_____
_____	$_____	_____
_____	$_____	_____
_____	$_____	_____
_____	$_____	_____
_____	$_____	_____
_____	$_____	_____
_____	$_____	_____
_____	$_____	_____
_____	$_____	_____
_____	$_____	_____
_____	$_____	_____
_____	$_____	_____
_____	$_____	_____

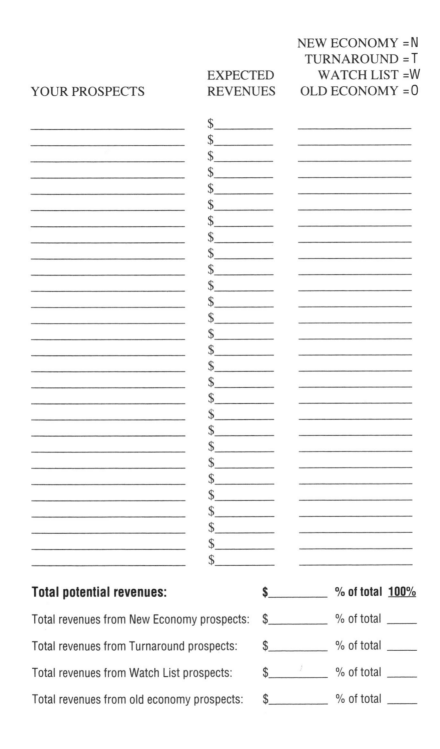

		NEW ECONOMY =N
		TURNAROUND =T
	EXPECTED	WATCH LIST =W
YOUR PROSPECTS	REVENUES	OLD ECONOMY =O

_____	$_____	_____
_____	$_____	_____
_____	$_____	_____
_____	$_____	_____
_____	$_____	_____
_____	$_____	_____
_____	$_____	_____
_____	$_____	_____
_____	$_____	_____
_____	$_____	_____
_____	$_____	_____
_____	$_____	_____
_____	$_____	_____
_____	$_____	_____
_____	$_____	_____
_____	$_____	_____
_____	$_____	_____
_____	$_____	_____
_____	$_____	_____
_____	$_____	_____
_____	$_____	_____
_____	$_____	_____
_____	$_____	_____
_____	$_____	_____
_____	$_____	_____
_____	$_____	_____
_____	$_____	_____
_____	$_____	_____
_____	$_____	_____
_____	$_____	_____

Total potential revenues: $_____   % of total <u>100%</u>

Total revenues from New Economy prospects: $_____   % of total _____

Total revenues from Turnaround prospects: $_____   % of total _____

Total revenues from Watch List prospects: $_____   % of total _____

Total revenues from old economy prospects: $_____   % of total _____

Within a very short space of time, you have calculated the first and vital hard numbers about your company's future in the New Economy. And you also have a no-frills (and free!) overview of how your company is positioned.

While my firm always goes into much greater detail than the broad industry approach taken here, a bird's eye view is better than flying blind.

FINDING
NEW CUSTOMERS
IN THE NEW ECONOMY

Excelerate Mini-Workbook No. 4

Finding New Customers

There are probably a dozen or more industries that you could supply your products to, if you set your mind to it. Most companies have more than one product, which in turn has more than one application. In one of my firm's newsletters, we publish a list of "What's Growing and What's Not" in the New Economy with a monthly ranking of their growth rates. I have reproduced the latest list for you here. Take a close look at the New Economy industries and suppliers. Surely you can sell something to someone.

Step 1: Take a magic marker and highlight the industries that you could target *now*. Keep in mind that these industries are growing rapidly. They're in "buying mode," they're expanding and someone has to supply their needs. Why not you?

Step 2: Check a couple of business directories at the local library, and jot down the names and phone numbers of companies in these New Economy industries. (My firm took the largest data base of this kind in Canada and classified every industry into New Economy, old economy, Watch List and Turnaround. We then listed the name, telephone number, postal code and president's name of every company in each industry.)

Step 3: Generate some sales in the New Economy. Hit the ground running. Score some quick hits. That's probably all it will take to convince your colleagues that your company will be further ahead with a New Economy business plan than with an old economy one. One or two quick successes and you will also have quelled the skeptics in the crowd, who will try to convince you that *"there's nothing we can do. . . ."*

WHAT'S GROWING AND WHAT'S NOT

Fastest Growing New Economy Engines and Suppliers
Ranked by Percentage Change from a Year Ago
Based on Real GDP as of December 1994

RANK THIS MONTH	PERCENT CHANGE FROM 12 MONTHS AGO	RANK LAST MONTH	INDUSTRY	PERCENT CHANGE FROM 1 MONTH AGO	PERCENT CHANGE FROM 3 MONTHS AGO	PERCENT CHANGE FROM 6 MONTHS AGO
(1)	69.39	(1)	COMPUTERS	3.51	22.53	35.10
(2)	18.49	(4)	MACHINE SHOPS	3.20	-1.46	9.19
(3)	18.02	(5)	QUARRIES & SAND PITS	1.31	3.21	8.47
(4)	16.12	(20)	FRUITS & VEGETABLES	5.13	7.75	9.37
(5)	15.72	(3)	TRUCKS MANUFACTURING	-4.23	-0.87	2.73
(6)	15.67	(2)	STEEL PIPE & TUBE	-4.75	-3.07	3.71
(7)	15.17	(9)	FABRICATED METAL PRODUCTS	1.37	4.00	8.84
(8)	14.51	(18)	PLASTIC & SYNTHETIC RESINS	2.23	6.76	8.89
(9)	14.34	(14)	PLASTIC PRODUCTS	4.68	4.02	6.80
(10)	14.19	(7)	POULTRY PRODUCTS	1.71	8.45	13.10
(11)	14.11	(6)	NON-METALLIC MINERAL PRODUCTS NEC.	-2.74	3.85	9.26
(12)	12.85	(12)	PRE-FAB. BUILDINGS, DOORS & BEAMS	0.51	-0.43	-0.34
(13)	12.58	(11)	HARDWARE, TOOLS & CUTLERY	1.19	-0.92	1.70
(14)	12.29	(28)	ENTERTAINMENT	2.89	1.30	3.96
(15)	10.67	(8)	SALT MINES	-1.33	7.84	2.48
(16)	10.62	(24)	PAINT & VARNISH	-1.07	0.88	1.06
(17)	9.82	(27)	PIPELINE TRANSPORT	1.69	1.70	2.29
(18)	9.27	(45)	COAL MINES	4.29	0.67	6.99
(19)	8.46	(19)	TRUCK TRANSPORT	1.37	4.08	5.52
(20)	8.17	(17)	TELECOMMUNICATIONS CARRIERS	0.86	2.04	3.36
(21)	7.40	(52)	NON-METAL MINES EX. COAL & ASBESTOS	7.58	-10.52	-9.41
(22)	7.22	(22)	ACCOMMODATIONS & FOOD SERVICES	0.53	0.05	1.78
(23)	7.07	(40)	PHARMACEUTICALS	0.13	-2.91	-0.50
(24)	5.96	(25)	OTHER WOOD	3.29	5.58	11.78
(25)	4.99	(32)	HEATING EQUIPMENT	0.00	1.80	6.90

FINDING NEW CUSTOMERS
IN THE NEW ECONOMY

New Economy industries that you could sell to <u>now</u>

Consult Mini-Workbook No. 1 for a list of New Economy engines and supplier industries. Then select ten industries that you could sell your existing goods or services to *now*.

1._____

COMPANIES IN THE INDUSTRY:

    1._____TEL:_____
    2._____TEL:_____
    3._____TEL:_____
    4._____TEL:_____
    5._____TEL:_____

2._____

COMPANIES IN THE INDUSTRY:

    1._____TEL:_____
    2._____TEL:_____
    3._____TEL:_____
    4._____TEL:_____
    5._____TEL:_____

3._____

COMPANIES IN THE INDUSTRY:

    1._____TEL:_____

    2._____TEL:_____

    3._____TEL:_____

    4._____TEL:_____

    5._____TEL:_____

4._____

COMPANIES IN THE INDUSTRY:

    1._____TEL:_____

    2._____TEL:_____

    3._____TEL:_____

    4._____TEL:_____

    5._____TEL:_____

5._____

COMPANIES IN THE INDUSTRY:

    1._____TEL:_____

    2._____TEL:_____

    3._____TEL:_____

    4._____TEL:_____

    5._____TEL:_____

6._____

COMPANIES IN THE INDUSTRY:

    1._____TEL:_____

    2._____TEL:_____

    3._____TEL:_____

    4._____TEL:_____

    5._____TEL:_____

7._____

COMPANIES IN THE INDUSTRY:

    1._____TEL:_____
    2._____TEL:_____
    3._____TEL:_____
    4._____TEL:_____
    5._____TEL:_____

8._____

COMPANIES IN THE INDUSTRY:

    1._____TEL:_____
    2._____TEL:_____
    3._____TEL:_____
    4._____TEL:_____
    5._____TEL:_____

9._____

COMPANIES IN THE INDUSTRY:

    1._____TEL:_____
    2._____TEL:_____
    3._____TEL:_____
    4._____TEL:_____
    5._____TEL:_____

10._____

COMPANIES IN THE INDUSTRY:

    1._____TEL:_____
    2._____TEL:_____
    3._____TEL:_____
    4._____TEL:_____
    5._____TEL:_____

*   *   *

I am sick and tired of companies saying, "We're in the old economy, and there's nothing we can do. Our only option is to wait until the dollar drops to forty cents, or interest rates are cut in half, or the government gets its house in order so it can afford to pick up the bill for us to clean up ours." Worse yet, these companies run whining to their Members of Parliament, provincial or federal and often both, pleading, begging, threatening, cajoling. Have they no pride whatsoever?

There are thousands of companies that have a real future in the New Economy. They're producing new products that people want to buy. They're vital suppliers to mighty engines that are creating growth and wealth for all Canadians. They embrace new technologies and adapt. They have a magic ability to find new markets, wherever those markets might be. There is a world of difference between corporate strategy and corporate sniveling.

FIVE SMART STRATEGIES FOR THE NEW ECONOMY

There's more to business planning than setting out a New Economy marketing plan. After all, many companies will decide to grow through acquisition, others will decide to sell out or diversify into other businesses. Here are five of the many strategies your company may wish to consider.

Strategy 1: A useful strategy is to expand into businesses that have a lower-knowledge base than your own. Why? Because it is often possible to inject your higher-knowledge base into a lower-knowledge business and run rings around the existing competition. Wal-Mart has done just that in the U.S. retailing business, and in the process it has set the standard against which retailing today is measured.

Strategy 2: Think carefully before you acquire a company that is smarter than you are. Check out the Knowledge Ratio *before* you make an acquisition, rather than after the ink is dry. I know one New Economy communications equipment manufacturer that wishes it had. It was doing exceedingly well in its own rapidly growing market and decided to go upscale. It bought a small software company, and had further plans to buy two more in rapid succession.

What was so interesting to me about their woes was that we weren't dealing with a low-knowledge player who was trying to take a flying leap into a high-knowledge industry. This was a high-knowledge player to begin with. Its Knowledge Ratio was in the sixties, but the company it had acquired was over twenty points ahead, with a Knowledge Ratio of 83.7 percent. No wonder the fit was disastrous. The two companies didn't even share a common corporate language. The new acquisition regarded the parent company as a bunch of bozos who were genetically incapable of understanding what the software people were doing. Resentment built on both sides and the relationship deteriorated rapidly. By the time

101

we were asked to become involved, you could barely put the two companies in the same room together.

Strategy 3: If you're going to diversify into a higher-knowledge business than the one you're in now, set the right ground rules. Either put the new folks in charge, or let your own managers know that they're supposed to learn from the newcomers, and let the newcomers know that they're supposed to teach the old dogs all their new tricks.

Strategy 4: Don't sell your company to an old economy player with a Knowledge Ratio lower than your own unless you'll be in the driver's seat (which you probably won't be). Many companies want to grow by being acquired by someone with deep pockets, but they make the mistake of selling to someone with a knowledge base far below their own. At every turn, they meet resistance to their new ideas and new products, and it grinds them to dust.

Strategy 5: When building your business through acquisition, be on the lookout for hidden values—for cheap innovation, and for the companies and divisions with very high patent activity. You can often acquire a company with a sky-high rate of return on knowledge assets for next to nothing. Take Mitel, the New Economy manufacturer of telecommunications equipment, or Moore Corporation, a producer of business forms. While calculating the rate of return on innovation for TSE 300 companies recently, we were pleasantly surprised by one of the ratios that determines the level, pace and cost of acquiring a high-knowledge company. Mitel's patent-to-stock price ratio is unbelievably attractive—it's the cheapest place to buy patents on the TSE 300. Moore Corp. is quietly scoring numbers on the innovation front that stopped us dead in our tracks. Companies can often be their own worst enemies by undervaluing their innovative capabilities. Why? Because they just don't have the tools to measure their true worth.

The stock market is littered with examples of companies that are undervalued by the yardsticks of the New Economy. But it's equally true that many old economy players on the TSE 300 have little to offer their shareholders but the memories of their former stature as the movers and shakers of a bygone world.

The Twenty-Minute Workout

At your company's or department's next planning session take an extra twenty minutes to share with your colleagues some of the opportunities and challenges you identified as you completed the mini-workbooks in this chapter. As a starting point to your discussion, here are eight questions your group can focus on as you draw up your company's road map to the New Economy:

- What are some of the potential New Economy markets that could be available to our organization? What challenges would we face if we tried to bring our current products to these markets?
- What current technology could our organization utilize that would improve our quality and delivery time and make our products more attractive to New Economy buyers?
- If we were starting this company from scratch, which of our current products or services would we agree *not* to introduce in today's economy?
- Which products or services can form our company's New Economy core strengths in the marketplace?
- Do our customers see our organization as a New Economy type of company, or are we perceived as an old economy player? (Take a few moments to identify the old economy symbols or signals that you may be sending to the marketplace.) How can our company's communications strategy be changed or modified to show a commitment to the New Economy?

103

- Every company has good and bad customers. Good customers are part of the growing New Economy and have the resources to buy, and are becoming more knowledge-intensive. From our list of customers, which ones can we identify as good and bad? Would our suppliers consider us a good or bad customer?

- Knowledge is the asset of the 1990s and beyond. What management practices would likely "turn off" the knowledge workers that our company will need to attract in the years ahead? What new management practices can we change or modify quickly?

- For our company to function better in a high-knowledge economy, what kind of training programs will our company need? (Describe the training programs currently available within your organization.) How can our employees get the training they will require outside of work?

5

INVESTING IN THE NEW ECONOMY

If you asked around for the words that best characterize Canadians, a "nation of wild gamblers" would probably be far down the list. We may line up (in single file, no less) and wait politely, patiently, at the lottery counter each week to enjoy the little flurry that only two bucks can buy, but that's a far cry from the big impulse to gamble our retirement savings with wild-eyed abandon on the Chicago futures market. We may be many, many things in Canada today, but "a nation of wild gamblers" isn't the first description that comes to my mind, either.

New Canadians also don't seem to have an appetite for taking big risks. If they did, most would probably have opted to stay in their homelands, where "risk" is too often synonymous with the loss of life or limb, never mind a pension plan or a couple of hundred dollars on a penny stock. We're conservative, cautious, careful and deliberate. And in the New Economy, there is no reason on earth why we need to change those traits.

Why? Because "new" doesn't mean "risky" any more than

"old" means "secure." Investing is, or should be, about *future* security, and that means taking stock of where the world is heading. You can never make money by investing in what used to be.

I gave a speech in Montreal on these very themes one evening, and afterwards a nice couple in their mid-fifties, who were waiting patiently for a private moment, came up to have a word with me. They introduced themselves and, with great candor, they explained their bewilderment to me. Paul had been offered a separation package from the company he had been with for almost thirty years. He described in vivid detail how the company had tried, without much lasting success, to become competitive. Some other company always seemed to outdo them and become even more competitive in a bizarre game of industry one-upmanship. On and on it went, with round after round of downsizing, in one division after the next.

Paul described his severance package as a generous one, and told me that he had even started his own business, one that he hoped would see him through the years ahead. Although he didn't tell me what this business was, and I certainly didn't want to pry, it was enough to see the obvious joy in his face and the look of pride in his eyes as he mentioned that he was now working for himself. You can tell a lot from a person's eyes.

Their needs weren't great, he told me, and the mortgage was paid. But they desperately needed to invest the funds they had as wisely as possible. He made it very clear that they couldn't afford to take big chances. He handed me a piece of paper, which I recognized instantly as a photocopy of a mutual funds portfolio, a fund I had never heard of, but one he had obviously considered carefully, and asked me, "Do these companies look risky to you"? As I looked down the list of names, old names, venerable names, names of companies that our grandparents would have recognized and respected, I felt raw anger rise in me. The very company that could no longer afford to pay Paul's salary was on that list of names. In fact, the portfolio had a huge weighting, a grotesque weighting, in an industry that could no longer even afford to pay its rent. I

instantly decided to catch a later flight home that night, and invited
Paul and his wife to join me for a cup of coffee.

You Know Where Your Kids Are . . . But Do You Know Where Your Money Is?

There is only a handful of things in this world that make me really
angry—spitting mad, in fact. People who abuse their children or
loved ones, Third World governments that remain intentionally
oblivious to the wretched poverty around them, judges who give
young offenders a little slap on the wrist and the excuse to make a
mockery of justice in this country: they're enough to make my
blood boil. And any mutual fund that dares to pretend that it's
investing your hard-earned money and mine in a world that no
longer exists fits right up there on my list.

The old generation of industrial leaders is no longer creating the
jobs, no longer creating the growth and certainly no longer creating the wealth the way it did in the past. That's dispiriting, because
if people like Paul and his wife had a better understanding of what
was growing and what wasn't, and what these changes and sweeping trends meant for them, they would never invest their money in
some of the places they do.

We all know someone who has lost a job in the old economy: a
brother, a sister, a neighbor, a friend. We all know people whose lives
have been turned upside down by changes that they didn't cause. If
an industry can't even provide the job security that you need today,
why are you investing in it? How on earth can you expect that same
industry to provide you with the income security you are going to
need in *your* retirement years? You know where your kids are, but,
good grief, do you actually know where your money is?

Take a look at the chart on the following page. You can see for
yourself that the old economy is vastly overweighted on the TSE

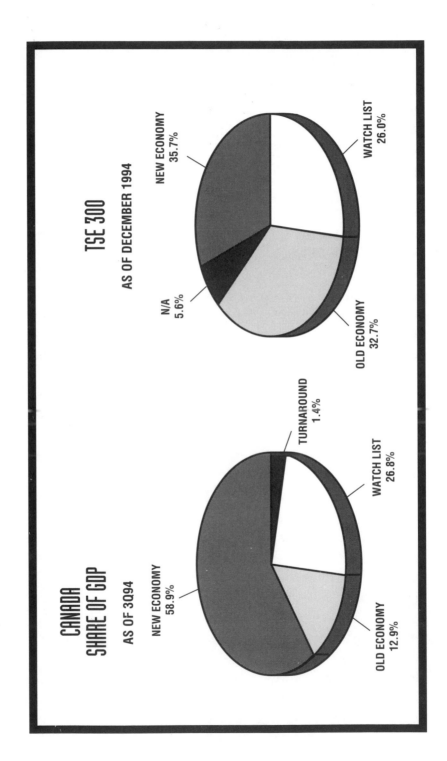

CANADA
SHARE OF GDP

AS OF 3Q94

NEW ECONOMY
58.9%

TURNAROUND
1.4%

WATCH LIST
26.8%

OLD ECONOMY
12.9%

TSE 300

AS OF DECEMBER 1994

NEW ECONOMY
35.7%

N/A
5.6%

WATCH LIST
26.0%

OLD ECONOMY
32.7%

300 (the Toronto Stock Exchange index of three hundred compa-nies that investment managers and others use as their barometer of the stock market). The old economy accounts for 32.7 percent of the TSE 300, but only 12.9 percent of the Canadian economy. Does the stock market adequately reflect the very real changes that we have been going through? No, you bet it doesn't! Will it one day? Of course it will.

Like most things, change doesn't occur at an even or measured pace. It's a rough and rocky road we're traveling, and some things are changing at a faster pace than others. An investment manager once asked me *how* the TSE 300 might eventually become a better reflection of the economy that underpins it. I said, "That's easy to answer. Why, the old economy companies on the TSE 300 will get delisted. They'll get knocked off the list, just as slower joggers in a marathon race will fall winded by the roadside." Sure, it's a hell of a way for the TSE 300 to change, but make no mistake about it: the cold winds of change will whistle through that index.

Now, take a look at the Watch List sectors of the TSE 300. These are the industries that could either tumble into the old economy or leap into the new. They're risky business. I often advise people that instead of investing in Watch List companies, they should go to Las Vegas. At least they'll get a free drink in Vegas.

At 26.0 percent of the market's capitalization, the Watch List is a big part of the stock market, but at least these industires are evenly matched, size-wise, with their percentage weighting in our economy.

Now, do some simple math.

Add up the old economy on the TSE 300 (the 32.7 percent rep-resenting the industries that have already gone tumbling into the old economy) and the Watch List of the TSE 300 (the 26.0 percent representing the sectors that could go either way). What number do you get? The hard cold fact is that 58.7 percent of the TSE 300 is already in the old economy or awfully close to the edge.

Anytime I hear someone say: "I don't need a stockbroker, a financial adviser or an investment manager—I can do this all by myself!" a shudder runs right through me. The simple odds are that, if you *don't* get some decent professional advice, you stand an almost 60 percent chance of committing your life's savings to companies whose main mission in life is, or soon might be, to move into a *broom closet.* I don't know about you, but I have better things to do with my money.

If you want to build a nostalgia portfolio, go right ahead, but you won't get my help to do so. Far too many people just ask around, get a smattering of well-meaning advice, a couple of hot stock tips and hope that they'll be able to sleep well until next season's RRSP deadline rolls around. For those of you who want to invest wisely, it's worthwhile getting professional advice. I know one doctor who should have.

Many years ago, when I was running the research department of a major investment dealer, I took a few days off to get some simple surgery attended to. It was a reasonably quiet time, and I knew that I wouldn't be missed for the few days. Surgery was scheduled for mid-morning, so I didn't even have to spend the night in hospital, which added to my comfort level. I was guided through the usual confusing process of forms, a blood test and the little empty bottle . . . you get the drift. I was all set for surgery, and I had even been given that injection of "happy juice." Man, did I feel great! But I was quickly jolted out of my blissful state by the doctor, who was shaking my shoulder in obvious agitation and asking me what he should do with his shares of Dome Petroleum. Can you believe it? There I was, half-unconscious on the operating room table, and this doctor was trying to wake me up because the shares of the late 1970s energy behemoth had dropped a couple of points on his way into the operating room! I can still remember his frenzied questions: "Should I buy more, or should I sell it all?" Dome Petroleum subsequently went bankrupt, and I have no idea whether I shook my head from side to side or up and down.

What's Growing and What's Not

The New Economy accounts for 35.7 percent of the TSE 300, and although it's now the single largest component of the stock market, its percentage is still far less than its share of the Canadian economy. Why is it so underweighted on the TSE 300? Here are two reasons:

- Many old economy companies have been around for a dog's age and have attracted huge followings. They take up space on the TSE 300, and their market capitalizations take time to decline.
- A lot of New Economy companies are still privately held. They're hugely profitable, but may not need outside capital at this stage. Or, they're eager to go public, but discover that it's difficult to find a major investment dealer who "understands" knowledge-based businesses.

Every three months, we publish for our clients the table you see on page 113. It lets them know which industries are in the New Economy, which sectors of the stock market are in the old economy, and which ones are on the Watch List and could go either way. While the list doesn't change drastically from one quarter to the next, it's important for you to keep an eye on big structural changes and not let them sneak up on you when you least expect it. And, if an industry has peaked, you don't want to be the last one to know. Some people in the investment industry express surprise when they study this list. I don't know what they expect to find in the New Economy: strange-sounding bio-things, run by nerds who live in their parents' basements?

Let me tell you what's on it and why. Then, after you have finished studying the list, take a couple of minutes to see what percentage of *your* portfolio, or the mutual funds that you have invested in, are tied to the New Economy, the old economy or the Watch List.

111

If you find that you have a vested interest in the old economy, and that you have based your future on the return of the 1970s, you have two obvious options: either invest in memorabilia, or start making some changes in your investment holdings and building security for the future, *now*.

New Economy Industry Groups in the TSE 300

- **Fabricating & Engineering**. This sector continues to grow in structural terms and is on the list for two reasons. First, it relies intensely on instrumentation, one of the four major engines that are driving the New Economy (the other three engines are computers and semiconductors, health and medical, and communications and telecommunications). Second, as a high-knowledge sector of the TSE 300, fabricating & engineering has become an integral part of our new high-knowledge economy.
- **Transportation Equipment**. On the TSE 300, this industry is synonymous with Bombardier, the company that grew from snowmobiles into a global giant in the world of modern transportation. It revitalized an old industry by using new technologies and finding new markets.
- **Technology—Hardware**. This sector's about as New Economy as it gets.
- **Technology—Software**. Ditto.
- **Chemicals & Fertilizers**. While not every part of this industry is in the New Economy, important segments of it, such as pharmaceuticals, plastic and synthetic resins, industrial chemicals, and paint and varnish continue to grow in structural terms. If more than 51 percent of an industry is in the New Economy, I classify it as New Economy, even though some old economy companies within the industry may be highly leveraged to all the wrong things.

TSE 300 CLASSIFICATIONS

4Q94

NEW ECONOMY	OLD ECONOMY	WATCH LIST
Fabricating & Engineering	Integrated Mines	Gold & Precision Metals
Transportation Equipment	Mining	Auto Parts
Technology—Hardware	Oil & Gas Producers	Real Estate
Technology—Software	Oil & Gas Services	Banks & Trust Companies
Chemicals & Fertilizers	Paper & Forest Products	Insurance
Business Services	Food Processing	
Transportation & Environmental Services	Tobacco	
Pipelines	Distilleries	
Biotech & Pharmaceutical	Breweries & Beverages	
Gas/Electric Utilities	Household Goods	
Cable & Entertainment	Steel	
Publishing & Printing	Building Materials	
Wholesale Distribution	Broadcasting	
Food Stores		
Department Stores		
Specialty Stores		
Hospitality		
Investment Companies & Funds		
Financial Management Companies		
Telephone Utilities		

- **Business Services**. Companies in this sector are leveraged to the New Economy, and, for the most part, they're very knowledge-intensive and technology-intensive players.
- **Transportation & Environmental Services**. This industry is classified as New Economy thanks to the waste management and environmental services components. Airline transportation, however, is on the Watch List because of its great dependence on business travel (read the high-margin side of the business). Knowledge workers now have other alternatives to traveling halfway across the continent for a sales meeting. These people can e-mail or Internet or video conference their way around the globe before you or I can hail a cab to the airport.
- **Pipelines**. These are the people who transport the natural gas to market, and they're downright lucky. Natural gas is the fuel of choice in the New Economy, just as oil was the fuel of choice in the old one. I just wish that the TSE would split the two, instead of lumping oil and gas together. If they were separate, I could keep oil in the old economy column of this list and shift natural gas into the New Economy column, where it belongs.
- **Biotech & Pharmaceutical**. Here's a New Economy engine that will ride the wave of demographic and technological change. The simple truth behind the long-term growth awaiting this industry is that the older we get, the more prescriptions we fill. Canada is particularly well placed as a clinical trial site because of our multicultural population, which allows pharmaceutical and biotech companies to test their new cures on a microcosm of the global village.
- **Gas/Electric Utilities**. The main drivers in this group are the gas utilities. They sell the gas from the New Economy natural gas producers, which the pipeline industry transports to market.
- **Cable & Entertainment**. Surprisingly, cable is in the old economy, having peaked in 1985, but entertainment is as New Economy as it gets. Canadian companies are making major inroads into U.S. television programming and films, and must

be rubbing their hands in glee at the prospect of five hundred channels to come.

- **Publishing & Printing**. In the information age, this sector is obviously well positioned, but some companies are adapting faster to the dramatically changing technological landscape than others are. In any period of great change, some companies will adapt, while others will fail to do so.
- **Wholesale Distribution**. While obviously not an engine, this group is a vital supplier to the New Economy of just-in-time production and distribution.
- **Food Stores**. This sector has rapidly globalized before our eyes. Canadians have traveled more in the last ten years than ever before, and have come to enjoy the exotic taste treats that they have sampled around the world. Aggressive companies will find markets abroad as well.
- **Department Stores**. Think of the deep-discount New Economy retailers, and you can understand why this industry is getting a whole new lease on life—at the expense of slower-moving retailers, who have been reluctant to adapt to shopping realities in the '90s.
- **Specialty Stores**. This sector includes both New Economy and old economy retailers; like the department stores sector, it's in the New Economy, but not all companies are adapting.
- **Hospitality**. Here's a New Economy sector with a sense of humor. It includes both luxury hotel chains, such as the Four Seasons Hotels, *and* Loewen Group, the funeral home people who are the final and ultimate stop in the hospitality cycle!
- **Investment Companies & Funds**. This industry group is riding the powerful demographic trends that drove housing to dizzying heights of prosperity through the 1950s and 1960s. As baby boomers age, their need for housing will decline, but their need for investment products and advice will soar.
- **Financial Management Companies**. Although this group is a mixture of old and new, most of the sector has some holdings in the New Economy.

• **Telephone Utilities**. In this information and communications age, it should come as no surprise that telephones, cellphones and wireless communications are an integral part of the New Economy, despite the relentless pressure on traditional monopoly players in the business.

Why Invest in the New Economy?

If you have the desire to make money over any long period of time, then invest in the New Economy. Of course, if you hold your breath long enough, old economy industries might have a good quarter. They might even have a good year. But don't mistake a dead cat bounce for the real thing called growth. Take a long, hard look at the numbers for yourself. Over the last ten years, the New Economy generated a total return of 267.0 percent, head and shoulders above the TSE 300's total return of 142.1 percent. The old economy, meanwhile, generated a total return of only 105.8 percent.

But don't kid yourself. The New Economy is not the land of Oz. I remember a New Economy company that went public a few years back. This young, aggressive company had parlayed its way onto Bay Street, and its information package looked terrific—*PRINTED CIRCUIT BOARDS!* "Now, that's an industry with a future," you could hear the unsuspecting brokers say. Although my colleagues and I are not in the business of assessing these new issues, we should be because when we took a look at the company out of curiosity what did we find? The company was in the New Economy all right, but at the very bottom of the class. In an industry that demanded a knowledge ratio of 57.7 percent, this company had a knowledge ratio of only 35.9 percent. Its stock dropped from over $18 to less than $6, reinforcing one of my deeply held beliefs: *Never invest in anything that has an IQ lower than room temperature!*

Pick the wrong company and, no matter how hot the industry or how secure its future, you will lose money. The chart on page 121 is

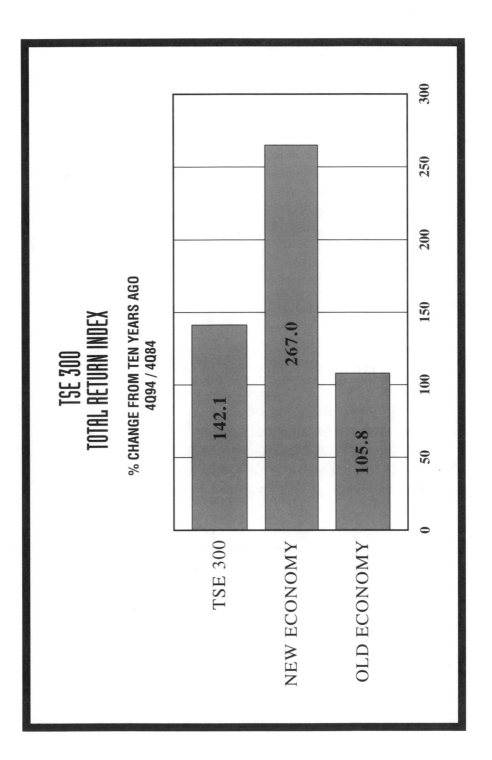

TSE 300
TOTAL RETURN INDEX

% CHANGE FROM TEN YEARS AGO
4Q94 / 4Q84

TSE 300 — 142.1

NEW ECONOMY — 267.0

OLD ECONOMY — 105.8

a useful and necessary reminder that the New Economy *will not be a stellar performer in every month or in every year.* After all, the business cycle isn't dead, and with anything that is tied to economic performance, good times will be followed by bad times. But, in the New Economy, you stand a far better chance that there will be more good than bad. And I have the hard numbers to prove it.

- Over the last ten years, the New Economy index of the TSE 300 rose in 101 months and fell in 19 months; 84 percent of the time, or 101 months out of 120, New Economy investors made money. But these statistics still mean that, 16 percent of the time, the New Economy index declined, and investors lost money. *Great* returns aren't the same thing as *perfect* returns, which, in all my years of research, I have yet to find.
- Over the last ten years, the New Economy index, with its ups and downs generated a total return of 267 percent. In comparison, the TSE 300 returned 142.1 percent.
- In 1994—a year of tough markets by anybody's yardstick—the New Economy index of the TSE 300 generated a total return of 6.1 percent, while the TSE 300 fell 0.2 percent.
- In 1994, the New Economy index outperformed the TSE 300 in nine of those twelve months, or 75 percent of the time. In good markets and bad, the New Economy isn't a bad place to be!

But all the fancy statistics in the world can't match the hard and simple truth: if you had invested $10,000 in the New Economy ten years ago, it would be worth $47,371.73 today. Investing in the TSE 300 would have turned your $10,000 into $25,098.58. Investing $10,000 in the old economy would have produced a nest egg of only $18,799.99. Why it comes as a stark revelation to some people that investing in growing New Economy companies makes simple sense, I'll never know.

If at this point you're *still* looking for a good reason *not* to invest in the New Economy, I'll do you a favor and give you the following five reasons:

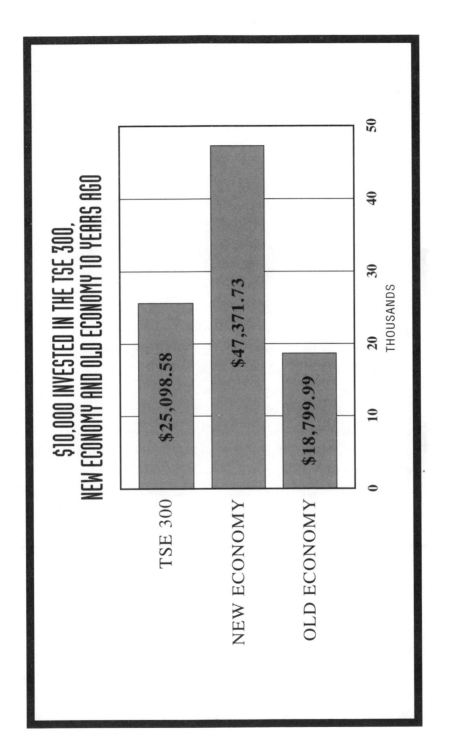

$10,000 INVESTED IN THE TSE 300,
NEW ECONOMY AND OLD ECONOMY 10 YEARS AGO

1. I saw *Jurassic Park* and decided to build a theme portfolio for the 1990s.
2. I got used to investing in stocks that collapse, and old habits are hard to break.
3. I bought a book on short-selling and I want to get my money's worth.
4. Red is my favorite color.
5. 'Tis better to give than to receive.

What's Risky and What's Not

There is good volatility and there is bad volatility, and it's worth taking a moment to understand the simple difference between the two. Good volatility is what happens above the zero line, where you make money. Bad volatility comes from living your financial life below the zero line, where you lose money.

Take a look at the first chart on page 121. The bold line shows the percentage change year-by-year in the New Economy index; the other line shows the percentage changes calculated for the TSE 300 index. Look at where the zero line is. The New Economy enjoys longer periods of growth; it moves up and down, but a lot of that movement is *good* volatility, above the zero line, where you want volatility to be. That's called growth, and that's why most people invest their money in the first place.

Now, I'll be the first to acknowledge that not every investor has the desire to make money. Some people—no more than a very few—have what I am sure is the financial equivalent of Münchhausen's syndrome, a condition that leads seemingly normal people to injure themselves so they can go to hospital and be cured! (If you think *that's* nuts, just read the Revenue Canada rules for the treatment of tax losses in this country.)

But, wackos aside, most people have a genuine desire to make

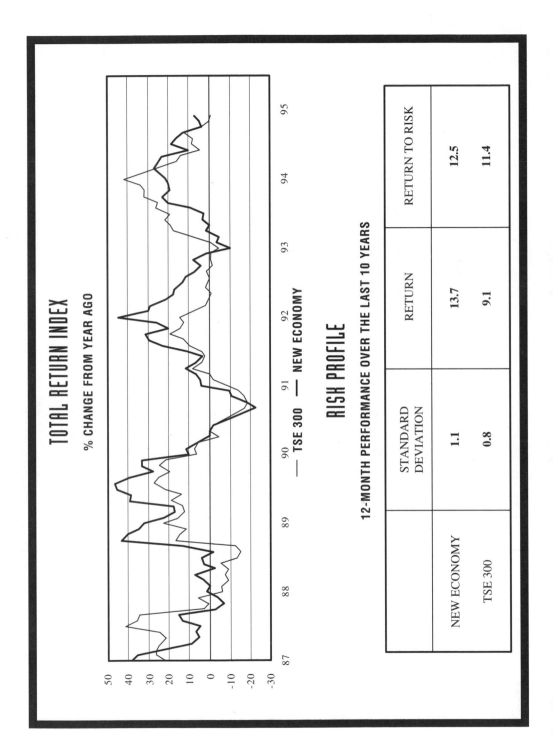

TOTAL RETURN INDEX

% CHANGE FROM YEAR AGO

— TSE 300   — NEW ECONOMY

RISK PROFILE

12-MONTH PERFORMANCE OVER THE LAST 10 YEARS

	STANDARD DEVIATION	RETURN	RETURN TO RISK
NEW ECONOMY	1.1	13.7	12.5
TSE 300	0.8	9.1	11.4

money commensurate with their tolerance for risk. A higher upside, without proportionately greater risk, counts as a good investment in most people's book. In the New Economy, the volatility is only slightly higher, the investment returns are much larger and the ratio of return to risk means that you're exposed to greater upside without proportionately greater risk.

INVESTMENT STRATEGY IN THE NEW ECONOMY

There are first-rate investment management and mutual fund companies in this country. Many of the best and largest have been clients of my firm for many years, and I know them very well. They're staffed by talented and sincere people, the kind of folks you would value as your neighbors or friends. The fact that these people know how to manage money, in what can be the most mystifying of markets, is a wonderful bonus. They're the pros, the "A" team. And they have earned our trust.

I don't manage money—I never have and I never will. That's not the business I'm in. My firm advises the people who manage your money and mine. We are experts in strategy, and we serve as advisers to about 55 percent of the pension fund assets in this country. The rest of my company's business focuses on management consulting (which I affectionately call the real world) and consulting for an assortment of government departments and agencies. This work keeps me and my colleagues busy, and we rarely have time to play in traffic.

So what are we advising investment managers to do these days? Here's the short version of our 1995 interpretations of omens, prognostications and divinations—in short, our investment outlook.

The Stock Market. We think the stock market will be very volatile for the next eighteen months, and it's the time in a business cycle to get stock selection strategy *really right*. Some years, when almost everything is heading straight up and almost everybody will have a good year, you can afford to be wrong or, at the very least, not too fussy about what you buy. But this will not be the case for the next year to eighteen months. That's why we're advising the advisers to concentrate their investments around core holdings in the New Economy.

Once upon a time, the core holdings in a well-balanced investment portfolio would have included pig iron, buggy whips, railroad stocks and cotton, but those days are long over. Why, to even dabble in cotton, we're talking big volumes . . . a major investment in space. Nowadays, you're better off with New Economy industries that have a future, instead of industries that have a past.

We are also advising our clients to invest very cautiously in Watch List sectors. Remember, they could go either way. It really concerns me when I see people leaping into large holdings in *little* Watch List companies. When the Watch List is on a roll, it dazzles, but when it goes, there is just no way to sell out in time, especially if the companies you picked only trade a few thousand shares a week. If you're going to invest in a Watch List sector, stick with big companies. Believe me, when the Watch List declines, it invariably collapses. *Snap* . . . and down it goes.

We continue to advise our clients to keep an eye on the old economy sectors of the market, because you don't want to be filing your nails, or sleeping at the switch when they have their day in the sun, as they do from time to time. After all, if the price of pig iron doubles because the only truck carting the stuff to market has a flat tire, that's called a "shortage in the market," and share prices will climb on the bad—read *good*—news. And I would guarantee you that precious few investors would think to stop and ask, "Exactly how big is the market for pig iron, anyway?" The smell of a shortage is sure to excite them.

Inflation. Forget inflation. I know, the U.S. Federal Reserve Board thinks it's going to be a big problem. But these are the people who thought the oil shocks of the 1970s would never drive inflation rates higher! We all know how that story ended in the early '80s with inflation rates of 12 percent and interest rates of 20 percent.

Oops! Sorry, never mind. In short, they have a sorry track record and an even sorrier sense of direction. The reason why they have scared themselves out of their wits is that they are fixated on old economy price trends. And because some bottlenecks are obvious in certain industries of the old economy, the Federal Reserve Board is issuing dire warnings about the fate of the free world. But just because the truck carrying pig iron has broken down and one little piggy won't make it to market on time . . . Has anybody at the Fed bothered to ask, "Exactly how big is the old economy, anyway?"

Alan Greenspan was quoted in a November 1994 issue of *Business Week* as saying that "the list of shortcomings in U.S. economic data is depressingly long." The report goes on to comfort us with news that "the Fed relies heavily on anecdotal evidence of inflation, hiring, and other economic trends." *Hearsay*—just what we need running U.S. monetary policy and dictating the direction of global capital markets! You would need to be stark raving mad not to adopt a cautious approach to capital markets, and not to have professionals manage your money.

But, sooner or later, the powerful underlying trends that are quietly at work will dictate the direction we're really heading in. And it's important to note that our U.S. composite leading indicator of inflation in the New Economy is only up by 0.8 percent from its level of one year ago. *Oops! Sorry, never mind.* Sooner or later the Federal Reserve folks will find something else to fuss about.

Interest Rates. With the Fed as your friend, who needs the bond market to be your enemy? Our only question is when, not if, interest rates decline. But we could be waiting a long time. In the meantime, what you make on bonds, you could blow on Rolaids. If you think that interest rates are high in real terms (when the inflation rate has been subtracted), just take a peek at the next chart, which shows U.S. interest rates in *really* "real" terms, using the New Economy's non-existent rate of inflation instead of the Consumer Price Index! A lot of people will eventually make a small fortune when the Fed quits yanking interest rates up to ridiculous levels.

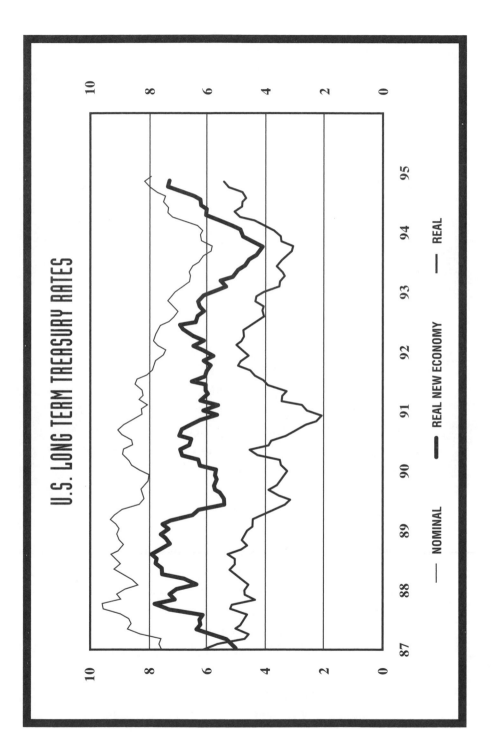

U.S. LONG TERM TREASURY RATES

NOMINAL — REAL NEW ECONOMY — REAL

6
A ROAD MAP FOR COMMUNITIES

Location, location, location . . . it's a wonderful old saying in real estate and economic development circles. And many communities still, to this day, believe that their location can be a magical source of strategic and competitive advantage in the New Economy. But they couldn't be more wrong. In the New Economy, location, in the traditional sense, simply doesn't matter nearly as much as it used to. Other factors matter a whole lot more.

Communities can be located way off the beaten track, without a divided highway or airport in sight; but as long as they have that all-important up-link to a satellite network, they are effectively located in the fast lane of any New Economy superhighway they choose to cruise. There are hundreds of thousands of companies across North America that are thriving today—while breaking all the old rules of economic development. One of my favorite examples is a Newfoundland company located in a tiny hamlet on the coast, miles from nowhere. There isn't even a road into the community—all comings and goings are by boat. And yet, with its up-link to a satellite, this company is in the very center of a global New Economy, with high-knowledge products that the world wants to buy. Does this company need an industrial park in which to conduct its business? *No*. Does it need to be located in a strip mall on the way into town to announce that it's where the action is? *Hardly.* In fact, the opposite is true. Companies like this one don't want to be where the action is, especially when it isn't their action.

Why did Bill Gates locate Microsoft in Redmond, Washington? Had anyone out of state ever heard of Redmond before Gates sprawled his thriving empire out there? Economic development officers in the New Yorks, Chicagos and Torontos of this world must agonize over the question: "What does Redmond have that we don't?" I'll tell you: it has a high-knowledge base, a beautiful natural setting, low taxes, peace and quiet, a low crime rate, nice neighbors and civilized living in an environment where every day can be a "casual Friday" if you so choose. While proximity to a first-rate university is a huge competitive advantage in the New Economy, Bill Gates and his kind know that knowledge workers can be attracted from far-flung places—such as the University of Waterloo in Ontario—to peaceful places like the outskirts of Seattle, as long as the conditions for interesting work are there. Communities that begin with a high-knowledge base have a leg up on everyone else. And that is why the knowledge base of a community is one of the most important strategic advantages in the New Economy.

The Changing Nature of Strategic Advantage

The nature of what constitutes a strategic advantage has changed enormously through the ages. It used to be a big deal to have a canal running through your town, but in the New Economy, who cares? Few New Economy companies would seriously consider sending their high-knowledge goods or services to the marketplace by barge, anyway! It used to be a major advantage for a community to have a railway line and, later, a highway to insure rapid transportation of products to market. Today, the only highway that really counts is the information superhighway you can't see. That's why provinces like New Brunswick have a huge advantage. New Brunswick realizes that access to information (not to waterways, railroad tracks or tarmac) is a powerful strategic advantage today. If this Maritime province plays its cards right in the New Economy, it stands a very good chance of becoming the knowledge capital of Canada. Its enviable telecommunication strategy stands to pay enormous dividends.

Of course, not every company in the New Economy has the luxury of being accessible only by dinghy. But the nature of a town's competitive advantage has changed dramatically, and it pains me when I see well-meaning and hardworking economic development officers plugging old economy advantages that used to count for a great deal, but are falling by the wayside today.

Here's a Top 10 list of old economy strategic advantages that used to be a community's ticket to economic development, but no longer count for very much.

1. **Cheap energy**. With co-generation springing up all over the place, cheap hydro rates are still important, but they're not the key factor that they used to be. One after another, utilities are losing their technological monopoly on electricity generation.

2. **Skilled work force**. In a new high-knowledge economy, we've upped the ante on education and skills. Each community needs to take inventory of the skill sets that it has to offer. Are they the skills much prized among old economy industries, the industries with the massive lay-off rates? Or are they the skills that meet the needs of a new and higher-knowledge-based economy?

3. **Excellent transportation**. Goods and services in the New Economy have different transportation needs. Miniaturization and the clear trend toward producing higher-knowledge goods that are shipped just-in-time mean that traditional, low-knowledge modes of transport are being rapidly displaced by high-

knowledge, computer-tracked transportation, such as courier services and air freight. If FedEx can't service your community before 10:00 a.m., you have an automatic disadvantage.

4. **Tax breaks**. Communities that are as lean as the New Economy companies they seek to attract are in a better position to offer low taxes—rather than short-lived tax breaks in what are probably outrageously high tax jurisdictions in the first place.

5. **Serviced land**. A very important consideration if you're bent on attracting plants the size of football fields, popular yesteryear. Serviced land isn't high on the shopping list of knowledge-based companies.

6. **Industrial parks**. I shake my head every time I pick up a glossy brochure that extols the virtues of a community's half-empty industrial park. The space needs of the New Economy are just plain different.

7. **Low hourly wage rates**. While low wage rates are still a key factor, they scarcely count at the high-knowledge end.

8. **Access to major markets**. Markets are changing. Among the fastest-growing markets in the world economy, today and into the foreseeable future, are India, China and scores of other Pacific Rim countries. It is pointless for North American communities to describe access to markets (like Detroit or Buffalo) in an old economy sense.

9. **Cheap land**. The New Economy is a world of product miniaturization, and it requires less space than the old economy did.

10. **Low workers' compensation premiums**. A decided plus for old economy employers, but hardly a reason for New Economy high-knowledge companies to pull up roots and move.

GHOST TOWNS OF THE 1990s

There are thousands of communities across this country that stand a good chance of becoming the ghost towns of the 1990s unless they start getting it right.

And it wouldn't cost them a loonie more to build a secure future for themselves and for their children. Why, in the long run, they could save millions of dollars that they don't even have.

I remember a meeting I had with one community, which I have come to think of as Riskyville. As I was ushered into the foyer, like most visitors, I was impressed by the cheery opulence of City Hall. It was beautifully decorated and had lots of open, airy spaces filled with (real) plants. The mayor was a nice man, full of bonhomie. As he guided me into his office, he pointed out the wingback chairs flanking his desk, and told me that they had been purchased at the local discount furniture store out by the highway. The message was clear enough: Look at these $250 wingback chairs that we got on sale for $199. We're doing our job in this community, and we pride ourselves on the fact that we're minding the store.

Some store. I had done my homework before the visit and had been shocked to discover that 87 percent of the tax base in the town was tied up with old economy industries or, in one way or another, with various levels of government. Governments, as you'll recall, are on the Watch List, and when you know where to look, you can see the downsizing coming for miles. Like many communities that are dangerously dependent on government departments or initiatives that have outlived their useful lives, this town was sitting there waiting for the shoe to drop. With only 13 percent of its tax base tied to the New Economy or New Economy suppliers, what hope did the town really have of weathering the winds of change?

At least the people in Riskyville had an inkling that their future wasn't as stable as they hoped. Other communities know their vulnerability, and frankly don't seem to give a damn. Hopelessville, for example, had been chugging along since the days of the Industrial Revolution, or so it seemed. No one over the age of eighteen bothered to stay because they couldn't see a future there. The biggest building on Main Street was an old supermarket converted into a bingo hall, as bingo had become the main economic event in town. Most of the people seemed to be on welfare; their unemployment checks had long since run out.

What really angered me was how they were living in the past. The local council talked incessantly about the industries that used to dominate the landscape; they took me for a day-long tour of the town, and, hour after miserable hour, I saw the ruins of the textile mills, a few old metal forging shops and a dilapidated shipbuilding facility that hadn't stored anything but bats in its storage lofts for decades.

The townspeople had a perverse sense of pride in the prosperity that they used to enjoy, as if, all of a sudden, a great heritage had been unfairly stripped away. But no one had stopped to ask what the hell had happened—everyone just felt that it was somehow unfair. The presumption of powerlessness was staggering to behold. And worse, these people were betraying the industriousness and hard work of their past by giving up on their community and themselves. Communities have no right to do that.

When I got back to my office, my colleagues and I spent weeks sorting out the town's strengths and weaknesses, and tailoring a proposal that we knew would meet their needs. We worked like mad fools putting it together. But the day before we were scheduled to present the proposal, we got a frantic call from one of the town's aldermen. "Hold everything!" he said. "We've got to put a freeze on any economic development work."

"Why?" I asked, not unreasonably.

The premier, he said, was scheduling a visit to the area, and there was a rumor that a program and some money might be coming down the pipeline from the provincial government for a winter jobs initiative. "It looks like they're going to do it for us," he said, with obvious excitement in his voice. The premier duly visited, nothing came down and that community, like thousands of others, sits frozen in its past, waiting for a bus that's never going to come. Meanwhile, there's a whole world of growth and opportunity around them that they could, and should, strive to become a part of.

What Do Foreign Companies Know That We in Canada Don't?

I had been particularly intrigued by the numbers we track on foreign investment into Canada, and had been astounded to see the huge inflows of business investment dollars. In the last five years alone, business investment into Canada had risen sharply: foreign companies had invested over $34 billion during what we would all agree had been tough recession years, not just here but around the world. As a nation, we are so often surprised when the world pays us a compliment or singles us out for praise. We're even more stunned when someone wants to invest in us! The numbers we track had piqued my curiosity, and I was delighted when we were asked to undertake a study on this very topic.

Our mandate was to study New Economy companies that had moved to Canada and had made substantial investments in operating here. With so many headlines about disaffected companies moving south, our job was to find out what had brought other companies here. Not the wintry clime, obviously, unless they were members of a weird corporate ski cult.

We were asked to concentrate on American firms that had established themselves in various locations across Canada. As we interviewed people from a sample of fifty New Economy companies, which represented a cross section of big and small producers of both goods and services, our mission was to identify what strategic advantages might exist in Canada that Canadians might not be aware of. In other words, what do foreign companies know that we in Canada don't? What an eye-opener those interviews were!

In meeting after meeting, we recorded the constant reference to personal safety and security. One CEO put it rather bluntly. The biggest attraction was that his kids could go for a walk in the park, his wife could ride a subway, and he didn't have to live in a heavily gated and guarded community that felt like an "us-versus-them" armed camp. And he and his wife liked the fact that they didn't have to carry a gun in the glove compartment of their car.

I was instantly reminded of a recent trip my husband and I had made to Boca Raton, and how nerve-racking the ride from Miami airport had been. I had been invited to give the keynote address at a conference, and was happy that Frank could fit a few vacation days into his own busy schedule. The limo was waiting to whisk us away to the lovely resort that we had seen many times on TV in a credit card advertisement—the one that shows the young couple driving up to this glorious pink-hued, palm-treed hotel and deciding, on the spur of the moment, to spend "just one night." We could feel ourselves relax as we sped along the highway, and we chatted amicably with the driver. But as we pulled off the highway, obviously nearing our destination, we froze in shock when we came to a red light and the driver said, nonchalantly, "I know you'll feel a lot safer, folks, if I just slip one in the chamber." He loaded the gun under his seat, and we rode the few remaining miles, with our knees shaking, to the safety and security of a heavily guarded resort. Needless to say, we were happy to arrive back at the airport in one piece a few days later, and *go home*.

But safety and security weren't the only eye-openers in those interviews. Many CEOs told me candidly how the quality of Canada's work force was a distinct advantage to them; they weren't as worried in Canada about drugs in the workplace and dealing with the nightmare of the "crack-head" who commandeers the customer service line when the company least expects it. Other executives cited the multicultural advantage to doing business in

Canada and how easy it was to hire highly skilled people who spoke languages such as German, Italian, Polish, Korean . . . and how big an advantage that was when dealing with the company's global customer base. One company couldn't quite believe its luck in having hired a marketing manager whose mother was Russian, whose father was German, and who spoke those languages fluently, plus English and French. A melting pot may have had many advantages in the old economy, but a multicultural workforce gives companies and communities a leg up in this global New Economy.

If We Build It, They Will Come

Many well-meaning towns have heard that travel and tourism is the world's largest industry today, and they believe that tourism can be their salvation. If all else fails, there are always tourist dollars to attract. On a visit to one such town I was asked if it would be a good idea to open a railroad museum. The town council members thought it might be a great local initiative, and that it might attract significant tourist activity to the area. They proceeded to recite the number of permanent and part-time summer jobs they thought this museum could generate. Now, I'm all for museums, including railway museums, but for a small town with little else going for it, this plan was simply a waste of taxpayer dollars. Here's why.

Although tourism has been around since before the days of the *Queen Mary*, it is a New Economy industry with strong links to the global growth in entertainment and communications. Long gone are the days when mother, father and their 2.7 children were content to take their two-week annual holiday at a motel miles from nowhere, just so the kids could get to swim in a pool. Nowadays, people expect to be entertained. Take one look at the roaring success of Orlando, with its massive entertainment focus, or Las Vegas, with its newly built theme parks for families, singles and every configuration in between, and it becomes patently obvious that most local initiatives on a shoestring stand very little chance of doing much more than breaking even—at best. At worst, they'll suck valuable tax dollars away from the tax base or away from better projects for years into the future. Unfortunately, a pretty view, a clean motel and the local pizza parlor don't cut it in the New Economy.

Knowledge workers want and expect more. They want entertainment that is every inch as technologically advanced as they are—as the cruise industry discovered to its dismay when it booked third-rate comedy acts on first-rate cruises. Cruise lines came to recognize that there was no sense leaving the entire passenger list wishing it was back at home watching David Letterman.

Active vacations and educational travel are also major trends in tourism. Witness the boom in eco-tourism as knowledge workers revel in the wonders of the natural environment. And, while there won't be a growing market for squash or racquetball holidays as baby boomers get older and their knees give out, there will be a bustling business in birdwatching and whale-watching and fishing holidays, whose pleasures boomers have already discovered. The secret is to serve the needs of the burgeoning mass of people working in high-knowledge industries, who already have the disposable income to spare.

Tourism can be enhanced in places where tourists already go, but it cannot be created out of thin air without a huge financial investment. Universal Studios' Orlando theme park cost over $600 million to build and lost money for years; it survived because it was backed by MCA, a giant in the industry. Few provincial or federal grants could match even a fraction of that financial support.

Drive along any highway, especially in the Maritimes or in Alberta, and you will see all of the leftover tourism initiatives of the past: motels whose neon "no vacancy" lights haven't flickered in years, little museums that few people visit anymore, mini-golf or go-cart courses that haven't seen a lineup since the '60s. But a lot of communities haven't gotten the message yet. And, some, unfortunately, never will.

Instead of lamenting a glorious past, communities have to look to the future. Town councils have a responsibility to the folks who pay them to insure that their community thrives. But, as ordinary citizens, we have a responsibility as well to make sure our cities and towns are on the right track. I see young mothers wheeling baby carriages through small towns across this country, and the children of this land have a right to a community with a future. Instead of dwelling on a community's old strategic advantages from a bygone era, we must focus on the new needs of our rapidly changing economic base, and figure out how we can meet them. Read on to find out what you can do in your community to insure that it's following a road map to the New Economy.

How to Build a New Economy Community

The first vital step is for communities to develop a strategic vision at the top. Leaders are paid to lead, so it's not at all unreasonable to insist that they do their jobs. But they need your input. After all, *whose town is it, anyway*? What does the community actually want to become? What is its mission, its goals? What targets should it set? How can it achieve those goals? Does your community have a strategic plan and the relevant benchmarks to judge its journey through the New Economy? If not, it's time to suggest that your leaders create one, because any community that tries to fly blind through this period of monumental change runs a high risk of hitting the wall. Holding a series of monthly town hall meetings, or running a week-long series of local radio call-in programs on the future of your community in the New Economy, is a useful first step to creating a shared vision. Chances are that a vision of sorts is already in place, but is it realistic? And is it a vision that is widely shared by the community?

I had a conversation with a teacher in a small town out west who, in his spare time, served on the local town council. The teacher expressed grave concern for the future of his graduating class because there were no jobs to be had, and most of the young people had no choice but to pull up roots and move away. I agreed that it was indeed a very sad state of affairs, and I went on to list several options that the community might consider to create jobs with a real future. The town was particularly picturesque and had a high-knowledge base to begin with, so I was quite sure that it would have little trouble developing further if the people set their minds to it. But I was shocked when this teacher dismissed each suggestion out of hand. I couldn't figure out why there was no pleasing him until he solved the puzzle for me. "I guess some of us folks in town don't fancy the place growing or changing much," he said. "Maybe it's better that the kids move away, after all." There was a strategy in place all right, but it was a silent and insidiously selfish one.

For a community to succeed in the New Economy, the second important step is to change old attitudes about what gets done, how it gets done and who does it now and in the future. Just as many companies need to re-engineer their operations, many towns need to streamline as well. They have to peel away the layers upon layers of red tape, eliminate all that duplication and change the attitude that practically screams, "No, I don't do that here, that's not my job." Or, "You'll need to see another department for another signature, on another form." Or, "That's the regulation." Or, "Fill this out and I'll pass it along. . . ." Or, "We'll mail it to you in six weeks (or six months)."

Take yourself on a tour of your town, and visit your various and sundry municipal departments. Ask the folks behind the counters what they do and how they do it. Ask them what they think needs to be streamlined, and what they think could be done away with altogether, without bringing the town to its knees. What new tools do they need to get their jobs done? If they're steeped in mindless paperwork and there's not a computer in sight, go to bat for them at your next town council meeting. *Just do it!*

For communities that have a *genuine* desire to insure their future for the next generation to come, there are straightforward and uncomplicated strategies to follow. Begin by taking stock of what your town's natural advantages are in the New Economy— the real cornerstones you may have for growth. Many communities overlook or are unaware of the New Economy advantages within their borders. Answering the questions in the following checklist is an important first step.

Does Your Community Have First-Rate Educational Facilities?

Having top-rated educational facilities in town or close by can give a town or city a real head start in the New Economy. Why? Because community colleges and universities are the natural resources of a high-knowledge economy. In the old economy, you would have expected a town to recognize and develop the riches in the ground beneath it—mineral deposits or oil wells, for example. In the New Economy, vast wealth and prosperity are created not just from minerals, but from the most natural and renewable of all resources— our brains. And it sure helps a community to have excellent educational facilities close at hand for all the lifelong learning we're supposed to do.

But having a handy supply of universities isn't the ticket to riches. Just look at Nova Scotia, a province well supplied with universities. Instead of sending students away the moment the ink is dry on their degrees, these university towns need to give young graduates a reason to stay and build their hopes and dreams. That's where entrepreneurial flair comes in, and it should be part of the mandate of every educational facility today, both for itself and for its students. If universities don't show their students how to combine the theory with the practice of creating wealth, like those Energizer bunnies in the battery ads, the students will just keep on going . . . and going . . . and going.

If entrepreneurial flair isn't a big feature at the university or local community college, don't despair. Once again, you can take matters into your own hands as a community, and you can offer community courses in entrepreneurship. You might be surprised at how eager your audience is—after all, these students either grew up in the community and might like to stay, or they chose your community for their education and came back to it after each school holiday. Who knows, you might even convince them to stay for good!

Do You Have the New Economy Infrastructure That Is Vital in Today's World?

Access to first-rate telecommunications is a source of enormous strategic advantage in the New Economy. Any community with a choice between a tarmac highway and an information highway would be well advised to pick the fiber optics. With the money a community makes from the strong New Economy tax base, it'll be able to afford as many of the old-fashioned highways as it wants.

A pretty town in Nova Scotia is on the right track to becoming a New Economy hotbed. A senior executive I know recently relocated to Lunenburg and runs a worldwide publishing empire, creating and operating magazines in Rome and Vienna, to name just two of this year's projects. Communications software, fax-modems and computers are the tools of his high-knowledge trade. Another small company in the same village develops and publishes books all over the world. One of its current projects involves input from Japan, France, England and Germany, made possible by simple access to a satellite system.

To encourage local initiative, why not offer every household and business in the community free trial access to the Internet for six months? And get the local high school or community college to run courses on "How to Cruise the Internet," with beginner, intermediate and advanced cruisin' courses. You could even go an important step further and encourage computer literacy in your community by allowing every home to deduct all or part of the cost of a home computer from its local tax bill. And it would be worthwhile to sweet-talk the provincial or federal government into doing a little cost-sharing for a New Economy initiative as vital as this one.

Does Your Community Have Access to the Global Village?

While a major airport can be an important advantage to a community, it's not at the top of the list. Software has been developing so fast that realistic teleconferencing is within our grasp. We'll soon look back on today's video conferencing technology and chuckle over the fish-eye view that is all too common today. Communities with an eye on the future would be well advised to contact their local telephone giant and offer to pilot whatever video conferencing and new technologies it plans to introduce. No community can expect to remain at the forefront without taking the initiative to do so.

Are Companies in Your Community Marketing to the New Economy?

Getting the existing companies in your community out of their shells is not as daunting a challenge as it might first appear. In fact, innovation can be downright infectious as companies begin to think larger thoughts than they're accustomed to. If a local company can sell to the guy down the street, there is no reason why it can't sell to people in other communities a few hundred or a few thousand kilometers away. Simple technologies such as faxes and modems and toll-free telephone lines allow market expansion to happen today with ease. A truly farsighted community would offer a free 1-800 telephone number to every business in town.

You can also start a New Economy marketing contest in conjunction with some local service clubs. Offer a community award to the company that manages to increase its out-of-town sales by the greatest percentage. Local libraries are stocked with business directories listing the names of companies far and wide, and by referring to Chapter Four of this book—which identifies the New Economy industries with a real future—companies in your community can become suppliers to what's growing beyond the borders. The local print shop, for example, could start marketing to a software company several communities away. After all, *someone* is going to have to get the contract for all that new product literature.

Are You a Clever Community?

With knowledge as the most important asset in the New Economy, it should come as little surprise that communities with a high Knowledge Ratio will have a wider range of opportunities and industries on their doorstep. But it's startling the number of communities that have no idea whether their knowledge base is high or low, rising or falling. Here's a low-cost and win-win suggestion for provinces with a real interest in raising the knowledge base of their cities and towns: give out annual awards to the communities that raise their Knowledge Ratios the most. Establish a "winner's circle" by issuing awards in a range of categories, such as one for northern communities, one for small communities, one for First Nations communities and so on.

If you can't convince your province to foster a rising knowledge base, don't be discouraged. Start such a program within your own community by measuring the knowledge base (refer to page 50 to find out how and to Appendix B for industry knowledge rankings) and by giving community awards to companies that have excelled in raising their Knowledge Ratio in the past year. Categories for awards might include small business, light manufacturing, large companies, owner-operated companies, retail stores and professional services. By putting into place programs to keep kids in school and to encourage lifelong learning, you can help your city or town become a high-knowledge community with a future.

Are You a New Economy Community?

Many communities have only a vague idea of how well they're positioned for change. Most communities have no clear idea what proportion of their economic base is tied to the New Economy, the old economy or to industries on the Watch List, which could go either way. Yet most communities have reasonable access to the numbers they need to determine this all-important information down to two decimal places.

Just as companies will flounder without a New Economy business plan, communities need a New Economy community plan. There's simply no point in running after semiconductor firms if you live in a low-knowledge–old economy town. It makes far better sense to become a New Economy–low-knowledge town, and attract New Economy industries that don't require the high-knowledge base that you don't have. If you discover that your community has a Knowledge Ratio of 24.3 percent, for example, then start by selecting New Economy industries that are in the 20 to 30 percent range. Leave the pharmaceutical companies with their industry Knowledge Ratios of 64 percent and up to someone else. Over time, you can gradually raise the knowledge base of the community, and go after anything that moves.

Communities should seek out New Economy companies that are compatible with their own skills and knowledge base. If you don't happen to have a ready supply of PhDs in advanced electronics in town, don't despair. The New Economy offers such a wide range of industries that it's not very difficult to find one, two or more industries that will be a fit.

In beleaguered provinces such as Newfoundland, communities need to build from established strengths by applying the knowledge base that's already in place. Most Newfoundlanders know the difference between port and starboard from a very early age, unlike mainland kids who take expensive summer sailing lessons and still can't distinguish the pointy end of the boat from the flat end. As

Newfoundlanders have a long and proud heritage in all things nautical, the cruise ship industry should be a natural target for economic development. After the enormous success of the Alaska run, cruise lines the world over are eager to replicate the experience, secure in their new-found knowledge that hundreds of thousands of free-spending passengers can be attracted to rugged coastlines and scenic spots, regardless of the weather.

The key to economic development is working with the advantages you already have. New Brunswick, for example, has been building a formidable industry in customer service and telephone ordering by recognizing its innate advantage as a bilingual population. Sadly enough, many communities overlook their obvious strengths.

Have You Abandoned Your Old Economy Companies?

In any community self-help program, it is important to remember the old economy companies in your town that may also need your help—perhaps more than ever. Don't just write them off because they're in the old economy, and think that the sooner they die off, the better you'll be. Every company can find its future in the New Economy by introducing new products, by finding new markets or by introducing new technologies to revitalize the whole industry.

You can take a small but vital step by encouraging the local community newspaper or newsletter to focus on the kinds of New Economy products that existing companies could actually produce. Ask readers to clip interesting articles on products that they read about or come across, and reprint these articles (with permission) in your community newspaper. Start a "World of Change" or "New Opportunities" column, and get everyone involved in finding the new products, new markets and new technologies, or the opportunities for strategic alliances and partnerships that are everywhere in this growing New Economy. Whatever you do, don't write off your old economy companies. They need a road map to the New Economy and they deserve better from you than that.

Are You Avoiding the Obvious Pitfalls?

Life is full of pitfalls, and I have fond memories of my teenage years when my mother shared a great deal of her wisdom with me. Of course, I still managed to give my parents frequent migraines, but like many of my generation, I chose to build my life on the solid values and sound advice that my well-meaning parents shared with me. In my years of economic research, I have found common sense to be every bit as applicable to economic development as it is to building a happy life.

Lesson No. 1: True love never runs smoothly—and neither does economic development. Recognize that every community will experience setbacks, but that it is worthwhile to stick with the companies you already have. Many communities make the mistake of believing that "somewhere out there" they will find the big employer who will move to town and save the community. Don't wait for that white knight to come charging into town when there are ways to build your community from within, by working with the companies you already have.

Lesson No. 2: Don't fall for a one-night stand—and stay away from footloose industries. Many communities have fallen for the charms of the company that whispered in their ear, "I'll be yours until the end of time." Footloose industries (such as car parts plants) can locate almost anywhere, and regularly relocate to the highest bidder—the community that offers the most incentives. Chasing after industries like that used to be a big feature of local economic development policy, and many a community has gone right to the brink of bankruptcy trying to attract the one-night stand—or, in the case of economic development, the company that shows up, collects its four or five years of tax incentives, and moves on down the road before it even becomes a tax-paying entity. What's worse, when the company moves to the next location, it petulantly demands even more incentives, which the next town can barely afford, either.

While footloose companies can reasonably argue that they are simply maximizing their returns to shareholders (after all, few companies would remain in the same old office building if better and cheaper space became available elsewhere), communities need to distinguish between a one-night stand and a lasting relationship.

Lesson No. 3: Marry a man you can rely on—and steer clear of industries on the Watch List. Too often, communities spend far too much time and money courting companies in industries that are on the Watch List—only to find that the company comes to town and then spends the next five years downsizing. In the entirely hopeless expectation of a reasonable return and a secure future, the community has spent money that it didn't really have.

Escape from Nowheresville

It can be very tempting to give up on a community—to pack your bags and move to another place where jobs and a future can be readily found. But there is another alternative. You can stay right where you are and build your community—a New Economy community with a *real* future. And, who knows, you might one day look back on your life and feel the sense of pride that so many people must have felt as they built this country, one community at a time, and left Canada a better, more prosperous and more enduring place for their children.

vision to create new wealth. And we need to recognize that, when all is said and done, we have three choices as a nation:

- Create wealth and prosperity for ourselves and for our children; or
- Maintain the wealth we have, but do not create any new wealth or prosperity; or
- Consume wealth by living off the prosperity that we created in the past.

If Canadians want their governments to create prosperity, then any re-engineering effort must prominently feature cost-efficient new processes, structures and technologies. The first step is to determine clear objectives, and then to address *how* these objectives will be implemented. All the wishful thinking in the world won't create prosperity for us: what we need is efficient growth. Sooner or later, we're going to have to work together as a nation to create it.

Here are ten road maps for government—examples of what governments can do to move us rapidly from wealth consumption or wealth maintenance to wealth creation. Each road map is based on a crucial shift in government's role. In the old economy, governments redistributed wealth, but in the New Economy governments create wealth.

1. Remodel Unemployment Insurance and Workers' Compensation

Canada has an enviable record in the life and health insurance field, and more companies and insurance brokers than not in the industry are solid players. In the old economy, governments were *in* the insurance business, with unemployment insurance and workers' compensation. In the New Economy, governments could partner or franchise with the private sector to offer and administer sweepingly better plans that meet our new and changing needs for personal protection. Government could set the terms of coverage and carefully regulate the industry, as they have actively regulated the delivery and quality of financial services for decades. There is no reason why governments couldn't mandate a basic level of required unemployment insurance coverage that every employee had to subscribe to, with premiums based on both the employee's and the employer's records. The rest of the decisions could then be left up to us, as we select (and pay for) a wide range of insurance options that we could tailor to our changing needs and circumstances.

New plan options would allow each of us to select the level of unemployment insurance coverage we need. A single parent with two children might want a higher level of protection than, say, a single person who is still living at home. On the other hand, a couple that has recently paid off its mortgage might decide that its insurance needs are now minimal, while a young couple raising a family on a single income would likely choose more coverage.

Retailers in the 1990s discovered (some the hard way) that consumers want more selection in the marketplace; they also learned that their success in the New Economy depends on bringing their cost structures into line with what consumers are now willing to pay. Governments need to learn these lessons as well because flexibility is the key to growth in this New Economy. Governments could serve a wide range of new needs if they replaced the old assumption that "one size fits all" with a new ethic of personal choice at affordable prices. Insurance companies and banks could also offer new products, such as retraining insurance that would allow us to finance our retraining and lifelong learning needs, and mortgage protection insurance that would protect our homes if we lost our jobs.

Instead of everyone paying UI premiums based solely on income level, as is the system today, a person could pay premiums according to the package of insurance products that he or she selected. Furthermore, the cost of new and broader insurance products would depend on whether the buyer is a high risk applicant—just as life insurance premiums are higher for people who smoke. For years, Canadians have taken personal responsibility for deciding whether they want term life or whole life insurance, and whether they require some level of disability coverage. Unemployment insurance need be no different.

Workers' compensation systems play a vital role in guaranteeing that injured workers receive disability income and rehabilitation. But why duplicate the private sector disability insurance plans that are already in place? Do we need—and can we afford—the parallel systems, when one less expensive system could suffice?

2. Insure the Integrity of the Canada Pension Plan

In the current pay-as-you-go system, our Canada Pension Plan money is lumped into government revenues and often spent as fast as it's collected. Instead, government could foster real wealth creation by phasing in our pension contributions to capital markets so that a large new pool of capital is available to finance the New Economy.

Even as private pension plan money has been invested judiciously and professionally for decades in stock and bond markets, so Canada Pension Plan money could be invested judiciously and professionally in New Economy companies. Rates of return for these companies are far higher than for the old economy corporations on the TSE 300, and, with the favorable return-to-risk profile of investing in the New Economy, governments could accomplish three worthy objectives.

First, they will insure that there will be money (and not just an accounting entry on the government books) to pay for our pensions when we retire. It is a national disgrace to expect our children to work until they drop to pay for the pensions that we have promised ourselves. Our generation could and should be creating wealth for our future and for theirs.

Second, they will get out of the subsidy and grant business by getting into the investment business. As an equity investor, governments—and that means you and me—would get to share in the growth and dividends of companies that haven't just seen the future . . . but *are* the future.

Third, they will free up billions of dollars to create wealth, growth and jobs by giving New Economy companies broader access to capital. This access to capital could be achieved in one or a combination of four ways:

- By using pension funds as partnering collateral to partially guarantee New Economy equity loans issued by chartered banks (a bank's allocation of guarantees would be reduced or eliminated if its loss experience exceeded federally mandated guidelines).
- By expanding the role of the Federal Business Development Bank to include an explicit New Economy mandate, according to minimum rate-of-return guidelines.
- By creating regional New Economy capital markets that are run like mutual funds, through which very small companies gain access to debt and equity capital.
- By expanding the role of credit unions to include a New Economy mandate for Canada Pension Plan contributions from the community, which would be recycled in the community to create wealth and growth according to minimum rate-of-return guidelines.

3. ELIMINATE INDEXATION

Federal indexation was a vital tool when inflation was high or rising, as it was in the old economy, where mature industries were a source of structural inflation. But inflation is not a problem in the

New Economy; nor will it be for decades until the New Economy
matures and becomes an old economy. As *Business Week* and other
publications have pointed out, the methods we use to calculate the
rate of inflation probably overestimate the rate of price increase,
which means that governments are paying large sums to protect us
from yesterday's threat. Eliminating indexation is a worthy step to
trimming expenditures that have outlived their original need and
use. Governments need to focus on the present and not the past,
because it is just too expensive to fight yesterday's battles when
today's challenges have created new needs.

4. Establish National Patriot Programs

Many Canadians might be willing to volunteer as government
appointees on a non-partisan basis. And the federal government
could save a bundle if it converted many appointments into volunteer positions in a series of national patriot programs that encourage Canadians to serve their country. The Canadian Senate is a
good example of how the government could transform a costly
institution into a volunteer corps; in fact, the vast majority of government appointments domestically and abroad could be reviewed.
If they advertised appointment vacancies, governments could cast
a wide net and potentially attract volunteers from a wide range of
backgrounds and talents. The principle of volunteerism is a worthy
one in any economy, old or new.

5. Create Pay-Your-Way Programs

In the New Economy, governments must consider how to replace
most taxpayer-financed operations with pay-your-way programs.
If hundreds of federal and provincial programs were run on a
cost-recovery basis, billions of dollars could be saved.

One of the best places where a pay-your-way program could work is in Canada's legal and judicial systems. To stop the judicial system from costing taxpayers billions a year, those who use the system could cover their own costs. For example, if you're found not guilty, then the government pays for the court costs; if you're found guilty, then the government grants you a *legal loan* that you must pay back, whether in or out of jail.

6. Create Franchise Opportunities

Private sector companies already do a good job running travel agencies, information services and many other services. There is no reason why new or existing companies couldn't do a fine job running a government franchise, on the condition that they offer expanded services at lower costs. Many government services are still vital to the national interest and could be expanded in new directions to serve new needs. Governments in the New Economy need to improve, commercialize and expand programs and services while cutting costs. Here are seven opportunities that spring instantly to mind:

- International trade marketing agencies that would insure that the services delivered were really relevant to the needs of a changing global market.
- A national travel and tourism agency to replace the myriad and often confusing programs in place today.
- Canada Employment Centers that are fully on-line with community and national help-wanted bulletin boards.
- A franchise with the private sector to collect and distribute economic and industry statistics.
- A franchise to run ports, marinas and harbors, either individually or nationally.
- A franchise to run airports according to federal standards.
- A franchise to run Canada's penal system according to federal

guidelines. Instead of taxpayers absorbing the horrendous costs of our penal system, penitentiaries could be run on a break-even basis by requiring inmates to provide more of their own services and be more self-supporting. Inmates could also learn valuable skills that might facilitate their re-entry into the labor force.

Management fees on these commercial franchises could be governed by formulas, in the same way that management fees in the mutual fund industry are well understood and subject to public disclosure. Governments could function like a board of directors to oversee the operations and serve the interest of Canadians—just as the directors of a company serve the interests of their shareholders by setting policy and strategy, and making management accountable for achieving the clear objectives in a business plan. If a franchisee failed to meet explicit government targets or operated outside of government regulations, then the franchise would be revoked and a new partner would be found. Hundreds of government programs at the federal and provincial levels could be renewed, expanded and made much more affordable if operated on this commercial basis. And there is no reason why governments couldn't charge commercial franchise fees and apply the proceeds to paying down the national debt.

7. Establish a Canadian Legacy Fund

There is nothing wrong with the government making money in the national interest, *if* those funds go directly to paying down Canada's national debt. If we have a genuine desire to create a legacy of hope for our children, we cannot kid ourselves that the national debt will somehow just go away. We must have the vision to move forward and fashion a new role for government.

There could be widespread national support for a Canadian legacy fund in which net revenues from certain "for profit" government programs were channeled directly into paying off our national debt. The goal would be for the baby boom generation to leave Canada debt-free for its children. As past issues of government bonds and treasury bills came due, they would be paid off from the balance in the fund.

The first priority would be to pay off foreign debt. Not only would we no longer be dependent on foreign investors to keep us afloat, but Canadian interest rates would fall much further and faster. With our national debt falling, Canada could then contemplate an independent monetary policy—something that we can't and shouldn't do now.

Revenues into the Canadian legacy fund could come from many sources, including franchise fees when existing programs and services are commercialized, and from annual director fees, for government's participation on the board of the franchise operations.

8. Encourage Job Creation Through Small Business

Entrepreneurs who have founded small businesses are the unsung heroes of the New Economy. Governments are already aware that entrepreneurs have created jobs for themselves and for others by accepting the risk of failure in exchange for a commitment to success. To stimulate job creation, governments could introduce an innovative entrepreneurial job creation–tax saving plan. Modeled on the RRSP program, this job creation initiative would allow small business owners who create net new jobs to deduct the T-4 federal tax payable by the new employee(s) from the small business owner's personal income taxes. A sliding scale with a limit of, perhaps, $10,000 in year one, $5,000 in year two and $2,500 in year three could be applied.

To ensure that the program has built-in revenue neutrality, the deduction would not be allowed to exceed the new employees' federal income taxes payable in any year. And, of course, to guarantee that an existing employee is not fired in favor of a new employee, only net new employees would be eligible for deduction. Finally, family members of the business owner would not be eligible.

9. Create Personal Tax Incentives for Lifelong Learners

Governments could go a long way to foster a well-trained New Economy work force by encouraging Canadians to take personal responsibility for lifelong learning. One way of achieving this goal is to provide a personal tax holiday for Canadians who upgrade their skills. For every day (or eight-hour period) that you attend a course at a registered educational or vocational institute, paid for out of personal funds, you could deduct one day of federal income tax payable from your income tax return, to a maximum of thirty days per year. If you don't pass the course, you don't qualify for the deduction.

10. Encourage Students to Stay in School

Governments are serious about the need to upgrade educational attainment in Canada, and I applaud them for taking this issue to heart because Canadians can no longer afford to carry the cost of unemployment and underemployment. In our high-knowledge economy, high school students should be encouraged to stay in school, and students who drop out should have only graduated access to unemployment insurance, in the same way that many jurisdictions are requiring that young drivers receive graduated driver's licenses. For example, if a high school student drops out, a percentage of UI benefits in years one to four could apply with full eligibility in the fifth year, providing no claims have been filed.

A Road Map for Education

Education, health care, law enforcement, immigration, missing children, government elections, dangerous offenders—at first, these words may seem out of place in the same sentence, but they're not odd bedfellows in the New Economy. The common link is that information technology can help all of these programs and systems to deliver better processes and products at a fraction of current costs.

When companies faced the cold winds of change, some made the mistake of believing that they would have to layer new tools and methods on top of the old systems already in place. To survive, they had to change, and in the process they came to realize that you can't *layer* the new on top of the old—you need to *replace* the old with the new.

In education alone, technology offers great opportunities to free up a teacher's time to teach. Instead of asking each teacher to create the modules, class notes and lessons for the week, the term or the year, the educational system could follow in the footsteps of industry and use teaching software (called courseware) on disk and CD-ROM. These programs can be customized with a mind-boggling assortment of button bars and individually selected features, just as any current version of Microsoft Word or Lotus 1-2-3 can be customized to fit the needs and preferences of the user. I'm not just talking about tools that allow teachers to track students' grades with ease. The technology goes far beyond that to include an exciting array of exercises, lessons and experiences for students at all grade levels. And it's not as complex as it sounds.

Microsoft can fit an entire encyclopedia of world knowledge on a CD-ROM, so it's not fanciful to think that *all* Grade One material or the entire course content for Grade Seven can fit on a library of CD-ROM disks, from which every Grade One or Grade Seven teacher could pick and choose. The same applies to Grade Ten chemistry and Grade Twelve economics. The truth is that we can

157

no longer afford the waste and inefficiency of every teacher duplicating every other teacher's modules and programs. And a CD-ROM system would be one way to get the set of national standards that Canada needs to compete in a global high-knowledge economy. If students in a particular class can't pass the test on the last disk in the package, then principals and parents have every right to ask the teacher what's going on.

Part of the problem is that many teachers today have only a slight familiarity with information technology and especially with the courseware that is rapidly making its multimedia debut. Some teachers have never seen or used software on CD-ROM, and many still think that Windows are something their students look out of when they get bored with the day's lessons! Computer literacy should be mandatory for every educator today.

Saving Money Is Too Expensive

I often hear the concerns that substantial educational changes can never come about because schools and universities don't have the money to introduce new programs or policies, or to effect change. They don't have enough money to buy computers for their students, and budgets cannot be stretched to afford what many old economy thinkers believe are wordprocessing toys. The simple truth is that you can walk into any store today and, for *less than $1,300*, buy a fully loaded 486/66 computer with a 340-megabyte hard drive, and a color monitor, math co-processor and keyboard with an operating system, ready to go. An entire school district or, heaven forbid, a province of school districts working together could certainly cut a better deal. Remodeling local school boards in favor of greater co-operation among school districts could be a vital first step.

Some schools are meeting the challenges in education today despite formidable roadblocks, and they seem to be getting it right. One school that has renewed my confidence in the Canadian educational system is located in St. Thomas, Ontario. I've never seen so many computers in a single school, and they were modern ones, too! As I was taken on a tour, I became increasingly impressed by the entrepreneurial spirit I saw all around me: the cafeteria was run by students taking hospitality courses, the school garage was run by students taking automotive mechanics and there was even a hair salon run by the kids who were studying how to become hairdressers. To this day, I have never seen as fine a technology group in any school or community college in the country. What impressed me most was that teachers and students were working as teams—the way knowledge workers work in the real world.

Looking beyond the benefits of schools working together to afford New Economy technologies, there are great merits to establishing a national strategy on education for the New Economy that focuses on one of the most important issues of all: training for jobs with a future. One of the saddest things that I have seen in this country is the hundreds and thousands of people who have been trained for jobs that either already don't exist or soon won't. That's why identifying jobs with a future is essential in Canada today, and why I developed the rating guide to five-star jobs in the New Economy (see Appendix A).

A Job for Life?

Tenure is another problem in education and, indeed, right across government today. A few years back, when some managers and workers insisted that they should be insulated from any change in the workplace, tenure certainly was a problem in business as well.

Years ago, when I joined a major investment dealer as a research economist, I was flown to Toronto and taken on a tour of the company to meet the people working in head office. I was impressed by the vigor of the place—the hundreds of bond traders, analysts and salespeople who were focused intently on doing their

159

jobs and being the best on Bay Street. But when I arrived in the afternoon for my 2:30 appointment with the corporate development department, there was hardly a soul in sight. As I waited patiently, I asked a secretary, "What does corporate development do?" She looked at me, clearly at a loss for words, and then admitted that, although she had been in the department for close to a year, she didn't quite know what the department actually did. "They're very senior gentlemen here, all directors of the firm, and they have been with the company for a long, long time. They have contacts, and I suppose it's their job to stay in touch with people they know." The plants on their desks were well tended, a whiff of expensive cigar smoke lingered in the air and I gathered that they took long lunches; it was half-past three when the first elderly gentleman toddled back to his desk, a smell of fine brandy drifting in after him.

Too often, tenure is used in education and government circles as it was in business—as protection for the out-of-date, the ineffective or the lazy. Many students have listened to the professor who drones on and on about the material that he or she specialized in as a grad student thirty or forty years ago. While tenure can rightfully protect the integrity of academic research, it should not be allowed to protect poor research or irrelevant research. Renewable employment contracts based on pay-for-performance are one answer.

A Road Map for Health Care

Teamwork is a concept well developed in health care. We've all seen the television dramas about the handsome, dedicated doctor in the emergency room surrounded by the high-tension team of nurses, sweat glistening on their brows, working seamlessly and feverishly to save the patient's life.

In the real world, nurses are among the most undervalued people in the medical system today—and this inefficiency is costing us a bundle. Most of the time, nurses (with graduate degrees, no less) are treated the way junior clerks used to be treated in corporations, before companies realized that they couldn't afford to underutilize their staff. Try asking a nurse in a hospital for some Tylenol—the stuff your ten-year-old can buy in any supermarket—and you will promptly be told that the nurse must first ask a doctor because nurses do not have the authority to issue any medication. Expanding the role of nurses into midwifery, and into licensed nurse practitioners who are allowed to treat many common ailments and issue prescriptions for routine medications, is part of the answer to a more efficient and lower-cost health care system. But what dismays me the most is seeing nurses deal with endless paperwork with barely a computer in sight. Their professional days are too often spent filling out forms, tending to the non-medical needs of their patients and caring for the elderly, who have no other place to go.

Patients also need to shoulder responsibility for the demands that they place on the medical system, and those who use the system unnecessarily must be advised of that fact. Sooner or later, doctors have to look some of their patients squarely in the eye and tell them, *"There's nothing really wrong with you."*

Computer registries that could tally our medical and prescription drug use each year and send each of us a personalized account of the costs that we have incurred would be a useful reminder to ourselves and our doctors that nothing in life is free. We are either net contributors to, or net users of, our system of health care, and the less we abuse it or allow people in the medical system to abuse it, intentionally or unintentionally, the more we will be able to preserve and improve our first-rate system for the people who need it the most.

Mother's Little Helper

Computer registries are vital New Economy helpers when it comes to personal safety and justice in this country. If I have the right to know what ingredients in my box of breakfast cereal could kill me, one ingredient at a time, surely I have a right to know what dangerous offenders, convicted pedophiles and rapists are in my neighborhood, municipality or province. And it tears my heart out when I hear about the plight of parents and their missing children. Why should an anguished parent have to resort to pictures on a milk carton when all children could be computer-registered right across the country? The same type of system could prevent the mess in immigration departments when bureaucrats manage to lose track of the deportation orders of convicted criminals.

Of course, I can hear the protests of the libertarians of the land, who deeply resent the intrusion of government into our lives. I believe, however, that the suffering of missing children and the personal safety of citizens supersede my rights to complete and total privacy. I want to live in a community where the rights of the society to safety, peace and security are held sacrosanct. In the New Economy, knowledge workers work in teams, and we need to work together outside as well as inside the workplace to achieve common goals for our country. Information technology is not the answer to all the world's problems, but it can certainly help us save the money we need to find solutions.

Workfare, Not Welfare

Workfare is not a particularly new idea but it is one that should be piloted more broadly in Canada to determine whether it can succeed better than welfare has in restoring people's self-sufficiency and self-esteem. Workfare simply requires that every able-bodied person who is drawing some kind of public assistance must work in his or her community to earn these funds. Just think of the huge opportunities and benefits to our society if people who *could* work, *did* work in a range of occupations—from education to health care to community and social service to child care and elder care. Here are some possibilities:

- A day-care program could be made possible with a national team of child minders. Workfare helpers would receive professional training in child-care skills, while working parents would have the comfort of knowing that their children were not sitting at home alone for part of each day, or spending time in a day-care program that may be understaffed.

- School hours could be extended to include homework hours after school for children who need the extra study time, or so that working parents have the peace of mind that homework isn't left to the last minute after the supper dishes have been cleared. Workfare helpers could supervise this important after-school activity.

- Seniors could benefit from having help at home, and could probably live independently for longer if they had the support of a workfare helper.

- Trained clerical helpers and nurse's aides could free up a nurse's time for medical work.

- Whole communities could benefit if parks and public recreation facilities were better staffed and better maintained.

- Transit systems would benefit if escorts were available to see single travelers safely home at night. This is a security service that many university campuses offer students.

But the biggest benefit of workfare would be to give people the training, dignity and self-esteem that come with having a job and playing a vital role in the community.

FINDING OUR OWN WAY HOME

The road map to the New Economy is straightforward enough. While there will always be a need for governments to step in and offer help to the disadvantaged, most of us can find our own way home, planting our feet firmly in the fertile ground of a New Economy. And, in the process, we can build a better future for ourselves and for our children.

163

8

WE'VE GOT TO GET BACK TO GROWTH

I'm on the edge of my seat waiting to see how the story of Canada's transition from old to new is going to end. It's the kind of high-tension real-life drama that could make Tom Clancy's *The Hunt for Red October* read like a children's storybook, and could make one of those sweeping biblical epics—the kind that Charleton Heston used to star in—seem lacking in context, empathy and compassion.

The place: Canada.
The mission: lead twenty-nine million Canadians, of all ages, races and creeds, safely into a world of prosperity.
Clear and present danger: special interest groups; federal, provincial and local governments who resist change.
Objective: growth.

If our leaders build a government that is shaped around the needs of Canada's New Economy, then they will deliver us safely from a world of old technologies and ideas and methods into a new paradigm of growth. Taking these final difficult steps will reward us beyond measure—the prize will be an unprecedented world of growth and opportunity.

The Prize

Picture our lives just ten years from now. After work, Laura heats the spaghetti sauce in the microwave oven that she and Peter bought eighteen years ago. It still works perfectly because the New Economy ushered in a new standard of product quality. We have more money to spend on *new* goods and services because we don't have to keep replacing what we've already paid good money for.

At seven o'clock, they sit down in front of the screen and tune into the House of Commons channel. People actually watch the debates now because technology has allowed the government to offer Canadians direct representation. Laura and Peter click on to the button bar for their riding and listen to their MP give a background briefing on tonight's votes. They indulge in a little channel surfing to see what some of the other MPs and some of the folks in Cabinet have to say about the first issue before Laura and Peter respond to whether they agree strongly, agree, disagree or disagree strongly—or whether they couldn't care less and think that the government has wasted its time and theirs on such a low priority concern. And God help any MP who votes against the wishes of his or her constituents. The last one who tried to pull that stunt was recalled by the people who elected her before she'd been in Ottawa long enough to unpack her bags.

Laura will probably see her daughter on TV again, interviewing one of the MPs during his background briefing and asking all the tough questions; she also fields the 1-800 calls better than Larry King ever did. It's amazing how many jobs in broadcast journalism were created when people began having a say in their own affairs, and these new positions sure pay better than those enumerator jobs ever did in the old economy, where people trudged door-to-door before federal elections or absurdly expensive referendums.

There will be two votes tonight. The second question is going to be the big one; the first vote is usually the least contentious and tonight it will deal with whether MPs and Cabinet ministers should get a government pension. Their pensions were abolished years ago, after the government had eyed people's RRSP contributions a little too covetously and taxpayers came close to revolt. Those were tough days then; Canada was so deep in debt it was frightening. People probably felt just as anxious after the Great Depression of the 1930s. What would have become of us or our parents if the future had been brushed aside in favor of the status quo: no New Deal, no unemployment insurance, no social security whatsoever?

It's hard to think back on how turbulent times used to be, and how afraid of the future we all were back in the mid '90s. I shudder to think what could have become of us if our governments hadn't had the courage and vision to adapt. But there's no sense dwelling on the past or on how close we came to the brink. Those monstrous federal deficits have since been eliminated, and the federal debt is on track and will be paid off in another five years. So will Laura's and Peter's mortgage. Today, Laura works from home almost as often as she works out of her downtown office. "I only go there when our team has a reason to meet. My husband likes the arrangement, too, especially since we bought our new home. We had found it just too frustrating to work in a house that had been designed around a world that no longer existed, and we wanted one of the 'smart homes' with the features everyone needs. Ours came pre-wired for Internet and satellite access, and the office space is soundproofed so I can't hear our dog barking when I'm on a conference call!" With interest rates at 3.5 percent, the mortgage is not a problem, and Laura and Peter are delighted that they decided to trade up—like millions of other Canadian baby boomers in the last eight years. But they are looking forward to the day when their dream house is paid for, lock, stock and barrel.

In the early 1990s, a lot of Canadians came close to losing everything when they or their partners—or both—lost their jobs and had no place to go. And it was so tough back then, especially when the kids were young. There was no day care in the schools, and parents positively hated calling into work and lying about being sick when it was the babysitter who was home in bed with a cold.

Politicians made some tough choices between 1993 and 1997, but we're all a lot better off now. Many Canadians have really gotten to know their representatives and most MPs are doing a good job. They'll get approval for their pension plan as long as it doesn't exceed what Canadians have.

The second vote tonight will probably stir things up a bit. We're going to vote on whether Canada's minimum wage should be raised to $15/hour. Can you still remember the hue and cry when it was increased to $10/hour in the year 2000? All the doom and gloomers said that the world would end, that companies would go bankrupt, that investment would leave Canada, and that inflation would come roaring back and drive interest rates through the roof. One industry association *still* runs on at the mouth about how government should abolish all minimum wage laws but double business subsidies "to foster lasting prosperity in this country." They just don't understand that knowledge is the asset of the twenty-first century, and that knowledge is a renewable natural resource. By raising the minimum wage, we had the chance to narrow a widening gap between incomes in this country, and it was the right thing to do. Most of the low-knowledge jobs have been transformed into higher-knowledge jobs, and the higher wages are simply rewarding people for their lifelong learning and skills upgrading. The nice thing about a higher-knowledge economy is that it always can and should translate into a higher-income economy.

But it is far easier now to keep up with new technologies and information. In the mid 1990s, we had no choice but to trudge out to classes held at high schools, colleges and universities. Today, distance learning is a blessing. Last term, Laura took an amazing chemistry course that is offered right across North and Central America from St. Francis Xavier University in Antigonish, Nova Scotia. Distance learning has helped millions of people to keep on top of developments in their industries and their companies—the ones they've worked in for years. So much for all the dire warnings that we would spend the rest of our life changing jobs faster than most husbands change their socks. But so much has changed in the work force since the New Economy began. Remember how wild an idea Casual Fridays were when companies started introducing them?

We're at a crossroads in Canada. We've shifted gears, and now we need to put our foot on the gas, move forward and *grow*. Our global New Economy, driven by information technology, has meant a world of change in where we work, how we work, what we work at and who we sell to. In short, *everything* in our world has changed. We're living through a transformation as tumultuous as the Industrial Revolution, and that's the truth of it. The prize that awaits us as a nation if we get on with the business of growth will include job security, growth, stability, a rising standard of living, access to low-cost education, a direct say in our country's future and in our own—and a future for our children.

Why the Future Will Be Different from the Past

What a lot of people couldn't see then, and a handful are probably too stubborn to admit now, is that so many old assumptions don't work in the New Economy. One of the biggest factors that is being overlooked is that when an industry's top line is growing rapidly, the industry can *afford* to pay more. And a higher level of national income fuels spending and savings. Only when an economy is mature and in the process of peaking structurally will higher wage rates ignite inflationary pressures—which in turn will eat away at savings and wealth.

The way things work in the first stages of any New Economy is that technology and innovation drive rates of return higher. That's called *wealth creation,* and you can keep this process feeding on itself to create growth as long as the rate of return on innovation continues to rise and governments don't consume wealth faster than the rest of us can create it.

If the minimum wage had been raised while the old economy was still struggling through the transition, the soothsayers would have been right in their dire predictions. What a disaster if the rates had been hiked while the top line was shrinking! But many old economy industries started raising their knowledge base by quantum leaps in the early 1990s, introducing new products and becoming suppliers to the New Economy here and abroad. In short, some are catching the next wave, while a lot more are trying.

Why some people can't seem to distinguish the difference between structural growth and decline, I'll never know. It's amazing how innovation can accelerate the growth rate of an economy. The labour productivity analysis of the 1970s and 1980s missed the point because it's a country's *innovation rate* and the *rate of return on innovation*—not the productivity growth rate—that are the key factors. Measuring how well Canada becomes more and more productive at making things that no one wants to buy anymore is like watching a nation of hamsters run faster and faster on little treadmills: in the end, they're exhausted, but exactly where they began. Unfortunately, that is all too common a feeling in old economy industries that have not yet raised their rate of return on knowledge and innovation.

The rules of the game are very different when an economy is underpinned by long-term structural growth, as every New Economy is at the beginning of every new era. It is time to put aside the old rule books, discard the old assumptions and embrace the opportunities. Armed with clear road maps, we can make our way to a better and more prosperous future.

169

APPENDIX A

JOBS WITH A FUTURE

Index of Industries

NEW ECONOMY JOBS

★ ★ ★ ★ ★

35.7% of all New Economy jobs are
in five-star industries.

★ ★ ★ ★

12.5% of all New Economy jobs are
in four-star industries.

★ ★ ★

22.7% of all New Economy jobs are
in three-star industries.

★ ★

6.9% of all New Economy jobs are
two-star industries.

★

20.2% of all New Economy jobs are
in one-star industries.

2% of the jobs are not classifiable.

OLD ECONOMY JOBS

11.4% of all old economy jobs are
in five-star industries.

0.9% of all old economy jobs are
in four-star industries.

18.2% of all old economy jobs are
in three-star industries.

20.1% of all old economy jobs are
in two-star industries.

36.1% of all old economy jobs are
in one-star industries.

13.3% of all old economy jobs could
not be classified.

INDUSTRY SCORES AND RANKINGS

Each industry has been ranked from best to worst for job security, advancement, average salary, salary change, knowledge base, industry knowledge changes and industry stability—and compared to all other industries for which data was available. Industries were then scored as follows:

JOB SECURITY

Very High	=	20 points
High	=	15 points
Moderate	=	10 points
Low	=	5 points
Very Low	=	0 points

ADVANCEMENT

Very Good	=	10 points
Good	=	7.5 points
Moderate	=	5 points
Poor	=	2.5 points
Very Poor	=	0 points

AVERAGE SALARY

Very High	=	20 points
High	=	15 points
Moderate	=	10 points
Low	=	5 points
Very Low	=	0 points

SALARY CHANGE

Very High	=	10 points
High	=	7.5 points
Moderate	=	5 points
Poor	=	2.5 points
Very Poor	=	0 points

KNOWLEDGE BASE

High (more than 40 knowledge workers per 100 employees)	=	10 points
Moderate (between 20 and 40 knowledge workers per 100 employees)	=	5 points
Low (fewer than 20 knowledge workers per 100 employees)	=	0 points

INDUSTRY KNOWLEDGE	Rising Very Sharply	=	10 points
	Rising Sharply	=	7.5 points
	Rising	=	5 points
	Reasonably Stable	=	2.5 points
	Declining	=	0 points
INDUSTRY STABILITY	Very High	=	10 points
	High	=	7.5 points
	Moderate	=	5 points
	Low	=	2.5 points
	Very Low	=	0 points

NEW ECONOMY industries that continue to grow in structural terms were awarded 10 points.

TURNAROUND industries that have begun to display long-term structural growth characteristics were awarded 7.5 points.

WATCH LIST industries that are developing many of the characteristics of an industry that may peak structurally were awarded 5 points.

OLD ECONOMY industries that have peaked structurally and are in long-term decline were awarded 2.5 points.

OVERALL SCORES were determined for each industry out of a possible 100 points. Star ratings were based on the following scores:

★ ★ ★ ★ ★   OVERALL SCORE OF 70 OR MORE

★ ★ ★ ★   OVERALL SCORE OF 60 – 69

★ ★ ★   OVERALL SCORE OF 50 – 59

★ ★   OVERALL SCORE OF 40 – 49

★   OVERALL SCORE OF 39 OR LESS

INDUSTRY KNOWLEDGE

Rising Very Sharply = 10 points
Rising Sharply = 7.5 points
Rising = 5 points
Reasonably Stable = 2.5 points
Declining = 0 points

INDUSTRY STABILITY

Very High = 10 points
High = 7.5 points
Moderate = 5 points
Low = 2.5 points
Very Low = 0 points

NEW ECONOMY industries that continue to grow in structural terms were awarded 10 points.

TURNAROUND industries that have begun to display long-term structural growth characteristics were awarded 7.5 points.

WATCH LIST industries that are developing many of the characteristics of an industry that may peak structurally were awarded 5 points.

OLD ECONOMY industries that have peaked structurally and are in long-term decline were awarded 2.5 points.

OVERALL SCORES were determined for each industry out of a possible 100 points. Star ratings were based on the following scores:

★ ★ ★ ★ ★ OVERALL SCORE OF 70 OR MORE

★ ★ ★ ★ OVERALL SCORE OF 60 – 69

★ ★ ★ OVERALL SCORE OF 50 – 59

★ ★ OVERALL SCORE OF 40 – 49

★ OVERALL SCORE OF 39 OR LESS

177

DATA SOURCES AND LIMITATIONS

- Every industry has been listed with its SIC code (Standard Industrial Classification). SIC codes are useful for job seekers because many business directories that list company names and addresses are organized by SIC code.

- Statistics Canada is the source of all data except industry Knowledge Ratio information, which is from Nuala Beck & Associates Inc. and is based on U.S. benchmark data.

- Industry volatility has been calculated on the basis of GDP. However, where GDP data for the industry was not available, employment statistics were used instead and have been noted as (empl.).

- Provincial employment data by industry is collected by Statistics Canada and is not available for all industries in every province.

- Data discrepancies may exist between provincial and national figures.

NEW ECONOMY ENGINES & SUPPLIERS

The following industries have not peaked structurally. While they ride the normal ups and downs of a business cycle, they are underpinned by long-term structural growth. Recession years are followed by strong and lengthy recoveries to new industry production records.

SOFTWARE & COMPUTER SERVICES

Canada's software industry employs more people than the mining industry and can no longer be described as "emerging." Although the principal occupations in this five-star industry revolve around programmers and systems personnel, there are job opportunities for "non-techies" as well: receptionists, accounting personnel, marketing and advertising people and personnel in distribution.

OVERALL
SCORE

87.5

Job security is very high, as demonstrated by the zero lay-off rate through the recession years of 1989–93. Job creation is also excellent, with 4,104 net new jobs added since 1989. The excellent average salary in this industry with a high and rapidly rising knowledge base was topped off with an 8.2 percent average increase in 1993.

HOW THE INDUSTRY COMPARES:

Job Security: Very High
Advancement: Very Good
Average Salary: Very High
Salary Change: Very High
Knowledge Base: High
Industry Knowledge: Rising Sharply
Industry Stability: Very Low

WHERE THE JOBS ARE:

TOTAL EMPLOYMENT	59,786
British Columbia	10,205
Alberta	4,233
Saskatchewan	n/a
Manitoba	542
Ontario	28,211
Quebec	13,983
New Brunswick	622
Nova Scotia	960
Prince Edward Island	n/a
Newfoundland	306
Northwest Territories	n/a
Yukon Territory	n/a

VITAL STATISTICS

Average Lay-off Rate, 1989–93: Zero
Net Job Creation, 1989–93: +4,104
Average Salary Level, 1993: $757/week
Salary Increase, 1993: +8.2%
Knowledge Workers per 100 Employees: 73
Knowledge Base Change: +8.2%
Industry Volatility: 11.6 (empl.)
SIC Code: 772

NATURAL GAS DISTRIBUTION SYSTEMS

The natural gas industry is a solid player in the New Economy, where natural gas is the fuel of choice. There are many reasons for the shift to natural gas: it's cleaner burning and has an important environmental appeal; it's cost-effective; and it's in abundant supply. For non-residential users, the promise of co-generation is an added appeal.

The gas distribution industry experienced a zero lay-off rate during the recession years of 1989–93; indeed, 2,434 net new employees were hired in that period.

Average salaries are very high, and wages in the industry rose 0.4 percent on average in 1993.

Another bonus is that the moderate knowledge base is rising sharply.

OVERALL SCORE

85

HOW THE INDUSTRY COMPARES:

Job Security: Very High
Advancement: Very Good
Average Salary: Very High
Salary Change: Moderate
Knowledge Base: Moderate
Industry Knowledge: Rising Sharply
Industry Stability: High

VITAL STATISTICS

Average Lay-off Rate, 1989–93: Zero
Net Job Creation, 1989–93: +2,434
Average Salary Level, 1993: $811/week
Salary Increase, 1993: +0.4%
Knowledge Workers per 100 Employees: 22
Knowledge Base Change: +8.6%
Industry Volatility: 5.6
SIC Code: 492

WHERE THE JOBS ARE:

TOTAL EMPLOYMENT	15,956
British Columbia	2,108
Alberta	3,804
Saskatchewan	n/a
Manitoba	n/a
Ontario	7,045
Quebec	n/a
New Brunswick	n/a
Nova Scotia	n/a
Prince Edward Island	n/a
Newfoundland	n/a
Northwest Territories	n/a
Yukon Territory	n/a

PHARMACEUTICAL MANUFACTURING

⭐ ⭐ ⭐ ⭐ ⭐

Pharmaceutical manufacturing is a five-star New Economy engine of growth. Despite pressures in the industry as several prized patents expire in coming years, the demographics and innovation base should support excellent long-term growth.

OVERALL SCORE

85

Two main factors are combining to create an exciting job future in this industry: the aging of our population (the older we get, the more prescriptions we fill) and the multicultural nature of our population, which makes Canada an ideal location for clinical trials.

Job security is very high and advancement prospects are good. Superior average salary increases of 10.7 percent and a high knowledge base make this New Economy industry a winner.

Occupations cover a broad spectrum in medical, scientific, managerial and clerical fields.

HOW THE INDUSTRY COMPARES:

Job Security: Very High
Advancement: Good
Average Salary: Very High
Salary Change: Very High
Knowledge Base: High
Industry Knowledge: Reasonably Stable
Industry Stability: Moderate

VITAL STATISTICS

Average Lay-off Rate, 1989–93: Zero
Net Job Creation, 1989–93: +536
Average Salary Level, 1993: $774/week
Salary Increase, 1993: +10.7%
Knowledge Workers per 100 Employees: 43
Knowledge Base Change: −0.8%
Industry Volatility: 6.6
SIC Code: 374

WHERE THE JOBS ARE:

TOTAL EMPLOYMENT	19,870
British Columbia	465
Alberta	n/a
Saskatchewan	n/a
Manitoba	356
Ontario	10,492
Quebec	8,063
New Brunswick	n/a
Nova Scotia	n/a
Prince Edward Island	n/a
Newfoundland	n/a
Northwest Territories	n/a
Yukon Territory	n/a

ELECTRIC POWER INDUSTRY

★ ★ ★ ★ ★

Despite the well-publicized layoffs at major power producers such as Ontario Hydro, electric power industry employees as a whole have enjoyed remarkable job security, thanks in large part to job security at the municipal level, and to the growth in other provincial power suppliers in Canada.

Indeed, the industry hired an additional 6,247 net new employees during the tough recession years of 1989–93, and has provided excellent advancement prospects to those already employed in this moderately knowledge-intensive field. However, the Knowledge Ratio of the industry —an average of 29 knowledge workers per 100 employees—has changed little in the last five years. This is a troubling development, given the technological change and competing sources of power that face the industry in the future.

Despite these negatives, the average salary in the industry is very high and recent wage increases have been very attractive.

OVERALL SCORE

82.5

HOW THE INDUSTRY COMPARES:

Job Security: Very High
Advancement: Very Good
Average Salary: Very High
Salary Change: High
Knowledge Base: Moderate
Industry Knowledge: Reasonably Stable
Industry Stability: High

VITAL STATISTICS

Average Lay-off Rate, 1989–93: Zero
Net Job Creation, 1989–93: +6,247
Average Salary Level, 1993: $947/week
Salary Increase, 1993: +2.5%
Knowledge Workers per 100 Employees: 29
Knowledge Base Change: +0.8%
Industry Volatility: 4.4
SIC Code: 491

WHERE THE JOBS ARE:	
TOTAL EMPLOYMENT	89,766
British Columbia	6,542
Alberta	7,296
Saskatchewan	2,666
Manitoba	4,478
Ontario	33,504
Quebec	27,298
New Brunswick	3,075
Nova Scotia	1,926
Prince Edward Island	n/a
Newfoundland	n/a
Northwest Territories	n/a
Yukon Territory	n/a

ELEMENTARY & SECONDARY SCHOOLS
★ ★ ★ ★ ★

Education is a big business—over half a million Canadians are employed in this high-knowledge, high-paying field. But the pressure to restructure education is intensifying for two reasons. First, government funding pressures are clearly on the rise, and second, there are increasing demands on educators to provide a higher quality of education that is geared more closely to the needs of this high-knowledge economy.

OVERALL SCORE

82.5

Elementary and secondary schools, which experienced a zero lay-off rate during the tough recession of 1989–93, provide a very high degree of job security. Advancement is well above average in this industry: 46,934 net new jobs were created between 1989–93 and provide an enviable degree of opportunity for advancement. At the very least, a flood of new entrants allows existing employees to move rapidly up the seniority scale.

While most of the job opportunities are in the high-knowledge field of teaching, there are many other job openings for support personnel in social work, administration, and maintenance, janitorial and food services.

HOW THE INDUSTRY COMPARES:

Job Security: Very High
Advancement: Very Good
Average Salary: High
Salary Change: Moderate
Knowledge Base: High
Industry Knowledge: Reasonably Stable
Industry Stability: Very High

VITAL STATISTICS

Average Lay-off Rate, 1989–93: Zero
Net Job Creation, 1989–93: +46,934
Average Salary Level, 1993: $744/week
Salary Increase, 1993: +1.4%
Knowledge Workers per 100 Employees: 65
Knowledge Base Change: −0.9%
Industry Volatility: 1.8 (empl.)
SIC Code: 851

WHERE THE JOBS ARE:

TOTAL EMPLOYMENT	559,643
British Columbia	67,556
Alberta	52,728
Saskatchewan	n/a
Manitoba	27,402
Ontario	221,906
Quebec	133,523
New Brunswick	13,959
Nova Scotia	n/a
Prince Edward Island	2,447
Newfoundland	n/a
Northwest Territories	n/a
Yukon Territory	850

PLASTICS & SYNTHETIC RESINS MANUFACTURING

This industry manufactures synthetic resins in the form of powders, granules, flakes and liquids, and is the principal supplier to manufacturers of plastic products.

Job security through the recession was very high, and the industry enjoyed a zero lay-off rate. Advancement prospects are good, with no net attrition of staff.

The very stable industry also pays very well, and offers current and prospective employees a high average salary and very large salary increases.

The one cause for concern is the moderate knowledge base of the industry. It is stable, but new technologies and processes may eventually require it to rise and may force companies in this industry to keep pace with change.

OVERALL SCORE

82.5

HOW THE INDUSTRY COMPARES:

Job Security: Very High
Advancement: Good
Average Salary: Very High
Salary Change: Very High
Knowledge Base: Moderate
Industry Knowledge: Reasonably Stable
Industry Stability: High

VITAL STATISTICS

Average Lay-off Rate, 1989–93: Zero
Net Job Creation, 1989–93: +161
Average Salary Level, 1993: $746/week
Salary Increase, 1993: +5.7%
Knowledge Workers per 100 Employees: 24
Knowledge Base Change: −1.6%
Industry Volatility: 5.8
SIC Code: 373

WHERE THE JOBS ARE:

TOTAL EMPLOYMENT	5,669
British Columbia	206
Alberta	633
Saskatchewan	n/a
Manitoba	n/a
Ontario	3,310
Quebec	1,377
New Brunswick	n/a
Nova Scotia	n/a
Prince Edward Island	n/a
Newfoundland	n/a
Northwest Territories	n/a
Yukon Territory	n/a

ELECTRICAL & ELECTRONIC EQUIPMENT WHOLESALERS

Suppliers can come and go, and products can gain or lose market favor. But wholesalers of electrical and electronic equipment—such as electrical wiring supplies, electrical generating equipment and electronic and communications equipment—are positioned with reasonable safety between a strongly rising demand for products and a wide range of manufacturers to buy from.

This "middleman" role has provided employees in the wholesale industry with enviable job security and a zero lay-off rate through the tough recession years of 1989–93. Salaries in this growing sector are very high relative to most industries in Canada, and advancement prospects are excellent. Salary increases are well above national averages.

The only negative in this industry is the low knowledge base. But low-knowledge industries can provide exciting opportunities for entrepreneurs to introduce new information technologies and modernize distribution channels.

OVERALL SCORE

80

HOW THE INDUSTRY COMPARES:

Job Security: Very High
Advancement: Very Good
Average Salary: Very High
Salary Change: Very High
Knowledge Base: Low
Industry Knowledge: Rising
Industry Stability: Moderate

VITAL STATISTICS

Average Lay-off Rate, 1989–93: Zero
Net Job Creation, 1989–93: +6,817
Average Salary Level, 1993: $757/week
Salary Increase, 1993: +5.6%
Knowledge Workers per 100 Employees: 19
Knowledge Base Change: +6.2%
Industry Volatility: 7.1 (empl.)
SIC Code: 574

WHERE THE JOBS ARE:	
TOTAL EMPLOYMENT	63,360
British Columbia	5,772
Alberta	5,845
Saskatchewan	885
Manitoba	1,370
Ontario	33,621
Quebec	13,666
New Brunswick	644
Nova Scotia	1,120
Prince Edward Island	n/a
Newfoundland	308
Northwest Territories	n/a
Yukon Territory	n/a

WASTE MANAGEMENT

Waste management has evolved rapidly in the New Economy, from the low-knowledge old economy field of garbage collection and sewage disposal into a moderate-knowledge industry that is experiencing explosive growth in its knowledge base.

Concern for the environment (a powerful trend that is here to stay) and rapidly changing technologies make this a five-star industry with a real future in the New Economy.

Average salaries are high and rising rapidly, job security is exceptional and advancement prospects are good in an industry where people are increasingly paid to think and not just "do."

Waste management offers a broad range of unskilled to highly skilled positions.

OVERALL
SCORE

80

HOW THE INDUSTRY COMPARES:

Job Security: Very High
Advancement: Good
Average Salary: High
Salary Change: High
Knowledge Base: Moderate
Industry Knowledge: Rising Very Sharply
Industry Stability: Moderate

VITAL STATISTICS

Average Lay-off Rate, 1989–93: Zero
Net Job Creation, 1989–93: +70
Average Salary Level, 1993: $641/week
Salary Increase, 1993: +4.9%
Knowledge Workers per 100 Employees: 26
Knowledge Base Change: +67.7%
Industry Volatility: 7.9
SIC Code: 499

WHERE THE JOBS ARE:

TOTAL EMPLOYMENT	14,860
British Columbia	1,619
Alberta	1,315
Saskatchewan	n/a
Manitoba	n/a
Ontario	8,469
Quebec	n/a
New Brunswick	317
Nova Scotia	369
Prince Edward Island	n/a
Newfoundland	n/a
Northwest Territories	n/a
Yukon Territory	n/a

COMMUNICATIONS EQUIPMENT

★ ★ ★ ★ ★

This New Economy engine manufactures semiconductors, satellite parts and components, microwave transmitting equipment, telephones, cellphones and a wide range of electronic components used in the communications and telecommunications industry.

Job security for the 51,889 people employed in the industry is high, with a lay-off rate between 1989 and 1993 of 10.3 percent. Because net job creation in recent years has been poor, opportunities for advancement are limited.

Average salaries are very high and raises averaged 14.2 percent in 1993.

In this industry that has a real future in the New Economy, knowledge workers figure prominently (46 out of every 100 employees), but many other positions are available in distribution, sales, accounting and clerical and administrative support.

OVERALL SCORE

77.5

HOW THE INDUSTRY COMPARES:

Job Security: High
Advancement: Poor
Average Salary: Very High
Salary Change: Very High
Knowledge Base: High
Industry Knowledge: Reasonably Stable
Industry Stability: High

VITAL STATISTICS

Average Lay-off Rate, 1989–93: 10.3%
Net Job Creation, 1989–93: −5,394
Average Salary Level, 1993: $796/week
Salary Increase, 1993: +14.2%
Knowledge Workers per 100 Employees: 46
Knowledge Base Change: −0.6%
Industry Volatility: 6.3
SIC Code: 335

WHERE THE JOBS ARE:

TOTAL EMPLOYMENT	51,889
British Columbia	n/a
Alberta	n/a
Saskatchewan	359
Manitoba	n/a
Ontario	26,236
Quebec	17,711
New Brunswick	179
Nova Scotia	n/a
Prince Edward Island	n/a
Newfoundland	n/a
Northwest Territories	n/a
Yukon Territory	n/a

COMMUNITY COLLEGES

Community colleges are the unsung heroes of the New Economy. They offer a wide and exciting array of courses geared to the skill sets that people need to function in the New Economy or to retrain for jobs that have a real future. It is little wonder that enrollment has risen sharply in recent years as the two messages of "stay in school" and "lifelong learning" affect the market for education.

OVERALL
SCORE

77.5

Job security is very high and advancement prospects are excellent in this large and diverse job sector. Beyond the obvious teaching occupations, opportunities abound for administrative and support personnel in areas such as accounts payable and receivable and maintenance and building management services.

The salary level is moderate, and people employed in this high-knowledge sector received a salary increase in 1993, albeit a modest one.

HOW THE INDUSTRY COMPARES:

Job Security: Very High
Advancement: Very Good
Average Salary: Moderate
Salary Change: Moderate
Knowledge Base: High
Industry Knowledge: Reasonably Stable
Industry Stability: Very High

VITAL STATISTICS

Average Lay-off Rate, 1989–93: Zero
Net Job Creation, 1989–93: +10,806
Average Salary Level, 1993: $621/week
Salary Increase, 1993: +0.4%
Knowledge Workers per 100 Employees: 68
Knowledge Base Change: −0.2%
Industry Volatility: 3.1 (empl.)
SIC Code: 852

WHERE THE JOBS ARE:

TOTAL EMPLOYMENT	115,225
British Columbia	14,697
Alberta	11,324
Saskatchewan	n/a
Manitoba	1,546
Ontario	41,023
Quebec	33,668
New Brunswick	3,250
Nova Scotia	n/a
Prince Edward Island	n/a
Newfoundland	n/a
Northwest Territories	n/a
Yukon Territory	211

MUSEUMS & ARCHIVES

★ ★ ★ ★ ★

The knowledge economy is translating itself into opportunities for museums on three counts. First, museums can benefit from a global economy by gaining access to collections from abroad (the success of the Barnes exhibit in Toronto is one such example).

Second, knowledge workers are creating a growth market for this high-knowledge industry with their rising level of interest in acquiring knowledge beyond their own fields.

Finally, technology is helping museums to create exciting visual and information displays that allow "virtual museums" to flourish. A museum in the New Economy can display a work of art electronically without actually owning the masterpiece. A sharply rising knowledge base in the industry is evidence of this fact.

With such widespread opportunities for museums and archives in the New Economy, it is little wonder that job security is high and that advancement is good. Although the salary base is low, increases are excellent.

OVERALL
SCORE

77.5

HOW THE INDUSTRY COMPARES:

Job Security: High
Advancement: Good
Average Salary: Low
Salary Change: Very High
Knowledge Base: High
Industry Knowledge: Rising Very Sharply
Industry Stability: Very High

VITAL STATISTICS

Average Lay-off Rate, 1989–93: 2.6%
Net Job Creation, 1989–93: –218
Average Salary Level, 1993: $537/week
Salary Increase, 1993: +7.5%
Knowledge Workers per 100 Employees: 52
Knowledge Base Change: +26.8%
Industry Volatility: 1.7
SIC Code: 855

WHERE THE JOBS ARE:	
TOTAL EMPLOYMENT	7,787
British Columbia	646
Alberta	280
Saskatchewan	n/a
Manitoba	305
Ontario	3,586
Quebec	2,265
New Brunswick	218
Nova Scotia	n/a
Prince Edward Island	n/a
Newfoundland	n/a
Northwest Territories	n/a
Yukon Territory	n/a

OFFICES OF OPTOMETRISTS, PHYSIOTHERAPISTS, CHIROPRACTORS & OTHER HEALTH PRACTITIONERS

Optometrists, physiotherapists, chiropractors and a wide range of other health practitioners provide excellent job security for their employees and very good advancement prospects. The only drawback to this otherwise high and rising knowledge-intensive field is that average salaries for support staff are very low. However, it is worth noting that salary increases of 14.5 percent rank this growing industry among the highest salary change sectors in Canada.

With a great deal of "unbundling" in the medical field (licensing of nurse practitioners, and a greater reliance on midwives, chiropractors, occupational and physical therapists), and as Canada's population ages and becomes a greater but more knowledgeable consumer of medical and related services, this industry should continue to grow rapidly.

OVERALL SCORE

77.5

HOW THE INDUSTRY COMPARES:

Job Security: Very High
Advancement: Very Good
Average Salary: Very Low
Salary Change: Very High
Knowledge Base: High
Industry Knowledge: Rising Sharply
Industry Stability: Very High

VITAL STATISTICS

Average Lay-off Rate, 1989–93: Zero
Net Job Creation, 1989–93: +3,511
Average Salary Level, 1993: $398/week
Salary Increase, 1993: +14.5%
Knowledge Workers per 100 Employees: 57
Knowledge Base Change: +8.7%
Industry Volatility: 2.7
SIC Code: 866

WHERE THE JOBS ARE:

TOTAL EMPLOYMENT	23,197
British Columbia	2,647
Alberta	2,709
Saskatchewan	n/a
Manitoba	764
Ontario	11,818
Quebec	3,916
New Brunswick	272
Nova Scotia	n/a
Prince Edward Island	n/a
Newfoundland	178
Northwest Territories	n/a
Yukon Territory	n/a

UNIVERSITIES

Universities are highly leveraged to the high-knowledge New Economy, and higher learning is Canada's new natural resource. But sweeping changes in Canada's education delivery systems are imminent as information and communications technologies introduce new levels of efficiency. It is not far-fetched to imagine the day when the "virtual" university will be as commonplace as the sprawling campus was in the 1980s.

OVERALL
SCORE

77.5

Universities that embrace New Economy technologies may win the reward of potentially major domestic and export earnings, which could reduce the heavy reliance on dwindling government subsidies. Canadian universities have an exciting opportunity to become global New Economy providers of a high quality– low cost education.

Job security is very high at universities, and the industry has enjoyed a zero lay-off rate through the recession years of 1989–93. Job creation at universities is also very high as rising enrollments require teaching and support staff additions.

HOW THE INDUSTRY COMPARES:

Job Security: Very High
Advancement: Very Good
Average Salary: Moderate
Salary Change: Moderate
Knowledge Base: High
Industry Knowledge: Reasonably Stable
Industry Stability: Very High

VITAL STATISTICS

Average Lay-off Rate, 1989–93: Zero
Net Job Creation, 1989–93: +11,382
Average Salary Level, 1993: $593/week
Salary Increase, 1993: +0.6%
Knowledge Workers per 100 Employees: 61
Knowledge Base Change: +2.7%
Industry Volatility: 1.6 (empl.)
SIC Code: 853

WHERE THE JOBS ARE:

TOTAL EMPLOYMENT	119,161
British Columbia	23,968
Alberta	16,585
Saskatchewan	n/a
Manitoba	7,746
Ontario	76,456
Quebec	46,271
New Brunswick	4,196
Nova Scotia	n/a
Prince Edward Island	n/a
Newfoundland	n/a
Northwest Territories	n/a
Yukon Territory	n/a

HOSPITALS

Despite serious cost cutting, which has resulted in fewer beds and shorter stays at most hospital facilities, this sector is highly leveraged to the health and medical engine, a key driver to the New Economy. Exciting medical breakthroughs, dazzling new medical equipment and new drug therapies will inevitably bring about even greater changes, and will raise the knowledge stakes in this already high-knowledge field.

Job security is very high, as shown by the zero lay-off rate in the sector as a whole. Advancement is very good thanks to the 10,082 net new employees, who have raised the seniority level and promotion prospects for current staff.

The major drawback to employment in this high-knowledge field, however, is the generally low average salary. With government funding constraints and the possibility of changes to medical care coverage, it is unlikely that salaries will rise appreciably in the near future.

OVERALL
SCORE

75

HOW THE INDUSTRY COMPARES:

Job Security: Very High
Advancement: Very Good
Average Salary: Low
Salary Change: Moderate
Knowledge Base: High
Industry Knowledge: Rising
Industry Stability: Very High

VITAL STATISTICS

Average Lay-off Rate, 1989–93: Zero
Net Job Creation, 1989–93: +10,082
Average Salary Level, 1993: $559/week
Salary Increase, 1993: +0.5%
Knowledge Workers per 100 Employees: 62
Knowledge Base Change: +4.6%
Industry Volatility: 2.4
SIC Code: 861

WHERE THE JOBS ARE:	
TOTAL EMPLOYMENT	557,335
British Columbia	63,721
Alberta	55,054
Saskatchewan	n/a
Manitoba	23,257
Ontario	175,023
Quebec	171,057
New Brunswick	15,304
Nova Scotia	n/a
Prince Edward Island	1,875
Newfoundland	11,213
Northwest Territories	1,167
Yukon Territory	375

MEDICAL & DENTAL OFFICES

★ ★ ★ ★ ★

The national concern over soaring medical costs has had little impact on staffing levels at the medical and dental office level: this high-knowledge sector has enjoyed a zero lay-off rate in recent years and employment levels have increased at a rapid rate.

The major drawback in a medical or dental office is the very low pay scale, although salary increases of 3.5 percent are high in comparison to the current low inflation/low salary environment of most other industries.

Advancement opportunities are very good in this business. The large number of new entrants will provide, at a minimum, supervisory opportunities for more senior staff members.

As the population ages, the demand for medical care will likely rise, and the demand for staff in the medical field will also probably increase.

OVERALL
SCORE

72.5

HOW THE INDUSTRY COMPARES:

Job Security: Very High
Advancement: Very Good
Average Salary: Very Low
Salary Change: High
Knowledge Base: High
Industry Knowledge: Rising
Industry Stability: Very High

VITAL STATISTICS

Average Lay-off Rate, 1989–93: Zero
Net Job Creation, 1989–93: +11,077
Average Salary Level, 1993: $433/week
Salary Increase, 1993: +3.5%
Knowledge Workers per 100 Employees: 59
Knowledge Base Change: +6.4%
Industry Volatility: 2.7
SIC Code: 865

WHERE THE JOBS ARE:

TOTAL EMPLOYMENT	125,270
British Columbia	21,148
Alberta	17,983
Saskatchewan	n/a
Manitoba	3,935
Ontario	49,478
Quebec	20,948
New Brunswick	2,977
Nova Scotia	n/a
Prince Edward Island	470
Newfoundland	1,403
Northwest Territories	139
Yukon Territory	n/a

PIPELINE TRANSPORTATION

★ ★ ★ ★ ★

Pipeline transportation is a powerful supplier industry in the New Economy, where the fuel of choice is natural gas.

The knowledge base is rising sharply and this five-star industry, leveraged to the New Economy, offers a wide range of opportunities for technicians and engineers. But the industry is not limited to technical jobs; many opportunities exist for clerical and support staff as well.

With the expected success of natural gas as a new Economy fuel (cleaner burning, less expensive), growth in the natural gas pipeline business is promising.

Meanwhile, job security is high and the net job loss during the recession was only 69 people. Advancement prospects are good and average salaries in the industry are very high. Salary increases in the 5.6 percent range make this high-paying field even more attractive.

OVERALL SCORE

72.5

HOW THE INDUSTRY COMPARES:

Job Security: High
Advancement: Good
Average Salary: Very High
Salary Change: Very High
Knowledge Base: Moderate
Industry Knowledge: Declining
Industry Stability: Moderate

VITAL STATISTICS

Average Lay-off Rate, 1989–93: 0.8%
Net Job Creation, 1989–93: −69
Average Salary Level, 1993: $1,014/week
Salary Increase, 1993: +5.6%
Knowledge Workers per 100 Employees: 20
Knowledge Base Change: −25.0%
Industry Volatility: 6.4
SIC Code: 461

WHERE THE JOBS ARE:

TOTAL EMPLOYMENT	7,853
British Columbia	1,169
Alberta	5,191
Saskatchewan	n/a
Manitoba	n/a
Ontario	797
Quebec	n/a
New Brunswick	n/a
Nova Scotia	n/a
Prince Edward Island	n/a
Newfoundland	n/a
Northwest Territories	n/a
Yukon Territory	n/a

SPECTATOR SPORTS, GAMBLING & RECREATIONAL FACILITIES

Despite the astronomical salaries paid to top-ranked athletes in professional sports, most segments of this broadly based industry offer decidedly low wage jobs. Bowling alleys, amusement parks, curling clubs, marinas, casinos and race tracks are not known for offering million-dollar salaries.

OVERALL SCORE

72.5

However, off-setting the low average wages in the industry is the zero lay-off rate, which has provided enviable job security to those not affected by baseball and hockey strikes. Advancement prospects are also very good, with plenty of newcomers boosting the seniority of those already employed in the industry. In addition, average salaries in this high-knowledge industry are rising rapidly, with salary increases far higher than the national average.

The aging of Canada's population in the decade ahead bodes well for the continued growth of the industry as spectator sports continue to gain ground among the middle-aged baby boomers who would rather watch than play.

HOW THE INDUSTRY COMPARES:

Job Security: Very High
Advancement: Very Good
Average Salary: Very Low
Salary Change: Very High
Knowledge Base: High
Industry Knowledge: Reasonably Stable
Industry Stability: Very High

VITAL STATISTICS

Average Lay-off Rate, 1989–93: Zero
Net Job Creation, 1989–93: +6,576
Average Salary Level, 1993: $397/week
Salary Increase, 1993: +6.8%
Knowledge Workers per 100 Employees: 43
Knowledge Base Change: −2.6%
Industry Volatility: 3.7
SIC Code: 960

WHERE THE JOBS ARE:	
TOTAL EMPLOYMENT	75,860
British Columbia	11,696
Alberta	10,601
Saskatchewan	n/a
Manitoba	1,997
Ontario	32,683
Quebec	11,683
New Brunswick	1,409
Nova Scotia	n/a
Prince Edward Island	n/a
Newfoundland	n/a
Northwest Territories	n/a
Yukon Territory	n/a

AGRICULTURAL CHEMICALS & FERTILIZER MANUFACTURING

Agriculture is shifting gears in Canada, and the agricultural chemical and fertilizer industry is leveraged to the New Economy. The knowledge base is rising very sharply, a trend that points to the future penetration of new markets, both domestically and abroad. Companies that fail to keep up with the fast pace of change in the industry's knowledge base will be left behind. Job seekers are well advised to pick the "smart" companies, which will benefit by being at the forefront of this high-knowledge field.

OVERALL
SCORE

67.5

Although the average salary in this type of manufacturing is very high, salary cuts have been the norm.

Job security is moderate, as demonstrated by the industry's 10.7 percent lay-off rate. Advancement prospects are good in this low-volatility sector.

HOW THE INDUSTRY COMPARES:

Job Security: Moderate
Advancement: Good
Average Salary: Very High
Salary Change: Very Poor
Knowledge Base: High
Industry Knowledge: Rising Very Sharply
Industry Stability: Very Low

VITAL STATISTICS

Average Lay-off Rate, 1989–93: 10.7%
Net Job Creation, 1989–93: −475
Average Salary Level, 1993: $748/week
Salary Increase, 1993: −6.8%
Knowledge Workers per 100 Employees: 41
Knowledge Base Change: +60.4%
Industry Volatility: 12.5 (empl)
SIC Code: 372

WHERE THE JOBS ARE:

TOTAL EMPLOYMENT	4,664
British Columbia	419
Alberta	827
Saskatchewan	n/a
Manitoba	302
Ontario	2,124
Quebec	633
New Brunswick	n/a
Nova Scotia	n/a
Prince Edward Island	n/a
Newfoundland	n/a
Northwest Territories	n/a
Yukon Territory	n/a

ENGINEERING, ARCHITECTURE & TECHNICAL & SCIENTIFIC SERVICES

Although advancement prospects are poor, this industry enjoys a high level of job security, as shown by the relatively low 4.7 percent lay-off rate.

The average salary level is very high in this high-knowledge-intensive industry, where 85 out of every 100 employees are knowledge workers. Ample opportunities exist for clerical, accounting and support staff as well.

The rising knowledge base of this already sky-high knowledge business bodes well for the industry, which is highly leveraged to the growing New Economy. Companies can benefit from numerous domestic and international opportunities.

OVERALL SCORE

67.5

HOW THE INDUSTRY COMPARES:

Job Security: High
Advancement: Poor
Average Salary: Very High
Salary Change: Moderate
Knowledge Base: High
Industry Knowledge: Rising
Industry Stability: Very Low

VITAL STATISTICS

Average Lay-off Rate, 1989–93: 4.7%
Net Job Creation, 1989–93: −4,498
Average Salary Level, 1993: $771/week
Salary Increase, 1993: +1.1%
Knowledge Workers per 100 Employees: 85
Knowledge Base Change: +4.4%
Industry Volatility: 11.5 (empl.)
SIC Code: 775

WHERE THE JOBS ARE:

TOTAL EMPLOYMENT	94,958
British Columbia	15,536
Alberta	14,884
Saskatchewan	n/a
Manitoba	2,982
Ontario	35,943
Quebec	19,066
New Brunswick	1,662
Nova Scotia	1,891
Prince Edward Island	117
Newfoundland	1,238
Northwest Territories	n/a
Yukon Territory	n/a

MOTION PICTURE, VIDEO & SOUND RECORDING INDUSTRY

Because it has a high innovation base, this industry is on its way to becoming a world-class player in the communications and telecommunications engine that drives the New Economy. A low Canadian dollar provides this high-knowledge industry with a powerful competitive advantage. With five hundred new channels coming soon to the TV set nearest you, the opportunity for Canadian players to grow internationally is extremely attractive.

OVERALL
SCORE

67.5

As the zero lay-off rate shows, job security in the industry is already very high, and advancement prospects for employees are excellent with so many newcomers entering the field.

Although the salary level is not as high as in other high-knowledge New Economy industries, salaries are rising. Strong growth ahead should make this attractive industry even more exciting for occupations ranging from production and technical staff to administrative and support staff.

HOW THE INDUSTRY COMPARES:

Job Security: Very High
Advancement: Very Good
Average Salary: Moderate
Salary Change: Moderate
Knowledge Base: High
Industry Knowledge: Reasonably Stable
Industry Stability: Very Low

VITAL STATISTICS

Average Lay-off Rate, 1989–93: Zero
Net Job Creation, 1989–93: +814
Average Salary Level, 1993: $580/week
Salary Increase, 1993: +2.0%
Knowledge Workers per 100 Employees: 69
Knowledge Base Change: −0.4%
Industry Volatility: 28.8 (empl.)
SIC Code: 961

WHERE THE JOBS ARE:

TOTAL EMPLOYMENT	12,130
British Columbia	1,372
Alberta	459
Saskatchewan	n/a
Manitoba	110
Ontario	4,868
Quebec	5,021
New Brunswick	n/a
Nova Scotia	n/a
Prince Edward Island	n/a
Newfoundland	n/a
Northwest Territories	n/a
Yukon Territory	n/a

RECREATIONAL SPORTS & CLUBS

Golfing, skiing, sailing and curling have gained in popularity and have driven the continued growth of this leisure industry. Job security is very high and advancement prospects are very good, as shown by the zero lay-off rate and the net addition of 5,137 people to the industry during the 1989–93 period. Although salary levels are generally very low, opportunities abound for people to make a living at their favorite leisure sport and receive a moderate raise.

The knowledge base of this very stable industry is only moderate, but it is rising sharply as new technologies are introduced.

OVERALL SCORE

67.5

HOW THE INDUSTRY COMPARES:

Job Security: Very High
Advancement: Very Good
Average Salary: Very Low
Salary Change: Moderate
Knowledge Base: Moderate
Industry Knowledge: Rising Sharply
Industry Stability: Very High

VITAL STATISTICS

Average Lay-off Rate, 1989–93: Zero
Net Job Creation, 1989–93: +5,137
Average Salary Level, 1993: $289/week
Salary Increase, 1993: +1.8%
Knowledge Workers per 100 Employees: 36
Knowledge Base Change: +10.6%
Industry Volatility: 3.7
SIC Code: 965

WHERE THE JOBS ARE:

TOTAL EMPLOYMENT	43,750
British Columbia	9,152
Alberta	5,210
Saskatchewan	n/a
Manitoba	n/a
Ontario	17,841
Quebec	7,739
New Brunswick	418
Nova Scotia	n/a
Prince Edward Island	n/a
Newfoundland	252
Northwest Territories	n/a
Yukon Territory	n/a

ACCOUNTING FIRMS & BOOKKEEPING SERVICES

★ ★ ★ ★

Accounting firms and bookkeeping services have faced the information age with mixed results. Competition in the industry has reduced fees for large audit accounts, the mainstay for many firms, while in-house accounting software at many small- and medium-sized companies has cut back the need for outside accounting expertise.

But the picture is not as bleak as it might first appear. The spectacular growth of New Economy companies has translated into rapid growth for those accounting firms and bookkeeping services that have been astute enough to build a New Economy clientele. As New Economy companies grow, audit revenues will rise; furthermore, small companies will continue to require a myriad of services designed to meet the needs of budding entrepreneurs.

As a result, accounting firms and bookkeeping services experienced a zero lay-off rate between 1989 and 1993; indeed, 4,272 new employees were hired. The main drawback, however, in this high-knowledge industry is that average salaries are low and salary increases are poor.

OVERALL SCORE

65

HOW THE INDUSTRY COMPARES:

Job Security: Very High
Advancement: Very Good
Average Salary: Low
Salary Change: Poor
Knowledge Base: High
Industry Knowledge: Reasonably Stable
Industry Stability: Moderate

VITAL STATISTICS

Average Lay-off Rate, 1989–93: Zero
Net Job Creation, 1989–93: +4,272
Average Salary Level, 1993: $548/week
Salary Increase, 1993: −1.3%
Knowledge Workers per 100 Employees: 67
Knowledge Base Change: +2.5%
Industry Volatility: 7.8 (empl.)
SIC Code: 773

WHERE THE JOBS ARE:

TOTAL EMPLOYMENT	49,899
British Columbia	6,986
Alberta	5,735
Saskatchewan	n/a
Manitoba	1,718
Ontario	19,975
Quebec	12,371
New Brunswick	746
Nova Scotia	881
Prince Edward Island	132
Newfoundland	303
Northwest Territories	n/a
Yukon Territory	n/a

COMMUNITY-BASED SOCIAL SERVICES

★ ★ ★ ★

The demand for social services from child care, family planning and meals-on-wheels to crisis centers and adult day care has risen dramatically in Canada. This growing sector now employs over 100,000 Canadians. Consequently, job security is very high; in fact, the industry experienced a zero lay-off rate throughout the 1989–93 recession. Advancement opportunities for employees are also very good, as evidenced by the over 19,000 people who entered this field in the last five years.

The major job disadvantage in the community-based social service sector is the low pay of these moderately knowledge-intensive jobs. The average salary—less than $400 a week—ranks this industry among the lowest paying in the country. Salary increases are unattractive compared to those in numerous other sectors that are leveraged to the New Economy. With government funding severely constrained, it is unlikely that social service workers will see significant raises anytime soon.

OVERALL SCORE

65

HOW THE INDUSTRY COMPARES:

Job Security: Very High
Advancement: Very Good
Average Salary: Very Low
Salary Change: Moderate
Knowledge Base: Moderate
Industry Knowledge: Rising
Industry Stability: Very High

VITAL STATISTICS

Average Lay-off Rate, 1989–93: Zero
Net Job Creation, 1989–93: +19,137
Average Salary Level, 1993: $365/week
Salary Increase, 1993: +0.1%
Knowledge Workers per 100 Employees: 37
Knowledge Base Change: +6.3%
Industry Volatility: 2.7
SIC Code: 864

WHERE THE JOBS ARE:

TOTAL EMPLOYMENT	113,931
British Columbia	16,990
Alberta	12,559
Saskatchewan	n/a
Manitoba	4,770
Ontario	39,648
Quebec	25,878
New Brunswick	3,493
Nova Scotia	n/a
Prince Edward Island	538
Newfoundland	2,256
Northwest Territories	179
Yukon Territory	171

CONSUMER & BUSINESS FINANCING

★ ★ ★ ★

The demand for equipment financing, leasing, consumer loan and business inventory financing and factoring has continued to grow in structural terms, and has resulted in a reasonably high level of job security for the people employed in this financial services business. Advancement prospects, however, are moderate.

Average salaries make this industry attractive for business-oriented individuals who are interested in a broad range of occupations from finance and marketing to clerical and support staff. But salary increases have tended to be poor at best.

This moderately stable industry enjoys only a moderate knowledge base, but the Knowledge Ratio is rising sharply.

OVERALL SCORE

65

HOW THE INDUSTRY COMPARES:

Job Security: High
Advancement: Moderate
Average Salary: High
Salary Change: Poor
Knowledge Base: Moderate
Industry Knowledge: Rising Sharply
Industry Stability: Moderate

VITAL STATISTICS

Average Lay-off Rate, 1989–93: 9.4%
Net Job Creation, 1989–93: −1,870
Average Salary Level, 1993: $725/week
Salary Increase, 1993: −0.3%
Knowledge Workers per 100 Employees: 34
Knowledge Base Change: +11.8
Industry Volatility: 6.6 (empl.)
SIC Code: 710

WHERE THE JOBS ARE:

TOTAL EMPLOYMENT	19,072
British Columbia	1,651
Alberta	1,380
Saskatchewan	789
Manitoba	495
Ontario	10,404
Quebec	2,966
New Brunswick	299
Nova Scotia	684
Prince Edward Island	n/a
Newfoundland	283
Northwest Territories	n/a
Yukon Territory	n/a

TELEPHONE COMPANIES & TELECOMMUNICATIONS CARRIERS

This New Economy engine is rapidly becoming the site of a play-off match as an old economy industry structure gives way to giants fighting for a share of this explosively growing market. Technology convergence and the costs of being a winner have raised the stakes. The game has moved into overtime, and players can afford to make few mistakes for fear of sudden death. But the prize for companies who make it to the winner's circle will be immense growth and profitability in the New Economy.

OVERALL SCORE

65

With so much jockeying for market power, job security is moderate at best, and advancement prospects are very poor as restructuring continues at a rapid pace. Between 1989 and 1993, 15.4 percent of the people employed in the industry lost their jobs.

Average salaries in the telephone and telecommunications carrier business are very high by Canadian industry standards, but salary increases have tended to be poor, with average wage cuts of 1.2 percent in 1993.

One of the most exciting aspects of working in this moderately knowledge-intensive industry is the sharply rising knowledge base.

HOW THE INDUSTRY COMPARES:

Job Security: Moderate
Advancement: Very Poor
Average Salary: Very High
Salary Change: Poor
Knowledge Base: Moderate
Industry Knowledge: Rising Very Sharply
Industry Stability: High

VITAL STATISTICS

Average Lay-off Rate, 1989–93: 15.4%
Net Job Creation, 1989–93: −16,277
Average Salary Level, 1993: $787/week
Salary Increase, 1993: −1.2%
Knowledge Workers per 100 Employees: 34
Knowledge Base Change: +18.0%
Industry Volatility: 4.4
SIC Code: 482

WHERE THE JOBS ARE:

TOTAL EMPLOYMENT	103,539
British Columbia	13,298
Alberta	9,997
Saskatchewan	3,997
Manitoba	5,175
Ontario	37,796
Quebec	23,914
New Brunswick	n/a
Nova Scotia	n/a
Prince Edward Island	n/a
Newfoundland	n/a
Northwest Territories	n/a
Yukon Territory	n/a

WATER TRANSPORTATION SERVICES

★ ★ ★ ★

Harbor and port operations, shipping agencies and marine handling operations have continued to grow in structural terms. But funding and subsidies to the sector will be increasingly constrained as government spending tightens further in Canada.

To date, however, the industry has enjoyed high job security and a very low lay-off rate of only 2.9 percent. Advancement prospects will remain good only so long as government funding remains high.

Average salaries are very high, but salary increases are poor; average salaries declined by 2 percent in 1993.

This moderate-knowledge industry enjoys only low stability. An additional cause for concern is the declining knowledge base, which does not bode well for the future of water transportation services in an increasingly high-knowledge economy.

OVERALL SCORE

62.5

HOW THE INDUSTRY COMPARES:

Job Security: High
Advancement: Good
Average Salary: Very High
Salary Change: Poor
Knowledge Base: Moderate
Industry Knowledge: Declining
Industry Stability: Low

VITAL STATISTICS

Average Lay-off Rate, 1989–93: 2.9%
Net Job Creation, 1989–93: −303
Average Salary Level, 1993: $779/week
Salary Increase, 1993: −2.0%
Knowledge Workers per 100 Employees: 22
Knowledge Base Change: −12.5%
Industry Volatility: 10.6 (empl.)
SIC Code: 455

WHERE THE JOBS ARE:

TOTAL EMPLOYMENT	10,709
British Columbia	4,195
Alberta	n/a
Saskatchewan	n/a
Manitoba	n/a
Ontario	1,140
Quebec	4,334
New Brunswick	289
Nova Scotia	484
Prince Edward Island	n/a
Newfoundland	n/a
Northwest Territories	n/a
Yukon Territory	n/a

BUSINESS SERVICES

★ ★ ★ ★

Security services, credit and collection agencies, customs brokers and business services such as photocopying services are enjoying long-term structural growth in the New Economy.

This industry provides very high job security, as demonstrated by the zero lay-off rate during the recession years of 1989–93.

Advancement in this diverse industry is very good, with occupations spanning many different fields. Some segments of the industry offer franchising opportunities as well.

Salary levels, however, are very low and salary increases have been only moderate in this moderately stable industry.

OVERALL SCORE

60

HOW THE INDUSTRY COMPARES:

Job Security: Very High
Advancement: Very Good
Average Salary: Very Low
Salary Change: Moderate
Knowledge Base: Low
Industry Knowledge: Rising Very Sharply
Industry Stability: Moderate

VITAL STATISTICS

Average Lay-off Rate, 1989–93: Zero
Net Job Creation, 1989–93: +2,581
Average Salary Level, 1993: $438/week
Salary Increase, 1993: +2.0%
Knowledge Workers per 100 Employees: 10
Knowledge Base Change: +42.2%
Industry Volatility: 7.4 (empl.)
SIC Code: 779

WHERE THE JOBS ARE:

TOTAL EMPLOYMENT	120,067
British Columbia	11,668
Alberta	9,559
Saskatchewan	n/a
Manitoba	3,671
Ontario	54,445
Quebec	32,039
New Brunswick	2,366
Nova Scotia	2,622
Prince Edward Island	122
Newfoundland	972
Northwest Territories	109
Yukon Territory	n/a

HAIRDRESSING BUSINESSES

★ ★ ★ ★

The knowledge base in the hairdressing business is low but rising sharply as smart beauty salons and barber shops take advantage of information technology to broaden their range of services and enlarge their clientele. Hairdressers also enjoy an enviable degree of job security: witness the large number of new employees hired on to payrolls during the difficult recession years of 1989–93. The industry offers very good prospects for advancement to supervisory, managerial or owner/operator levels.

OVERALL SCORE

60

The one drawback to current and prospective employees is the very low average salary in the business. However, this income is often supplemented by tips.

A sharply rising knowledge base, albeit from a very low level, may translate into some improvement in earnings in the years ahead.

HOW THE INDUSTRY COMPARES:

Job Security: Very High
Advancement: Very Good
Average Salary: Very Low
Salary Change: High
Knowledge Base: Low
Industry Knowledge: Rising Sharply
Industry Stability: Moderate

VITAL STATISTICS

Average Lay-off Rate, 1989–93: Zero
Net Job Creation, 1989–93: +1,587
Average Salary Level, 1993: $292/week
Salary Increase, 1993: +2.4%
Knowledge Workers per 100 Employees: 1
Knowledge Base Change: +7.5%
Industry Volatility: 7.4 (empl.)
SIC Code: 971

WHERE THE JOBS ARE:

TOTAL EMPLOYMENT	47,917
British Columbia	7,196
Alberta	4,997
Saskatchewan	n/a
Manitoba	1,138
Ontario	16,888
Quebec	12,832
New Brunswick	761
Nova Scotia	n/a
Prince Edward Island	252
Newfoundland	839
Northwest Territories	n/a
Yukon Territory	n/a

LOGGING & FORESTRY

Although many sectors within the logging and forestry business are decidedly old economy, the industry as a whole is leveraged to the growing New Economy and will benefit from the information age because of the demand for many grades of new and recycled paper and wood products. As concern for the environment continues, however, dwindling supplies of fiber will constrain strong growth.

Despite the challenges ahead, job security has remained high—the lay-off rate between 1989 and 1993 was only 6.3 percent—but advancement is only moderate.

This high-paying industry has generated moderate wage gains, and the rising knowledge base bodes well for salaries in the future.

The major negative in logging and forestry is the volatile nature of growth. Industry stability is very low.

OVERALL SCORE

60

HOW THE INDUSTRY COMPARES:

Job Security: High
Advancement: Moderate
Average Salary: High
Salary Change: Moderate
Knowledge Base: Moderate
Industry Knowledge: Rising
Industry Stability: Very Low

VITAL STATISTICS

Average Lay-off Rate, 1989–93: 6.3%
Net Job Creation, 1989–93: –3,975
Average Salary Level, 1993: $667/week
Salary Increase, 1993: +1.2%
Knowledge Workers per 100 Employees: 36
Knowledge Base Change: +6.8%
Industry Volatility: 14.5
SIC Code: 05T

WHERE THE JOBS ARE:

TOTAL EMPLOYMENT	58,969
British Columbia	25,873
Alberta	3,123
Saskatchewan	831
Manitoba	660
Ontario	10,002
Quebec	12,271
New Brunswick	3,424
Nova Scotia	1,875
Prince Edward Island	n/a
Newfoundland	774
Northwest Territories	n/a
Yukon Territory	n/a

NON-METAL MINING

★ ★ ★ ★

Potash-, salt-, gypsum- and peat-mining operators provide moderate job security in a highly volatile industry known for its large cyclical fluctuations.

But advancement is reasonably good and average salaries are very high, thanks to the long-term structural growth of the industry.

Recently, however, salary increases have been poor, with employees receiving an average wage cut of 1.8 percent.

The knowledge base in the non-metal mining business is low, but has been rising sharply as new technologies are introduced and as new mining processes make their way into the industry.

OVERALL
SCORE

60

HOW THE INDUSTRY COMPARES:

Job Security: Moderate
Advancement: Good
Average Salary: Very High
Salary Change: Poor
Knowledge Base: Low
Industry Knowledge: Rising Sharply
Industry Stability: Low

VITAL STATISTICS

Average Lay-off Rate, 1989–93: 15.7%
Net Job Creation, 1989–93: −1,528
Average Salary Level, 1993: $767/week
Salary Increase, 1993: −1.8%
Knowledge Workers per 100 Employees: 15
Knowledge Base Change: +13.2%
Industry Volatility: 10.2
SIC Code: 062

WHERE THE JOBS ARE:

TOTAL EMPLOYMENT	8,886
British Columbia	n/a
Alberta	280
Saskatchewan	3,014
Manitoba	n/a
Ontario	1,442
Quebec	2,507
New Brunswick	n/a
Nova Scotia	n/a
Prince Edward Island	n/a
Newfoundland	n/a
Northwest Territories	n/a
Yukon Territory	n/a

COMMERCIAL PRINTING

★ ★ ★

The commercial printing industry is leveraged to the information economy. Rising rates of innovation in the New Economy translate into rising demand for new and revised product literature, which in turn creates demand for commercial printing.

The industry offers high job security because of its reasonably low lay-off rate. But advancement is poor.

Average salaries are moderate and salary changes have been equally modest, but the knowledge base is rising sharply. This indicator provides good reason to expect that average salary levels will begin to increase, as the knowledge base expands in step with technological change and an unrelenting pressure in the industry to compete.

OVERALL SCORE

57.5

HOW THE INDUSTRY COMPARES:

Job Security: High
Advancement: Poor
Average Salary: Moderate
Salary Change: Moderate
Knowledge Base: Moderate
Industry Knowledge: Rising Sharply
Industry Stability: Low

VITAL STATISTICS

Average Lay-off Rate, 1989–93: 6.5%
Net Job Creation, 1989–93: −4,312
Average Salary Level, 1993: $594/week
Salary Increase, 1993: +0.9%
Knowledge Workers per 100 Employees: 32
Knowledge Base Change: +13.6%
Industry Volatility: 10.3 (empl.)
SIC Code: 281

WHERE THE JOBS ARE:	
TOTAL EMPLOYMENT	65,691
British Columbia	5,377
Alberta	4,068
Saskatchewan	891
Manitoba	2,186
Ontario	28,793
Quebec	21,977
New Brunswick	1,413
Nova Scotia	742
Prince Edward Island	n/a
Newfoundland	161
Northwest Territories	n/a
Yukon Territory	n/a

HEAVY ENGINEERING & INDUSTRIAL CONSTRUCTION

The heavy engineering and construction industry is a high-knowledge industry that designs and builds thermal and nuclear generating stations, oil and gas structures such as Hibernia and constructs pipelines.

For job seekers who desire a rising knowledge base in a highly technical field, but who can live with the reality of low job security, this well-paying industry is certain to appeal.

Although advancement prospects are moderate, salary increases are attractive at an average of 4.5 percent a year.

While most jobs are in engineering and construction, opportunities also exist for payroll, accounting, clerical and support staff.

OVERALL SCORE

57.5

HOW THE INDUSTRY COMPARES:

Job Security: Low
Advancement: Moderate
Average Salary: High
Salary Change: High
Knowledge Base: High
Industry Knowledge: Rising
Industry Stability: Very Low

VITAL STATISTICS

Average Lay-off Rate, 1989–93: 20.8%
Net Job Creation, 1989–93: −2,880
Average Salary Level, 1993: $742/week
Salary Increase, 1993: +4.5%
Knowledge Workers per 100 Employees: 84
Knowledge Base Change: +4.3%
Industry Volatility: 16.8
SIC Code: 411

WHERE THE JOBS ARE:

TOTAL EMPLOYMENT	12,183
British Columbia	1,368
Alberta	4,916
Saskatchewan	643
Manitoba	121
Ontario	1,954
Quebec	1,129
New Brunswick	240
Nova Scotia	n/a
Prince Edward Island	n/a
Newfoundland	n/a
Northwest Territories	n/a
Yukon Territory	n/a

LAWYERS' & NOTARIES' OFFICES

Law firms in the New Economy face two major challenges: changing fields of specialization and a more sophisticated and knowledge-intensive client base. So far, access to on-line legal services and to software are having only a marginal impact on industry revenues. But as information technologies and expert systems are applied more broadly across professional services, they could erode revenues at a potentially rapid rate.

Average salaries are moderate in the legal industry, and salary increases have been modest, averaging 1.9 percent.

The industry's Knowledge Ratio is high—63 out of every 100 employees in the legal business are knowledge workers—and the knowledge base increased 6.4 percent in the past five years.

OVERALL SCORE

57.5

HOW THE INDUSTRY COMPARES:

Job Security: Moderate
Advancement: Poor
Average Salary: Moderate
Salary Change: Moderate
Knowledge Base: High
Industry Knowledge: Rising
Industry Stability: Moderate

VITAL STATISTICS

Average Lay-off Rate, 1989–93: 13.2%
Net Job Creation, 1989–93: −7,594
Average Salary Level, 1993: $580/week
Salary Increase, 1993: +1.9%
Knowledge Workers per 100 Employees: 63
Knowledge Base Change: +6.4%
Industry Volatility: 7.0 (empl.)
SIC Code: 776

WHERE THE JOBS ARE:

TOTAL EMPLOYMENT	55,653
British Columbia	8,553
Alberta	7,223
Saskatchewan	n/a
Manitoba	1,183
Ontario	24,220
Quebec	9,742
New Brunswick	847
Nova Scotia	1,507
Prince Edward Island	157
Newfoundland	504
Northwest Territories	121
Yukon Territory	n/a

LIBRARIES

★ ★ ★

Since knowledge is the asset of the 1990s and the twenty-first century, libraries are leveraged to the New Economy. Despite funding pressures and an explosion of information sources, the challenge for libraries will be to embrace information technologies and employ them to advantage.

"Smart" libraries have an amazing ability to transform themselves from old economy repositories of information (piled high with books and microfiche) into information distributors and "virtual" libraries, providing access to information around the globe.

With more and more people seeking information on the Internet, libraries will have to increase their own knowledge base from the industry's current high level.

Job security is high, advancement is good, but the average salary is very low as libraries emerge from an old paradigm in which knowledge was an undervalued asset.

OVERALL
SCORE

57.5

HOW THE INDUSTRY COMPARES:

Job Security: High
Advancement: Good
Average Salary: Very Low
Salary Change: High
Knowledge Base: High
Industry Knowledge: Reasonably Stable
Industry Stability: Moderate

VITAL STATISTICS

Average Lay-off Rate, 1989–93: 5.2%
Net Job Creation, 1989–93: −1,063
Average Salary Level, 1993: $412/week
Salary Increase, 1993: +3.7%
Knowledge Workers per 100 Employees: 46
Knowledge Base Change: −0.6%
Industry Volatility: 7.1 (empl.)
SIC Code: 854

WHERE THE JOBS ARE:

TOTAL EMPLOYMENT	20,003
British Columbia	2,696
Alberta	1,817
Saskatchewan	n/a
Manitoba	721
Ontario	10,132
Quebec	2,091
New Brunswick	240
Nova Scotia	n/a
Prince Edward Island	n/a
Newfoundland	229
Northwest Territories	n/a
Yukon Territory	n/a

213

METAL & METAL PRODUCTS WHOLESALERS

★ ★ ★

Job security in the wholesale metal and metal products industry has remained high and the lay-off rate is low at 4.6 percent. Given the continued long-term growth of the industry, advancement prospects remain attractive.

Average salary levels are high, and the average wage increase of 4.9 percent is high by Canadian industry standards.

The knowledge base of the industry is low and one cause for concern is that the knowledge base has fallen sharply.

OVERALL
SCORE

57.5

HOW THE INDUSTRY COMPARES:

Job Security: High
Advancement: Good
Average Salary: High
Salary Change: High
Knowledge Base: Low
Industry Knowledge: Declining
Industry Stability: Low

VITAL STATISTICS

Average Lay-off Rate, 1989–93: 4.6%
Net Job Creation, 1989–93: −482
Average Salary Level, 1993: $690/week
Salary Increase, 1993: +4.9%
Knowledge Workers per 100 Employees: 10
Knowledge Base Change: −21.7%
Industry Volatility: 9.3 (empl.)
SIC Code: 561

WHERE THE JOBS ARE:

TOTAL EMPLOYMENT	10,755
British Columbia	1,706
Alberta	757
Saskatchewan	446
Manitoba	270
Ontario	5,608
Quebec	1,805
New Brunswick	n/a
Nova Scotia	n/a
Prince Edward Island	n/a
Newfoundland	n/a
Northwest Territories	n/a
Yukon Territory	n/a

214

NEWSPAPER & MAGAZINE
PUBLISHING & PRINTING

Newspapers and magazine publishers and printers have been facing major challenges. They are seeking to define their new role in the information age, where global telecommunications capabilities provide their subscriber base with information content and delivery choices that were unimaginable only a few short years ago.

But change is also a breeding ground for opportunity. Many successful magazine publishers have secured strong growth by appealing to important niche markets (sports, travel, computers, gourmet cooking, etc.), and by shifting away from the old economy approach of reporting the news to the New Economy approach of providing more in-depth interpretation that can't be found in a sixty-second sound bite.

OVERALL
SCORE

57.5

HOW THE INDUSTRY COMPARES:

Job Security: High
Advancement: Moderate
Average Salary: Moderate
Salary Change: Very Poor
Knowledge Base: Moderate
Industry Knowledge: Rising
Industry Stability: High

VITAL STATISTICS

Average Lay-off Rate, 1989–93: 6.5%
Net Job Creation, 1989–93: −2,438
Average Salary Level, 1993: $632/week
Salary Increase, 1993: −3.0%
Knowledge Workers per 100 Employees: 37
Knowledge Base Change: +6.7%
Industry Volatility: 5.2 (empl.)
SIC Code: 284

WHERE THE JOBS ARE:

TOTAL EMPLOYMENT	36,752
British Columbia	3,884
Alberta	3,504
Saskatchewan	1,565
Manitoba	1,944
Ontario	17,217
Quebec	5,230
New Brunswick	800
Nova Scotia	1,603
Prince Edward Island	207
Newfoundland	680
Northwest Territories	n/a
Yukon Territory	n/a

NON-FERROUS SMELTING & REFINING

★ ★ ★

End-use markets for non-ferrous metals such as aluminum, nickel, zinc, copper and gold are changing rapidly. Nickel is the metal of the New Economy, followed by copper and aluminum.

OVERALL SCORE

57.5

The smelting and refining industry stands at the forefront of a rapidly rising technological base in which mining technologies bear little resemblance to past practices. Indeed, over the last five years, the knowledge base has risen 24.2 percent, which ranks among the highest increases of any industry in Canada.

But job security is low; the lay-off rate of 23.1 percent between 1989 and 1993 shows how hard this transition has been on the industry's work force. Not surprisingly, although salary levels are very high and raises are moderate, advancement prospects remain poor.

HOW THE INDUSTRY COMPARES:

Job Security: Low
Advancement: Poor
Average Salary: Very High
Salary Change: Moderate
Knowledge Base: Low
Industry Knowledge: Rising Very Sharply
Industry Stability: Moderate

VITAL STATISTICS

Average Lay-off Rate, 1989–93: 23.1%
Net Job Creation, 1989–93: −4,887
Average Salary Level, 1993: $887/week
Salary Increase, 1993: +1.8%
Knowledge Workers per 100 Employees: 16
Knowledge Base Change: +24.2
Industry Volatility: 8.5
SIC Code: 295

WHERE THE JOBS ARE:

TOTAL EMPLOYMENT	20,374
British Columbia	n/a
Alberta	n/a
Saskatchewan	n/a
Manitoba	n/a
Ontario	4,935
Quebec	9,557
New Brunswick	n/a
Nova Scotia	n/a
Prince Edward Island	n/a
Newfoundland	n/a
Northwest Territories	n/a
Yukon Territory	n/a

PAINT & VARNISH MANUFACTURING

★ ★ ★

Paint and varnish manufacturers that keep pace with the evolving needs of the New Economy should fare well both domestically and in emerging markets abroad.

Although job security is presently very low—witness the 28.9 percent lay-off rate over the course of the 1989–93 recession—advancement prospects in the industry are reasonable.

High average salaries and a sharply rising knowledge base constitute the prime attractions in this moderately knowledge-intensive industry, which should set its sights on growth within NAFTA and beyond.

OVERALL
SCORE

57.5

HOW THE INDUSTRY COMPARES:

Job Security: Low
Advancement: Moderate
Average Salary: High
Salary Change: Moderate
Knowledge Base: Moderate
Industry Knowledge: Rising Very Sharply
Industry Stability: Low

VITAL STATISTICS

Average Lay-off Rate, 1989–93: 28.9%
Net Job Creation, 1989–93: −1,887
Average Salary Level, 1993: $641/week
Salary Increase, 1993: +0.6%
Knowledge Workers per 100 Employees: 38
Knowledge Base Change: +50.1%
Industry Volatility: 9.6
SIC Code: 375

WHERE THE JOBS ARE:

TOTAL EMPLOYMENT	6,152
British Columbia	788
Alberta	n/a
Saskatchewan	n/a
Manitoba	219
Ontario	3,321
Quebec	1,638
New Brunswick	n/a
Nova Scotia	n/a
Prince Edward Island	n/a
Newfoundland	n/a
Northwest Territories	n/a
Yukon Territory	n/a

ASSOCIATIONS, UNIONS &
RELIGIOUS ORGANIZATIONS

This industry represents the interests of others and provides its employees with a reasonably high level of job security. Between 1989 and 1993, 7.4 percent of the people in this sector lost their jobs, for a net job loss of 6,923 people. In light of these high levels of attrition, job advancement is poor.

OVERALL SCORE

Another major drawback to employment in this field is the low average salary level. Salary cuts have been the norm.

55

However, the knowledge base is high and rising very sharply, which may appeal to some job seekers.

HOW THE INDUSTRY COMPARES:

Job Security: High
Advancement: Poor
Average Salary: Low
Salary Change: Very Poor
Knowledge Base: High
Industry Knowledge: Rising Sharply
Industry Stability: Moderate

WHERE THE JOBS ARE:

TOTAL EMPLOYMENT	86,846
British Columbia	12,561
Alberta	6,876
Saskatchewan	n/a
Manitoba	2,957
Ontario	37,498
Quebec	17,664
New Brunswick	1,710
Nova Scotia	n/a
Prince Edward Island	n/a
Newfoundland	1,184
Northwest Territories	n/a
Yukon Territory	n/a

VITAL STATISTICS

Average Lay-off Rate, 1989–93: 7.4%
Net Job Creation, 1989–93: −6,923
Average Salary Level, 1993: $450/week
Salary Increase, 1993: −4.6%
Knowledge Workers per 100 Employees: 51
Knowledge Base Change: +11.7%
Industry Volatility: 7.0 (empl.)
SIC Code: 980

MACHINE SHOPS

★ ★ ★

This industry manufactures machine parts and equipment, rebuilds engines and undertakes a wide range of custom and repair work.

OVERALL
SCORE

55

The knowledge base is moderate, but moving in the right direction with a 5.3 percent increase in the industry's Knowledge Ratio over the last five years.

Job security is high; employees experienced a 6.1 percent lay-off rate, which is low by national standards, thanks to continued structural growth in the demand for specialized machining, parts and engine rebuilding work. Volatility in the industry is moderate, and advancement prospects are reasonably good.

The principal drawbacks to employment in the industry are the low average salary level and the poor increase in base salaries. In fact, people employed in the business experienced an average 2.5 percent wage cut in 1993.

HOW THE INDUSTRY COMPARES:

Job Security: High
Advancement: Good
Average Salary: Low
Salary Change: Poor
Knowledge Base: Moderate
Industry Knowledge: Rising
Industry Stability: Moderate

VITAL STATISTICS

Average Lay-off Rate, 1989–93: 6.1%
Net Job Creation, 1989–93: −1,290
Average Salary Level, 1993: $553/week
Salary Increase, 1993: −2.5%
Knowledge Workers per 100 Employees: 22
Knowledge Base Change: +5.3%
Industry Volatility: 6.5
SIC Code: 308

WHERE THE JOBS ARE:	
TOTAL EMPLOYMENT	20,860
British Columbia	1,953
Alberta	1,837
Saskatchewan	685
Manitoba	486
Ontario	10,954
Quebec	4,286
New Brunswick	383
Nova Scotia	211
Prince Edward Island	n/a
Newfoundland	n/a
Northwest Territories	n/a
Yukon Territory	n/a

219

PHARMACIES & DRUG STORES

Pharmacies and drug stores are low on the salary scale, but rank exceptionally well in terms of job security and advancement. The knowledge base in this moderately knowledge-intensive business is rising sharply and may translate into better income prospects in the future. Salary cuts, however, are the norm at present.

The demand for prescription medicine is destined to rise sharply as Canada's population ages because the older we get, the more prescriptions we fill. The main challenges facing pharmacies and drug stores will likely come from two directions. First, as information technology provides increasing access to 1-800 ordering, customers will take fewer trips to the local pharmacy. Second, the rising concentration of major drug store chains will challenge the future of the small pharmacy, which may lack the ability to offer deep discounts on many non-prescription products.

OVERALL SCORE

55

HOW THE INDUSTRY COMPARES:

Job Security: Very High
Advancement: Very Good
Average Salary: Very Low
Salary Change: Poor
Knowledge Base: Moderate
Industry Knowledge: Rising Sharply
Industry Stability: Very Low

VITAL STATISTICS

Average Lay-off Rate, 1989–93: Zero
Net Job Creation, 1989–93: +18,224
Average Salary Level, 1993: $339/week
Salary Increase, 1993: –2.2%
Knowledge Workers per 100 Employees: 29
Knowledge Base Change: +9.7%
Industry Volatility: 14.8 (empl.)
SIC Code: 603

WHERE THE JOBS ARE:

TOTAL EMPLOYMENT	98,501
British Columbia	13,869
Alberta	6,910
Saskatchewan	n/a
Manitoba	n/a
Ontario	39,694
Quebec	24,835
New Brunswick	2,476
Nova Scotia	n/a
Prince Edward Island	n/a
Newfoundland	n/a
Northwest Territories	n/a
Yukon Territory	n/a

COMPUTER MANUFACTURING

⭐ ⭐ ⭐

A rapid pace of technological change, which has diverted computer demand away from old economy mainframes, has resulted in enormous lay-offs and very low job security for people employed in the manufacturing end of this New Economy engine. An unrelenting shift to increasingly portable and wireless computing will change this industry even more.

But strong growth in the demand for computers has resulted in moderate stability in the industry as a whole, despite the well-publicized upheavals at many of the largest companies.

This high-knowledge business offers excellent salaries and raises, but advancement prospects are poor. Between 1989 and 1993, 4,742 people left the industry through layoffs and early retirement programs.

OVERALL SCORE

52.5

HOW THE INDUSTRY COMPARES:

Job Security: Very Low
Advancement: Poor
Average Salary: High
Salary Change: High
Knowledge Base: High
Industry Knowledge: Reasonably Stable
Industry Stability: Moderate

VITAL STATISTICS

Average Lay-off Rate, 1989–93: 40.9%
Net Job Creation, 1989–93: −4,742
Average Salary Level, 1993: $726/week
Salary Increase, 1993: +3.7%
Knowledge Workers per 100 Employees: 58
Knowledge Base Change: +1.0%
Industry Volatility: 7.3
SIC Code: 336

WHERE THE JOBS ARE:

TOTAL EMPLOYMENT	12,474
British Columbia	n/a
Alberta	350
Saskatchewan	230
Manitoba	n/a
Ontario	7,599
Quebec	1,915
New Brunswick	n/a
Nova Scotia	128
Prince Edward Island	n/a
Newfoundland	n/a
Northwest Territories	n/a
Yukon Territory	n/a

HEATING EQUIPMENT MANUFACTURING

★ ★ ★

Manufacturers of major heating equipment, air conditioning systems and combination heating and cooling units have provided only a low level of job security for their employees in recent years. Indeed, people working in this field experienced a 28 percent lay-off rate between 1989 and 1993.

Although the average salary is low, salary increases have been dramatic in this highly cyclical industry.

The knowledge base of the heating equipment industry is moderate, but the Knowledge Ratio is rising very sharply. This is a positive trend as the industry embraces new technologies and introduces new processes in a bid to increase its competitive position.

OVERALL
SCORE

52.5

HOW THE INDUSTRY COMPARES:

Job Security: Low
Advancement: Good
Average Salary: Low
Salary Change: Very High
Knowledge Base: Moderate
Industry Knowledge: Rising Very Sharply
Industry Stability: Very Low

VITAL STATISTICS

Average Lay-off Rate, 1989–93: 28.0%
Net Job Creation, 1989–93: −1,276
Average Salary Level, 1993: $560/week
Salary Increase, 1993: +9.7%
Knowledge Workers per 100 Employees: 25
Knowledge Base Change: +23.8%
Industry Volatility: 15.1
SIC Code: 307

WHERE THE JOBS ARE:

TOTAL EMPLOYMENT	4,480
British Columbia	n/a
Alberta	371
Saskatchewan	n/a
Manitoba	196
Ontario	2,086
Quebec	n/a
New Brunswick	n/a
Nova Scotia	n/a
Prince Edward Island	n/a
Newfoundland	n/a
Northwest Territories	n/a
Yukon Territory	n/a

RESTAURANTS & CATERING

★ ★ ★

In the New Economy, people don't dine, they graze—a lifestyle change that has created a mini-boom in job creation in this industry with a zero lay-off rate. Job security is very high, and salary changes offer modest pay increases.

OVERALL
SCORE

52.5

The big job negatives are the low pay (sometimes supplemented by tips) and the very low knowledge base of the industry, which can create a workplace climate of "don't think —just do." However, advancement prospects are very good, and opportunities for promotion and job changes within this growing business abound.

Although most jobs are for servers and kitchen staff, opportunities for management positions and nutritionists, and for corporate planners and managers in the larger chains, can provide interesting career paths in the restaurant and food service business.

HOW THE INDUSTRY COMPARES:

Job Security: Very High
Advancement: Very Good
Average Salary: Very Low
Salary Change: Moderate
Knowledge Base: Low
Industry Knowledge: Reasonably Stable
Industry Stability: Moderate

VITAL STATISTICS

Average Lay-off Rate, 1989–93: Zero
Net Job Creation, 1989–93: +9,342
Average Salary Level, 1993: $199/week
Salary Increase, 1993: +0.8%
Knowledge Workers per 100 Employees: 17
Knowledge Base Change: +2.4%
Industry Volatility: 6.4
SIC Code: 921

WHERE THE JOBS ARE:

TOTAL EMPLOYMENT	523,774
British Columbia	89,174
Alberta	51,184
Saskatchewan	n/a
Manitoba	20,250
Ontario	207,655
Quebec	111,367
New Brunswick	9,417
Nova Scotia	n/a
Prince Edward Island	1,980
Newfoundland	5,156
Northwest Territories	472
Yukon Territory	374

AIRCRAFT & PARTS MANUFACTURING

★ ★ ★

The aircraft and aircraft parts industry has been growing because of a combination of innovative design initiatives (the Canadair Challenger) and a high degree of political involvement. With government spending under pressure, this moderately knowledge-intensive industry—in which only 39 out of every 100 employees are knowledge workers—must increasingly look to international markets for its long-term growth.

OVERALL
SCORE

50

Lay-off rates between 1989 and 1993 rose to 16.2 percent; consequently, job security can be described as moderate at best in this industry that is known for its very high volatility. On a net basis, 5,819 people have already lost their jobs.

Average salaries are very high, but average salary cuts of 8.4 percent were the norm in 1993.

HOW THE INDUSTRY COMPARES:

Job Security: Moderate
Advancement: Poor
Average Salary: Very High
Salary Change: Very Poor
Knowledge Base: Moderate
Industry Knowledge: Reasonably Stable
Industry Stability: Very Low

VITAL STATISTICS

Average Lay-off Rate, 1989–93: 16.2%
Net Job Creation, 1989–93: –5,819
Average Salary Level, 1993: $797/week
Salary Increase, 1993: –8.4%
Knowledge Workers per 100 Employees: 39
Knowledge Base Change: +2.4%
Industry Volatility: 12.9
SIC Code: 321

WHERE THE JOBS ARE:

TOTAL EMPLOYMENT	34,475
British Columbia	804
Alberta	1,187
Saskatchewan	n/a
Manitoba	3,396
Ontario	10,444
Quebec	17,219
New Brunswick	n/a
Nova Scotia	1,255
Prince Edward Island	n/a
Newfoundland	n/a
Northwest Territories	n/a
Yukon Territory	n/a

NURSING HOMES & HOMES FOR PEOPLE WITH DISABILITIES

Despite the clear trend to home-based care, nursing homes and homes for people with disabilities are a big industry and employ almost 200,000 Canadians.

Job security is high, and the industry experienced only a 3.7 percent lay-off rate through the difficult recession years of 1989–93. However, advancement prospects are poor and could deteriorate further as government funding cuts speed up the shift to home-based care.

Additional drawbacks to employment in this industry are the very low average salary and the poor salary changes. In 1993, average wage cuts of 2.4 percent were the norm.

This very stable industry is moderately knowledge intensive and its knowledge base is rising.

OVERALL SCORE

50

HOW THE INDUSTRY COMPARES:

Job Security: High
Advancement: Poor
Average Salary: Very Low
Salary Change: Poor
Knowledge Base: Moderate
Industry Knowledge: Rising
Industry Stability: Very High

VITAL STATISTICS

Average Lay-off Rate, 1989–93: 3.7%
Net Job Creation, 1989–93: −7,122
Average Salary Level, 1993: $409/week
Salary Increase, 1993: −2.4%
Knowledge Workers per 100 Employees: 30
Knowledge Base Change: +6.6%
Industry Volatility: 2.7
SIC Code: 862

WHERE THE JOBS ARE:

TOTAL EMPLOYMENT	192,898
British Columbia	21,544
Alberta	6,277
Saskatchewan	n/a
Manitoba	11,124
Ontario	73,060
Quebec	48,011
New Brunswick	6,002
Nova Scotia	n/a
Prince Edward Island	1,775
Newfoundland	4,118
Northwest Territories	131
Yukon Territory	n/a

WATER TRANSPORTATION, SHIPPING & FERRIES

★ ★ ★

Although the industry continues to grow in structural terms, the future for many segments of the water transportation, shipping and ferry business is increasingly uncertain, as government funding constraints force a review of long-standing policies and subsidies.

Job security is low, as demonstrated by the 31.8 percent lay-off rate between 1989 and 1993, and advancement prospects are poor in this moderately knowledge-intensive industry.

High and rising salaries will prove increasingly difficult to sustain as the knowledge base declines.

OVERALL
SCORE

50

HOW THE INDUSTRY COMPARES:

Job Security: Low
Advancement: Poor
Average Salary: High
Salary Change: High
Knowledge Base: Moderate
Industry Knowledge: Declining
Industry Stability: Moderate

VITAL STATISTICS

Average Lay-off Rate, 1989–93: 31.8%
Net Job Creation, 1989–93: −4,537
Average Salary Level, 1993: $732/week
Salary Increase, 1993: +3.7%
Knowledge Workers per 100 Employees: 22
Knowledge Base Change: −12.5%
Industry Volatility: 7.2
SIC Code: 454

WHERE THE JOBS ARE:

TOTAL EMPLOYMENT	13,833
British Columbia	5,558
Alberta	n/a
Saskatchewan	n/a
Manitoba	n/a
Ontario	3,008
Quebec	2,017
New Brunswick	1,044
Nova Scotia	509
Prince Edward Island	749
Newfoundland	822
Northwest Territories	n/a
Yukon Territory	n/a

ADVERTISING AGENCIES

⭐ ⭐

Advertising agencies offer employees a high-knowledge and high-paying environment.

The only drawback is the very low level of job security. Between 1989 and 1993, an incredibly large number of people lost their jobs in the advertising business, which suffered a stunning lay-off rate of 66.1 percent, one of the highest in Canada.

For those who survived the carnage, average salary increases of 9.5 percent were the norm. But prospects for advancement are very poor.

Advertising agencies face enormous shifts in their traditional markets. Old economy advertisers cannot afford to maintain their spending allocations of the past. New advertising mediums have sprung up quickly and have left all but the most technologically savvy agencies grappling with their impact: the stable nature of the knowledge base is an ominous sign. But the real prize to agencies will come from the rapid rate of innovation inherent in the New Economy. New products (often information-technology related) are being introduced in droves, and provide an important opportunity for advertisers to thrive amid the challenges in their industry.

VITAL STATISTICS

Average Lay-off Rate, 1989–93: 66.1%
Net Job Creation, 1989–93: −17,195
Average Salary Level, 1993: $666/week
Salary Increase, 1993: +9.5%
Knowledge Workers per 100 Employees: 51
Knowledge Base Change: −1.3%
Industry Volatility: 17.9 (empl.)
SIC Code: 774

OVERALL SCORE

47.5

HOW THE INDUSTRY COMPARES:

Job Security: Very Low
Advancement: Very Poor
Average Salary: High
Salary Change: Very High
Knowledge Base: High
Industry Knowledge: Reasonably Stable
Industry Stability: Very Low

WHERE THE JOBS ARE:

TOTAL EMPLOYMENT	25,949
British Columbia	2,461
Alberta	1,657
Saskatchewan	n/a
Manitoba	1,109
Ontario	14,221
Quebec	5,608
New Brunswick	104
Nova Scotia	422
Prince Edward Island	n/a
Newfoundland	184
Northwest Territories	n/a
Yukon Territory	n/a

MANAGEMENT CONSULTING

★ ★

The management consulting industry is broadly based and covers a range of specialties from corporate planning and change management to customer service and production planning. The field consists of both large and small firms.

The industry offers moderate job security to current and future employees. It experienced a 12.8 percent lay-off rate over the course of the recession years of 1989–93, and job advancement is ranked very poorly compared to other industries in Canada.

The average salary level in management consulting is moderate, and salary cuts of 5.1 percent in 1993 were commonplace.

While the industry displays a low level of stability it boasts a very high knowledge base—79 knowledge workers per 100 employees. Even better news for the future of the industry is that the knowledge base is rising sharply.

OVERALL SCORE

47.5

HOW THE INDUSTRY COMPARES:

Job Security: Moderate
Advancement: Very Poor
Average Salary: Moderate
Salary Change: Very Poor
Knowledge Base: High
Industry Knowledge: Rising Sharply
Industry Stability: Very Low

VITAL STATISTICS

Average Lay-off Rate, 1989–93: 12.8%
Net Job Creation, 1989–93: −8,664
Average Salary Level, 1993: $609/week
Salary Increase, 1993: −5.1%
Knowledge Workers per 100 Employees: 79
Knowledge Base Change: +8.8%
Industry Volatility: 21.8 (empl.)
SIC Code: 777

WHERE THE JOBS ARE:

TOTAL EMPLOYMENT	61,536
British Columbia	7,396
Alberta	7,747
Saskatchewan	n/a
Manitoba	2,159
Ontario	23,912
Quebec	17,150
New Brunswick	883
Nova Scotia	608
Prince Edward Island	195
Newfoundland	603
Northwest Territories	n/a
Yukon Territory	n/a

FRUIT & VEGETABLE PROCESSING

Consumers' desire for higher vegetable and fruit content in their daily diets has underpinned the long-term growth of this industry, but job prospects are not particularly attractive.

Average salaries are low, and the high lay-off rate of 20.1 percent translates into low job security for the 15,000 people that the industry employs.

However, the knowledge base is rising, a positive sign in this low-knowledge field.

Technology may enable businesses in this sector to introduce new processes, and to develop new products that are more innovative than the ones that have served the industry well for many decades.

OVERALL SCORE

45

HOW THE INDUSTRY COMPARES:

Job Security: Low
Advancement: Moderate
Average Salary: Low
Salary Change: Very High
Knowledge Base: Low
Industry Knowledge: Rising
Industry Stability: Moderate

VITAL STATISTICS

Average Lay-off Rate, 1989–93: 20.1%
Net Job Creation, 1989–93: –3,308
Average Salary Level, 1993: $536/week
Salary Increase, 1993: +6.9%
Knowledge Workers per 100 Employees: 14
Knowledge Base Change: +7.1%
Industry Volatility: 6.9
SIC Code: 103

WHERE THE JOBS ARE:

TOTAL EMPLOYMENT	15,395
British Columbia	1,612
Alberta	728
Saskatchewan	n/a
Manitoba	n/a
Ontario	7,237
Quebec	2,119
New Brunswick	n/a
Nova Scotia	473
Prince Edward Island	n/a
Newfoundland	n/a
Northwest Territories	n/a
Yukon Territory	n/a

INVESTMENT DEALERS &
INVESTMENT MANAGEMENT

Investment dealers and managers are exceptionally well positioned to benefit from the aging of Canada's population. Baby boomers will save and invest more as they plan for their retirement years and a future in which government social security may not be able to provide for them. The rapid growth in the mutual fund industry is already evidence of this growing trend.

OVERALL SCORE

45

Corporate finance departments and pension funds are also well positioned to finance the New Economy, and even though markets will move up and down, a steady lineup of companies in growing industries will decide to offer their shares to the public or will place shares privately.

The volatility of this business, however, is a serious negative. The industry experienced a 42.8 percent lay-off rate between 1989 and 1993. Despite the growth ahead, job security is very low and advancement prospects limited.

The investment field has a moderate knowledge base at present, but the Knowledge Ratio is rising sharply. This fast-paced New Economy industry provides a work environment of rapid change.

HOW THE INDUSTRY COMPARES:

Job Security: Very Low
Advancement: Very Poor
Average Salary: High
Salary Change: High
Knowledge Base: Moderate
Industry Knowledge: Rising Sharply
Industry Stability: Very Low

VITAL STATISTICS

Average Lay-off Rate, 1989–93: 42.8%
Net Job Creation, 1989–93: –19,493
Average Salary Level, 1993: $695/week
Salary Increase, 1993: +2.5%
Knowledge Workers per 100 Employees: 34
Knowledge Base Change: +11.8%
Industry Volatility: 14.2 (empl.)
SIC Code: 720

WHERE THE JOBS ARE:	
TOTAL EMPLOYMENT	41,073
British Columbia	5,895
Alberta	5,332
Saskatchewan	1,311
Manitoba	3,295
Ontario	15,031
Quebec	8,458
New Brunswick	348
Nova Scotia	761
Prince Edward Island	n/a
Newfoundland	471
Northwest Territories	n/a
Yukon Territory	n/a

SAWMILLS, PLANING & SHINGLE MILLS

This wood-based industry displays moderate volatility, which translated into a moderate lay-off rate of 15.7 percent between 1989 and 1993. However, job advancement is poor, and average salaries are only moderate compared to other industries in Canada.

The low knowledge base of the industry is cause for concern; however, it has begun to rise, albeit at a rather slow pace. Recent salary changes have been poor.

OVERALL
SCORE

45

HOW THE INDUSTRY COMPARES:

Job Security: Moderate
Advancement: Poor
Average Salary: Moderate
Salary Change: Poor
Knowledge Base: Low
Industry Knowledge: Rising
Industry Stability: Moderate

WHERE THE JOBS ARE:

TOTAL EMPLOYMENT	51,953
British Columbia	28,747
Alberta	3,270
Saskatchewan	442
Manitoba	324
Ontario	5,682
Quebec	10,033
New Brunswick	2,147
Nova Scotia	1,087
Prince Edward Island	n/a
Newfoundland	160
Northwest Territories	n/a
Yukon Territory	n/a

VITAL STATISTICS

Average Lay-off Rate, 1989–93: 15.7%
Net Job Creation, 1989–93: −7,760
Average Salary Level, 1993: $633/week
Salary Increase, 1993: −0.3%
Knowledge Workers per 100 Employees: 11
Knowledge Base Change: +4.9%
Industry Volatility: 8.7
SIC Code: 251

COAL MINING

★ ★

Government funding kept the growth of the coal mining industry from peaking structurally, but pressures to reduce government spending have intensified and will place this industry at risk, should direct or indirect subsidies be reduced or eliminated. The already low level of job security could deteriorate even further, beyond the 31.7 percent lay-off rate that employees have already undergone.

OVERALL
SCORE

42.5

Few measures are being taken within the industry to encourage growth. The low knowledge base is declining and salary levels remain very high, two factors that are creating competitive pressures among coal mining companies.

Salary increases, however, are poor by national standards. Average salary cuts of 2.1 percent are the recent norm in this unstable industry.

HOW THE INDUSTRY COMPARES:

Job Security: Low
Advancement: Moderate
Average Salary: Very High
Salary Change: Poor
Knowledge Base: Low
Industry Knowledge: Declining
Industry Stability: Very Low

VITAL STATISTICS

Average Lay-off Rate, 1989–93: 31.7%
Net Job Creation, 1989–93: −2,470
Average Salary Level, 1993: $860/week
Salary Increase, 1993: −2.1%
Knowledge Workers per 100 Employees: 11
Knowledge Base Change: −4.6%
Industry Volatility: 18.6
SIC Code: 063

WHERE THE JOBS ARE:	
TOTAL EMPLOYMENT	8,093
British Columbia	3,169
Alberta	2,442
Saskatchewan	n/a
Manitoba	n/a
Ontario	n/a
Quebec	n/a
New Brunswick	n/a
Nova Scotia	1,901
Prince Edward Island	n/a
Newfoundland	n/a
Northwest Territories	n/a
Yukon Territory	n/a

HARDWARE, TOOLS & CUTLERY MANUFACTURING

★ ★

Manufacturers of hardware, metal dies, moulds, patterns, hand tools and basic cutlery have provided only moderate job security, and advancement prospects in this low-knowledge industry are not exceptionally attractive.

Average salary levels are also only moderate, and employees enjoyed only a 1.6 percent salary increase in 1993.

The industry is quite volatile, but of even more concern is that the already low knowledge base is declining. In the last five years, 16.4 percent fewer knowledge workers were employed in this manufacturing industry.

To continue the growth that the business has enjoyed in the past, manufacturers will need to focus on new technologies, new products and on developing new markets for existing products.

OVERALL
SCORE

42.5

HOW THE INDUSTRY COMPARES:

Job Security: Moderate
Advancement: Moderate
Average Salary: Moderate
Salary Change: Moderate
Knowledge Base: Low
Industry Knowledge: Declining
Industry Stability: Low

VITAL STATISTICS

Average Lay-off Rate, 1989–93: 15.2%
Net Job Creation, 1989–93: −2,483
Average Salary Level, 1993: $628/week
Salary Increase, 1993: +1.6%
Knowledge Workers per 100 Employees: 12
Knowledge Base Change: −16.4%
Industry Volatility: 10.4
SIC Code: 306

WHERE THE JOBS ARE:	
TOTAL EMPLOYMENT	20,066
British Columbia	1,116
Alberta	118
Saskatchewan	n/a
Manitoba	n/a
Ontario	15,854
Quebec	2,816
New Brunswick	n/a
Nova Scotia	n/a
Prince Edward Island	n/a
Newfoundland	n/a
Northwest Territories	n/a
Yukon Territory	n/a

PUBLISHING

★ ★

The publishing industry is leveraged to the information economy, and the sharply rising Knowledge Ratio reflects the introduction of new processes, products and technologies. Challenges and opportunities abound for publishers as new technologies open up a wide and exciting range of on-line, CD-ROM and multimedia options. Publishers who know how to take advantage of these opportunities in the New Economy will have a head start on everyone else.

The transition to new technologies and products has not been an easy one for Canadian publishing firms, as lay-off rates of 18.3 percent attest. Advancement prospects are poor and average salaries are at the low end for Canadian industries as a whole. The industry has a low degree of stability, but its sharply rising knowledge base proves that it is shifting gears into the New Economy.

OVERALL SCORE

42.5

HOW THE INDUSTRY COMPARES:

Job Security: Moderate
Advancement: Poor
Average Salary: Low
Salary Change: Very Poor
Knowledge Base: Moderate
Industry Knowledge: Rising Sharply
Industry Stability: Low

VITAL STATISTICS

Average Lay-off Rate, 1989–93: 18.3%
Net Job Creation, 1989–93: −4,770
Average Salary Level, 1993: $544/week
Salary Increase, 1993: −2.6%
Knowledge Workers per 100 Employees: 32
Knowledge Base Change: +13.6%
Industry Volatility: 9.3 (empl.)
SIC Code: 283

WHERE THE JOBS ARE:

TOTAL EMPLOYMENT	25,452
British Columbia	3,111
Alberta	1,239
Saskatchewan	568
Manitoba	164
Ontario	13,008
Quebec	6,775
New Brunswick	237
Nova Scotia	228
Prince Edward Island	n/a
Newfoundland	n/a
Northwest Territories	n/a
Yukon Territory	n/a

TRUCKING & TRANSPORT

★ ★

The trucking industry has benefited from a move to higher-value goods, miniaturization and a proliferation of New Economy products that require transportation to market. But the knowledge base of this already low-knowledge industry is declining, which is a cause for concern as the economy (and its customer base) moves up the knowledge scale.

Average salaries in the trucking and transport business are low, but have been supplemented recently by high wage increases in the order of 3.4 percent.

Job security is moderate. The industry's 18.1 percent lay-off rate over the 1989–93 period meant that 23,076 people lost their jobs. Advancement prospects are very poor at present.

OVERALL SCORE

42.5

HOW THE INDUSTRY COMPARES:

Job Security: Moderate
Advancement: Very Poor
Average Salary: Low
Salary Change: High
Knowledge Base: Low
Industry Knowledge: Declining
Industry Stability: Very High

VITAL STATISTICS

Average Lay-off Rate, 1989–93: 18.1%
Net Job Creation, 1989–93: −23,076
Average Salary Level, 1993: $565/week
Salary Increase, 1993: +3.4%
Knowledge Workers per 100 Employees: 9
Knowledge Base Change: −6.9%
Industry Volatility: 3.9
SIC Code: 456

WHERE THE JOBS ARE:	
TOTAL EMPLOYMENT	120,566
British Columbia	15,173
Alberta	16,250
Saskatchewan	4,822
Manitoba	7,103
Ontario	37,687
Quebec	29,861
New Brunswick	3,880
Nova Scotia	3,512
Prince Edward Island	474
Newfoundland	1,288
Northwest Territories	324
Yukon Territory	192

FOOD WHOLESALERS

Wholesalers of food in Canada employ 67,521 Canadians today after net layoffs of 9,806 employees between 1989 and 1993. Consequently, job security in the industry is moderate and advancement prospects are very poor.

The average salary in the field is low and salary increases averaged only 0.5 percent in 1993. However, the industry is very stable and is not known for wild fluctuations.

The knowledge base is low and declining—a worrying trend in this higher-knowledge economy.

While the major occupations involve sales and purchasing, other jobs in accounts payable, accounts receivable and customer service are also very important to the business.

OVERALL SCORE

37.5

HOW THE INDUSTRY COMPARES:

Job Security: Moderate
Advancement: Very Poor
Average Salary: Low
Salary Change: Moderate
Knowledge Base: Low
Industry Knowledge: Declining
Industry Stability: High

VITAL STATISTICS

Average Lay-off Rate, 1989–93: 13.9%
Net Job Creation, 1989–93: −9,806
Average Salary Level, 1993: $510/week
Salary Increase, 1993: +0.5%
Knowledge Workers per 100 Employees: 10
Knowledge Base Change: −12.7%
Industry Volatility: 5.5 (empl.)
SIC Code: 521

WHERE THE JOBS ARE:

TOTAL EMPLOYMENT	67,521
British Columbia	9,939
Alberta	5,438
Saskatchewan	2,099
Manitoba	2,720
Ontario	18,874
Quebec	20,394
New Brunswick	2,559
Nova Scotia	3,855
Prince Edward Island	n/a
Newfoundland	1,081
Northwest Territories	n/a
Yukon Territory	n/a

FOOD STORES & SUPERMARKETS

★

Food stores are a major employer in Canada, providing over 330,000 people with work. The industry offers a high degree of job security in a very low-knowledge, very low-wage environment.

Advancement in the food store business is poor as shown by the net job losses in the industry, as a whole, of over 8,000 people between 1989 and 1993.

Salary changes are poor, with average wage cuts of 1.6 percent from a salary base that is already very low.

Of greater concern is that the knowledge base is stable, despite the fact that food stores and supermarkets face potentially formidable competition in the future from on-line food shopping.

OVERALL SCORE

35

HOW THE INDUSTRY COMPARES:

Job Security: High
Advancement: Poor
Average Salary: Very Low
Salary Change: Poor
Knowledge Base: Low
Industry Knowledge: Reasonably Stable
Industry Stability: Low

VITAL STATISTICS

Average Lay-off Rate, 1989–93: 2.5%
Net Job Creation, 1989–93: –8,009
Average Salary Level, 1993: $290/week
Salary Increase, 1993: –1.6%
Knowledge Workers per 100 Employees: 3
Knowledge Base Change: +3.5%
Industry Volatility: 10.6 (empl.)
SIC Code: 601

WHERE THE JOBS ARE:

TOTAL EMPLOYMENT	330,109
British Columbia	48,185
Alberta	30,575
Saskatchewan	10,789
Manitoba	12,302
Ontario	121,227
Quebec	81,688
New Brunswick	9,153
Nova Scotia	7,420
Prince Edward Island	1,530
Newfoundland	6,434
Northwest Territories	499
Yukon Territory	307

HARDWARE, PLUMBING, HEATING & AIR CONDITIONING EQUIPMENT WHOLESALERS

Wholesalers of hardware, plumbing, heating and air conditioning equipment have struggled through the tough recession years of 1989–93, laying off 37 percent of their employees in the process. Advancement in the industry is very poor at best.

Average salary levels are moderate and salary increases are surprisingly high as the economy recovers.

The moderate stability of this low-knowledge industry is cause for some concern. The knowledge base is declining because wholesalers have apparently not made any major efforts to diversify their business with higher value-added and higher-knowledge goods.

OVERALL SCORE

35

HOW THE INDUSTRY COMPARES:

Job Security: Very Low
Advancement: Very Poor
Average Salary: Moderate
Salary Change: Very High
Knowledge Base: Low
Industry Knowledge: Declining
Industry Stability: Moderate

VITAL STATISTICS

Average Lay-off Rate, 1989–93: 37.0%
Net Job Creation, 1989–93: −9,562
Average Salary Level, 1993: $590/week
Salary Increase, 1993: +5.9%
Knowledge Workers per 100 Employees: 10
Knowledge Base Change: −21.7%
Industry Volatility: 8.4 (empl.)
SIC Code: 562

WHERE THE JOBS ARE:	
TOTAL EMPLOYMENT	24,376
British Columbia	3,485
Alberta	2,336
Saskatchewan	395
Manitoba	557
Ontario	10,238
Quebec	5,966
New Brunswick	547
Nova Scotia	493
Prince Edward Island	n/a
Newfoundland	n/a
Northwest Territories	n/a
Yukon Territory	n/a

BUS, TRUCK & VAN MANUFACTURING

★

Unlike other segments of the automotive industry, this sector offers employees very low industry and job stability. Between 1989 and 1993, 5,978 people lost their jobs and created an average lay-off rate of 61.8 percent in this essentially low-knowledge, low-paying field.

Of keen interest, however, is that the knowledge base of the industry is rising very sharply as manufacturers embrace new technologies and find new markets.

OVERALL
SCORE

32.5

HOW THE INDUSTRY COMPARES:

Job Security: Very Low
Advancement: Poor
Average Salary: Low
Salary Change: Moderate
Knowledge Base: Low
Industry Knowledge: Rising Very Sharply
Industry Stability: Very Low

VITAL STATISTICS

Average Lay-off Rate, 1989–93: 61.8%
Net Job Creation, 1989–93: −5,978
Average Salary Level, 1993: $515/week
Salary Increase, 1993: +1.3%
Knowledge Workers per 100 Employees: 19
Knowledge Base Change: +22.6%
Industry Volatility: 18.9
SIC Code: 324

WHERE THE JOBS ARE:

TOTAL EMPLOYMENT	9,672
British Columbia	1,747
Alberta	998
Saskatchewan	n/a
Manitoba	1,580
Ontario	2,502
Quebec	n/a
New Brunswick	n/a
Nova Scotia	n/a
Prince Edward Island	n/a
Newfoundland	n/a
Northwest Territories	n/a
Yukon Territory	n/a

DEPARTMENT STORES

⭐

General merchandisers such as department stores and variety stores provide moderate job security in an industry that faces enormous challenges and opportunities in the New Economy.

One challenge will be to compete effectively with the major discount chains that are making their way into Canada, and with the warehouse-style superstores that are dotting the landscape at an increasing rate. But the more serious challenge will be to face a proliferation of retailers who set up shop along the information highway and provide mind-boggling choice at rock-bottom prices.

Job security is only moderate, and the lay-off rate of 15.2 percent in this big industry has translated into the loss of over 29,000 jobs. Advancement prospects are very poor in this low-knowledge business.

The main drawbacks to employment are the very low average salary and the zero wage increase.

OVERALL SCORE

32.5

HOW THE INDUSTRY COMPARES:

Job Security: Moderate
Advancement: Very Poor
Average Salary: Very Low
Salary Change: Poor
Knowledge Base: Low
Industry Knowledge: Reasonably Stable
Industry Stability: High

WHERE THE JOBS ARE:

TOTAL EMPLOYMENT	200,287
British Columbia	22,973
Alberta	19,725
Saskatchewan	8,445
Manitoba	9,874
Ontario	86,102
Quebec	33,244
New Brunswick	5,714
Nova Scotia	8,046
Prince Edward Island	867
Newfoundland	4,175
Northwest Territories	n/a
Yukon Territory	n/a

VITAL STATISTICS

Average Lay-off Rate, 1989–93: 15.2%
Net Job Creation, 1989–93: −29,198
Average Salary Level, 1993: $293/week
Salary Increase, 1993: Zero
Knowledge Workers per 100 Employees: 11
Knowledge Base Change: −1.7%
Industry Volatility: 5.8 (empl.)
SIC Code: 641

COMMERCIAL & INDUSTRIAL BUILDERS & DEVELOPERS

Commercial and industrial development is known for its big fluctuations between boom and bust. The lay-off rate of the industry rings the bell at 75.3 percent between 1989 and 1993. Consequently, advancement prospects are very poor.

OVERALL SCORE

30

Commercial and industrial builders and developers have been somewhat slow to recognize the shift from an old economy into a new one, and have been caught squarely in the transition. But New Economy companies need office and warehouse space, too, and commercial developers who raise their knowledge base and become attuned to the space needs of growing industries will prosper. Commercial and industrial developers also need to pick their communities with great care and stay clear of the cities and towns that are highly leveraged to old economy or Watch List industries.

Salary levels are high, but salary increases of late have been rather poor, averaging cuts of 0.8 percent. Although the major occupations in the industry concern real estate, opportunities exist for accounting, clerical and administrative staff as well. The knowledge base of the business is low, but reasonably stable.

HOW THE INDUSTRY COMPARES:

Job Security: Very Low
Advancement: Very Poor
Average Salary: High
Salary Change: Poor
Knowledge Base: Low
Industry Knowledge: Reasonably Stable
Industry Stability: Very Low

VITAL STATISTICS

Average Lay-off Rate, 1989–93: 75.3%
Net Job Creation, 1989–93: −20,475
Average Salary Level, 1993: $674/week
Salary Increase, 1993: −0.8%
Knowledge Workers per 100 Employees: 15
Knowledge Base Change: −1.5%
Industry Volatility: 15.3 (empl.)
SIC Code: 402

WHERE THE JOBS ARE:

TOTAL EMPLOYMENT	26,669
British Columbia	4,308
Alberta	2,896
Saskatchewan	912
Manitoba	1,032
Ontario	9,517
Quebec	5,433
New Brunswick	322
Nova Scotia	782
Prince Edward Island	161
Newfoundland	1,081
Northwest Territories	208
Yukon Territory	n/a

EMPLOYMENT AGENCIES & PROFESSIONAL SEARCH FIRMS

The sad irony is that employment agencies suffered one of the highest lay-off rates for any industry during the 1989–93 recession: 11,788 Canadians lost their jobs at employment agencies and professional search firms over the period. Consequently, advancement prospects are very poor.

Average salaries in the business are very low, but employees enjoyed a high wage increase of 7.0 percent in 1993.

A longer term worry in the industry is the moderate knowledge base, which is declining.

OVERALL SCORE

30

HOW THE INDUSTRY COMPARES:

Job Security: Low
Advancement: Very Poor
Average Salary: Very Low
Salary Change: Very High
Knowledge Base: Moderate
Industry Knowledge: Declining
Industry Stability: Very Low

VITAL STATISTICS

Average Lay-off Rate, 1989–93: 21.3%
Net Job Creation, 1989–93: −11,788
Average Salary Level, 1993: $378/week
Salary Increase, 1993: +7.0%
Knowledge Workers per 100 Employees: 32
Knowledge Base Change: −8.3%
Industry Volatility: 21.6 (empl.)
SIC Code: 771

WHERE THE JOBS ARE:

TOTAL EMPLOYMENT	56,275
British Columbia	5,399
Alberta	5,697
Saskatchewan	610
Manitoba	1,112
Ontario	29,483
Quebec	11,810
New Brunswick	707
Nova Scotia	1,008
Prince Edward Island	n/a
Newfoundland	428
Northwest Territories	n/a
Yukon Territory	n/a

HIGHWAY & HEAVY CONSTRUCTION

★

In Canada, as in other industrialized countries, the emphasis has shifted rapidly from the old economy's infrastructure of highways to the New Economy's infrastructure of telecommunications. With government spending constrained in most jurisdictions across Canada, privately financed construction projects are becoming increasingly common.

Over the course of the recession, 16,991 layoffs in this volatile industry represented 37.5 percent of workers. Advancement prospects are consequently quite poor at present.

The average salary is high but salary cuts have been astronomic—25.8 percent in 1993.

On average, the industry employs only 15 knowledge workers per 100 staff. The stability of this low knowledge base is a cause for concern, given the technological changes that are sweeping across our industrial landscape.

OVERALL
SCORE

30

HOW THE INDUSTRY COMPARES:

Job Security: Very Low
Advancement: Very Poor
Average Salary: High
Salary Change: Very Poor
Knowledge Base: Low
Industry Knowledge: Reasonably Stable
Industry Stability: Low

VITAL STATISTICS

Average Lay-off Rate, 1989–93: 37.5%
Net Job Creation, 1989–93: −16,991
Average Salary Level, 1993: $640/week
Salary Increase, 1993: −25.8%
Knowledge Workers per 100 Employees: 15
Knowledge Base Change: −1.5%
Industry Volatility: 10.8 (empl.)
SIC Code: 412

WHERE THE JOBS ARE:

TOTAL EMPLOYMENT	32,127
British Columbia	3,958
Alberta	2,861
Saskatchewan	882
Manitoba	1,060
Ontario	11,437
Quebec	8,312
New Brunswick	909
Nova Scotia	1,482
Prince Edward Island	384
Newfoundland	n/a
Northwest Territories	n/a
Yukon Territory	n/a

243

HOTELS & MOTELS

★

The hotel and motel business has suffered from the recession. The high jobless rate in Canada has resulted in fewer holiday travelers. But business travel has also suffered—knowledge workers in the New Economy are more likely to teleconference and e-mail than to rely exclusively on face-to-face meetings. Nonetheless, travel and tourism are global industries and are positioned well in the New Economy over the longer term.

With a lay-off rate of 27.8 percent in the hotel and motel industry, job security is understandably low and advancement is very poor.

The average salary level is also very low, but recent salary changes have been quite high, averaging 2.8 percent.

This industry employs 18 knowledge workers on average per 100 employees. This low knowledge base is stable, which places the business at a competitive disadvantage to a customer base that is becoming increasingly more sophisticated.

OVERALL SCORE

30

HOW THE INDUSTRY COMPARES:

Job Security: Low
Advancement: Very Poor
Average Salary: Very Low
Salary Change: High
Knowledge Base: Low
Industry Knowledge: Reasonably Stable
Industry Stability: Moderate

VITAL STATISTICS

Average Lay-off Rate, 1989–93: 27.8%
Net Job Creation, 1989–93: –39,937
Average Salary Level, 1993: $274/week
Salary Increase, 1993: +2.8%
Knowledge Workers per 100 Employees: 18
Knowledge Base Change: +1.8%
Industry Volatility: 6.4
SIC Code: 911

WHERE THE JOBS ARE:

TOTAL EMPLOYMENT	136,519
British Columbia	26,912
Alberta	20,920
Saskatchewan	n/a
Manitoba	6,085
Ontario	44,559
Quebec	22,009
New Brunswick	2,393
Nova Scotia	n/a
Prince Edward Island	645
Newfoundland	1,430
Northwest Territories	813
Yukon Territory	653

MEN'S CLOTHING STORES

⭐

Retailing is leveraged to the New Economy, but remains a low-knowledge, low-paying field that will be threatened more and more as traditional shopping centers lose ground to on-line shopping malls springing up along the information highway.

OVERALL SCORE

27.5

The knowledge base of the men's clothing store business is declining from its already low level. This decrease is a source of concern since the real competition to the traditional shopping experience is decidedly high-tech.

Job security is low; 34.2 percent of the people in this low-wage industry have already lost their jobs, and for those who remain, advancement prospects are poor.

Of relevance to job seekers, however, is the high average wage increase of 7.2 percent.

HOW THE INDUSTRY COMPARES:

Job Security: Low
Advancement: Poor
Average Salary: Very Low
Salary Change: Very High
Knowledge Base: Low
Industry Knowledge: Declining
Industry Stability: Very Low

VITAL STATISTICS

Average Lay-off Rate, 1989–93: 34.2%
Net Job Creation, 1989–93: –5,372
Average Salary Level, 1993: $344/week
Salary Increase, 1993: +7.2%
Knowledge Workers per 100 Employees: 5
Knowledge Base Change: –7.9%
Industry Volatility: 11.6 (empl.)
SIC Code: 612

WHERE THE JOBS ARE:	
TOTAL EMPLOYMENT	17,030
British Columbia	2,511
Alberta	1,976
Saskatchewan	416
Manitoba	389
Ontario	5,890
Quebec	4,800
New Brunswick	n/a
Nova Scotia	455
Prince Edward Island	n/a
Newfoundland	108
Northwest Territories	n/a
Yukon Territory	n/a

ORNAMENTAL & ARCHITECTURAL METAL PRODUCTS MANUFACTURING

The introduction of new products has saved this industry from extinction. While the demand for metal doors and windows has seriously declined, wrought-iron furniture has now become all the rage.

The knowledge base is low, but it has risen sharply in the last five years, mirroring the pace of product development and innovation in the industry.

Nonetheless, the lay-off rate through the tough recession years rose to a staggering 68.9 percent: 9,920 people net lost their jobs. And, needless to say, advancement prospects in the industry are very poor at present.

The average salary is low, and salary increases rank as very poor, with the average wage cut in the order of 3.7 percent.

OVERALL SCORE

27.5

HOW THE INDUSTRY COMPARES:

Job Security: Very Low
Advancement: Very Poor
Average Salary: Low
Salary Change: Very Poor
Knowledge Base: Low
Industry Knowledge: Rising Sharply
Industry Stability: Moderate

VITAL STATISTICS

Average Lay-off Rate, 1989–93: 68.9%
Net Job Creation, 1989–93: –9,920
Average Salary Level, 1993: $562/week
Salary Increase, 1993: –3.7%
Knowledge Workers per 100 Employees: 19
Knowledge Base Change: +8.0%
Industry Volatility: 7.5
SIC Code: 303

WHERE THE JOBS ARE:

TOTAL EMPLOYMENT	12,715
British Columbia	n/a
Alberta	1,798
Saskatchewan	n/a
Manitoba	428
Ontario	6,302
Quebec	2,480
New Brunswick	138
Nova Scotia	n/a
Prince Edward Island	n/a
Newfoundland	n/a
Northwest Territories	n/a
Yukon Territory	n/a

PLASTIC PRODUCTS MANUFACTURING

★

Manufacturers of plastic products laid off 15,549 employees or 32.7 percent of their work force during the recession years of 1989–93. With such widespread restructuring, job security in the industry is low and advancement prospects are very poor.

The industry offers low average salaries, and people employed in the plastic products field received an average wage cut of 3.2 percent in 1993. This low-knowledge industry is struggling to regain a competitive footing.

However, the battle may not be lost. In the last five years, the knowledge base has risen sharply, increasing by 11.1 percent. This strong increase indicates that new technologies and processes are being introduced and that innovation is taking hold in this industry.

OVERALL
SCORE

27.5

HOW THE INDUSTRY COMPARES:

Job Security: Low
Advancement: Very Poor
Average Salary: Low
Salary Change: Very Poor
Knowledge Base: Low
Industry Knowledge: Rising Sharply
Industry Stability: Very Low

VITAL STATISTICS

Average Lay-off Rate, 1989–93: 32.7%
Net Job Creation, 1989–93: −15,549
Average Salary Level, 1993: $531/week
Salary Increase, 1993: −3.2%
Knowledge Workers per 100 Employees: 16
Knowledge Base Change: +11.1%
Industry Volatility: 18.6 (empl.)
SIC Code: 160

WHERE THE JOBS ARE:

TOTAL EMPLOYMENT	48,564
British Columbia	3,598
Alberta	1,706
Saskatchewan	n/a
Manitoba	1,751
Ontario	26,349
Quebec	13,960
New Brunswick	n/a
Nova Scotia	n/a
Prince Edward Island	n/a
Newfoundland	n/a
Northwest Territories	n/a
Yukon Territory	n/a

WOODEN PREFAB BUILDINGS, CABINETS, DOOR & WINDOW MANUFACTURING

Manufacturers of these wood products have weathered major restructuring across the industry and laid off 15,656 employees through the tough recession years of 1989–93. The lay-off rate of 54 percent is one of the highest in Canada. Advancement prospects are consequently very poor.

Average salaries in the industry are low and salary changes are discouraging: employees watched their wages decline an average of 1.4 percent in 1993.

The welcome sign is that the low knowledge base—only 11 out of 100 employees are knowledge workers—is rising. To survive in the New Economy, industries have no choice but to introduce new technologies. Manufacturers must be willing and able to employ new processes, develop new products and find new markets both domestically and abroad.

OVERALL
SCORE

27.5

HOW THE INDUSTRY COMPARES:

Job Security: Very Low
Advancement: Very Poor
Average Salary: Low
Salary Change: Poor
Knowledge Base: Low
Industry Knowledge: Rising
Industry Stability: Moderate

VITAL STATISTICS

Average Lay-off Rate, 1989–93: 54.0%
Net Job Creation, 1989–93: −15,656
Average Salary Level, 1993: $483/week
Salary Increase, 1993: −1.4%
Knowledge Workers per 100 Employees: 11
Knowledge Base Change: +4.9%
Industry Volatility: 8.7
SIC Code: 254

WHERE THE JOBS ARE:	
TOTAL EMPLOYMENT	26,582
British Columbia	5,537
Alberta	2,011
Saskatchewan	396
Manitoba	2,038
Ontario	8,661
Quebec	7,121
New Brunswick	493
Nova Scotia	171
Prince Edward Island	n/a
Newfoundland	144
Northwest Territories	n/a
Yukon Territory	n/a

WOMEN'S CLOTHING STORES

★

Significant challenges face the retail industry in the New Economy as shopping patterns shift from local malls to shopping centers along the information highway, accessed from the comfort of our own homes.

OVERALL SCORE

25

The decline in the knowledge base of this industry, from its already low level, is therefore cause for concern.

Job security is moderate, as shown by the industry's lay-off rate of 14.7 percent, and the net job creation indicator shows that 7,309 people lost their jobs in the business between 1989 and 1993.

Average salaries are very low and salary increases are very poor. In fact, average salary cuts of 2.6 percent prevailed in 1993.

HOW THE INDUSTRY COMPARES:

Job Security: Moderate
Advancement: Poor
Average Salary: Very Low
Salary Change: Very Poor
Knowledge Base: Low
Industry Knowledge: Declining
Industry Stability: Low

VITAL STATISTICS

Average Lay-off Rate, 1989–93: 14.7%
Net Job Creation, 1989–93: −7,309
Average Salary Level, 1993: $239/week
Salary Increase, 1993: −2.6%
Knowledge Workers per 100 Employees: 5
Knowledge Base Change: −7.9%
Industry Volatility: 10.2 (empl.)
SIC Code: 613

WHERE THE JOBS ARE:	
TOTAL EMPLOYMENT	54,027
British Columbia	6,914
Alberta	4,752
Saskatchewan	1,292
Manitoba	2,077
Ontario	20,174
Quebec	15,568
New Brunswick	1,098
Nova Scotia	1,282
Prince Edward Island	180
Newfoundland	671
Northwest Territories	n/a
Yukon Territory	n/a

CHILDREN'S CLOTHING STORES AND MISCELLANEOUS CLOTHING RETAILERS

Significant challenges face the retailing sector in the New Economy: consumers are demanding better customer service and greater choice at deeply discounted prices.

But the ultimate challenge to retailers comes from the potentially radical shift in how shoppers shop: the popularity of mail-order catalogues may be the simple first step on the road to burgeoning growth in on-line shopping with next-day delivery via FedEx. An ominous sign for children's clothing retailers is that the knowledge base of the industry has declined from its already low level.

Low job security, coupled with very poor advancement prospects, provide a poor future to employees in this field, where the average salary is very low and declining.

OVERALL SCORE

15

HOW THE INDUSTRY COMPARES:

Job Security: Low
Advancement: Very Poor
Average Salary: Very Low
Salary Change: Very Poor
Knowledge Base: Low
Industry Knowledge: Declining
Industry Stability: Very Low

VITAL STATISTICS

Average Lay-off Rate, 1989–93: 29.3%
Net Job Creation, 1989–93: –10,970
Average Salary Level, 1993: $259/week
Salary Increase, 1993: –4.6%
Knowledge Workers per 100 Employees: 5
Knowledge Base Change: –7.9%
Industry Volatility: 16.5 (empl.)
SIC Code: 614

WHERE THE JOBS ARE:	
TOTAL EMPLOYMENT	39,645
British Columbia	3,846
Alberta	3,816
Saskatchewan	1,320
Manitoba	1,630
Ontario	11,259
Quebec	15,308
New Brunswick	844
Nova Scotia	624
Prince Edward Island	279
Newfoundland	673
Northwest Territories	n/a
Yukon Territory	n/a

BEDDING, HOTEL & RESTAURANT FURNITURE MANUFACTURING

The hospitality business is firmly anchored in the New Economy, as travel and tourism emerge as major and rapidly growing international industries. As a supplier of bedding, hotel and restaurant furniture, this low-knowledge manufacturing industry has experienced difficulty adapting; the 20.8 percent lay-off rate has translated into low job security.

Advancement prospects are moderate compared to other industries, and the business provides low stability. Average salary data is not available.

The positive note for potential job seekers is that the knowledge base is rising very sharply, an indication that the industry is wide open to new ideas and to the introduction of new technologies and processes.

OVERALL
SCORE

N/A

HOW THE INDUSTRY COMPARES:

Job Security: Low
Advancement: Moderate
Average Salary: N/A
Salary Change: N/A
Knowledge Base: Low
Industry Knowledge: Rising Very Sharply
Industry Stability: Low

WHERE THE JOBS ARE:

TOTAL EMPLOYMENT	12,269
British Columbia	1,026
Alberta	483
Saskatchewan	n/a
Manitoba	516
Ontario	6,624
Quebec	3,254
New Brunswick	127
Nova Scotia	n/a
Prince Edward Island	n/a
Newfoundland	n/a
Northwest Territories	n/a
Yukon Territory	n/a

VITAL STATISTICS

Average Lay-off Rate, 1989–93: 20.8%
Net Job Creation, 1989–93: −2,641
Average Salary Level, 1993: N/A
Salary Increase, 1993: N/A
Knowledge Workers per 100 Employees: 14
Knowledge Base Change: +24.2%
Industry Volatility: 9.5 (empl.)
SIC Code: 269

251

Wholesalers of clothing and shoes provide good advancement prospects in a low-knowledge industry.

By national standards, job security is high, with the industry having undergone only a 6.7 percent lay-off rate during the difficult recession years of 1989–93.

A positive sign in the clothing and shoe wholesale industry is that the knowledge base is rising; it increased 4.2 percent over the last five years.

OVERALL SCORE

N/A

HOW THE INDUSTRY COMPARES:

Job Security: High
Advancement: Good
Average Salary: N/A
Salary Change: N/A
Knowledge Base: Low
Industry Knowledge: Rising
Industry Stability: Very Low

WHERE THE JOBS ARE:

TOTAL EMPLOYMENT	10,812
British Columbia	1,094
Alberta	571
Saskatchewan	n/a
Manitoba	n/a
Ontario	3,807
Quebec	4,923
New Brunswick	n/a
Nova Scotia	n/a
Prince Edward Island	n/a
Newfoundland	n/a
Northwest Territories	n/a
Yukon Territory	n/a

VITAL STATISTICS

Average Lay-off Rate, 1989–93: 6.7%
Net Job Creation, 1989–93: −837
Average Salary Level, 1993: N/A
Salary Increase, 1993: N/A
Knowledge Workers per 100 Employees: 14
Knowledge Base Change: +4.2%
Industry Volatility: 27.0 (empl.)
SIC Code: 531

ELECTRIC WIRE & CABLE MANUFACTURING

The fiber optic and electric wire and cable industry includes telephone wire as well as electric power cables. This high-wage industry is in transition because competitive pressures have raised the appeal of low-wage jurisdictions.

Job security has been abysmal, with an industry lay-off rate of 86.9 percent—unheard of in any economy, old or new. Needless to say, advancement prospects in the industry for the few employees that remain are poor.

Average salaries are very high and salary increases in 1993 were surprisingly high—5.5 percent on average.

OVERALL
SCORE

N/A

HOW THE INDUSTRY COMPARES:

Job Security: Very Low
Advancement: Poor
Average Salary: Very High
Salary Change: Very High
Knowledge Base: N/A
Industry Knowledge: N/A
Industry Stability: Low

VITAL STATISTICS

Average Lay-off Rate, 1989–93: 86.9%
Net Job Creation, 1989–93: −4,869
Average Salary Level, 1993: $754/week
Salary Increase, 1993: +5.5%
Knowledge Workers per 100 Employees: N/A
Knowledge Base Change: N/A
Industry Volatility: 10.3
SIC Code: 338

WHERE THE JOBS ARE:	
TOTAL EMPLOYMENT	5,158
British Columbia	n/a
Alberta	n/a
Saskatchewan	n/a
Manitoba	n/a
Ontario	3,451
Quebec	834
New Brunswick	n/a
Nova Scotia	n/a
Prince Edward Island	n/a
Newfoundland	n/a
Northwest Territories	n/a
Yukon Territory	n/a

This industry includes manufacturers of basic industrial inorganic chemicals (such as acids, alkalies, compressed gases and radioactive chemical elements) and industrial organic chemicals (such as alcohols, glycols, unsaturated monomers and petroleum additives). An important attraction of this industry is that employees have the opportunity to work in a high-knowledge environment where the knowledge base is rising sharply.

OVERALL
SCORE

N/A

Job security is very high, as the zero lay-off rate over the 1989–93 period indicates, and advancement prospects are very good. The industry continued to hire new employees right through the recession years of 1989–93.

Almost half of the job openings in this industry are located in Ontario.

HOW THE INDUSTRY COMPARES:

Job Security: Very High
Advancement: Very Good
Average Salary: N/A
Salary Change: N/A
Knowledge Base: High
Industry Knowledge: Rising Sharply
Industry Stability: Low

VITAL STATISTICS

Average Lay-off Rate, 1989–93: Zero
Net Job Creation, 1989–93: +1,793
Average Salary Level, 1993: N/A
Salary Increase, 1993: N/A
Knowledge Workers per 100 Employees: 40
Knowledge Base Change: +7.9%
Industry Volatility: 9.4 (empl.)
SIC Code: 371

WHERE THE JOBS ARE:

TOTAL EMPLOYMENT	15,768
British Columbia	741
Alberta	3,236
Saskatchewan	207
Manitoba	235
Ontario	7,906
Quebec	3,233
New Brunswick	n/a
Nova Scotia	n/a
Prince Edward Island	n/a
Newfoundland	n/a
Northwest Territories	n/a
Yukon Territory	n/a

MOVIE THEATERS

The entertainment industry is an integral part of the communications and telecommunications engine that is driving growth in the New Economy. But movie theaters will continue to be challenged by the New Economy's sweeping pace of technological advance, as movies on demand make their way into the households of the future. This convergence of technologies will increasingly blur the lines that once distinguished industries from each other, and companies with the greatest access to knowledge and capital will have a head start on everyone else.

OVERALL
SCORE

N/A

Movie theaters will have to find a more solid niche for themselves, and provide viewers with a reason to leave the comfort of their VCRs and satellite dishes.

As expected, job security is only moderate, but layoffs have not reached high enough levels to jeopardize advancement.

The obvious negative in this low-knowledge industry is that average salaries and raises are very poor.

HOW THE INDUSTRY COMPARES:

Job Security: Moderate
Advancement: Good
Average Salary: Very Low
Salary Change: Very Poor
Knowledge Base: Low
Industry Knowledge: N/A
Industry Stability: Low

VITAL STATISTICS

Average Lay-off Rate, 1989–93: 14.6%
Net Job Creation, 1989–93: −1,386
Average Salary Level, 1993: $249/week
Salary Increase, 1993: −4.2%
Knowledge Workers per 100 Employees: 19
Knowledge Base Change: N/A
Industry Volatility: 10.3 (empl.)
SIC Code: 962

WHERE THE JOBS ARE:	
TOTAL EMPLOYMENT	8,882
British Columbia	1,257
Alberta	1,224
Saskatchewan	n/a
Manitoba	n/a
Ontario	3,753
Quebec	1,691
New Brunswick	123
Nova Scotia	n/a
Prince Edward Island	n/a
Newfoundland	n/a
Northwest Territories	n/a
Yukon Territory	n/a

STEEL PIPE & TUBE MANUFACTURING

The steel pipe and tube industry has caught the next wave of growth in Canada's New Economy, thanks to the bright future for natural gas as the fuel of choice. And, as the demand for pipelines to transport gas to market increases, the steel pipe and tube industry is well positioned as a supplier.

The industry offers job seekers high average salaries and high wage increases, as well as superior job security and good advancement prospects.

Above-average job prospects exist in production, supervising, management and marketing, as well as in support staff roles.

OVERALL
SCORE

N/A

HOW THE INDUSTRY COMPARES:

Job Security: High
Advancement: Good
Average Salary: High
Salary Change: High
Knowledge Base: N/A
Industry Knowledge: N/A
Industry Stability: Very Low

VITAL STATISTICS

Average Lay-off Rate, 1989–93: 4.5%
Net Job Creation, 1989–93: –254
Average Salary Level, 1993: $742/week
Salary Increase, 1993: +4.2%
Knowledge Workers per 100 Employees: N/A
Knowledge Base Change: N/A
Industry Volatility: 22.7
SIC Code: 292

WHERE THE JOBS ARE:

TOTAL EMPLOYMENT	5,663
British Columbia	n/a
Alberta	1,293
Saskatchewan	n/a
Manitoba	n/a
Ontario	3,070
Quebec	n/a
New Brunswick	n/a
Nova Scotia	n/a
Prince Edward Island	n/a
Newfoundland	n/a
Northwest Territories	n/a
Yukon Territory	n/a

TURNAROUND INDUSTRIES

Although the following industries have peaked structurally, they have now started to turn around and display many of the characteristics of industries that are underpinned by long-term structural growth. Their future could be far better than their past, and they warrant close attention.

RUBBER PRODUCTS & TIRE MANUFACTURING

⭐ ⭐ ⭐ ⭐

The rubber products industry has caught the next wave of growth after being in long-term structural decline for over ten years. New products and technologies have helped to revitalize this industry and to transform old into new.

Job security is high and advancement is good—this is a business with a future in the New Economy.

Average salary levels are moderate, but average salary increases of 4.7 percent are enviable.

The low knowledge base of the industry is rapidly giving way as companies employ more technology and process control equipment. Consequently, the Knowledge Ratio is rising very sharply: 14.9 percent in the last five years.

OVERALL SCORE

60

HOW THE INDUSTRY COMPARES:

Job Security: High
Advancement: Good
Average Salary: Moderate
Salary Change: High
Knowledge Base: Low
Industry Knowledge: Rising Very Sharply
Industry Stability: Low

VITAL STATISTICS

Average Lay-off Rate, 1989–93: 7.6%
Net Job Creation, 1989–93: −1,466
Average Salary Level, 1993: $632/week
Salary Increase, 1993: +4.7%
Knowledge Workers per 100 Employees: 17
Knowledge Base Change: +14.9%
Industry Volatility: 9.5
SIC Code: 150

WHERE THE JOBS ARE:

TOTAL EMPLOYMENT	19,330
British Columbia	n/a
Alberta	n/a
Saskatchewan	n/a
Manitoba	157
Ontario	8,865
Quebec	n/a
New Brunswick	n/a
Nova Scotia	n/a
Prince Edward Island	n/a
Newfoundland	n/a
Northwest Territories	n/a
Yukon Territory	n/a

COSMETICS, PERFUMES & PERSONAL CARE PRODUCTS MANUFACTURING

★

The baby boom generation has had a major impact on this industry, as it has on many others. As the population ages, matures and wrinkles, the demand for cosmetics and personal care products has gotten a new lease on life. While job security is very low and lay-off rates of 42.0 percent prevailed between 1989 and 1993, prospects for long-term growth have improved.

Average salaries in the industry are low, however, and salary changes remain very poor.

The knowledge base of the industry is moderate, but it is encouraging to see a 5.3 percent increase in the Knowledge Ratio in the last five years.

OVERALL SCORE

27.5

HOW THE INDUSTRY COMPARES:

Job Security: Very Low
Advancement: Moderate
Average Salary: Low
Salary Change: Very Poor
Knowledge Base: Moderate
Industry Knowledge: Rising
Industry Stability: Very Low

VITAL STATISTICS

Average Lay-off Rate, 1989–93: 42.0%
Net Job Creation, 1989–93: −2,533
Average Salary Level, 1993: $568/week
Salary Increase, 1993: −5.0%
Knowledge Workers per 100 Employees: 32
Knowledge Base Change: +5.3%
Industry Volatility: 14.2
SIC Code: 377

WHERE THE JOBS ARE:

TOTAL EMPLOYMENT	6,124
British Columbia	110
Alberta	n/a
Saskatchewan	n/a
Manitoba	n/a
Ontario	3,461
Quebec	2,548
New Brunswick	n/a
Nova Scotia	n/a
Prince Edward Island	n/a
Newfoundland	n/a
Northwest Territories	n/a
Yukon Territory	n/a

STAMPED, PRESSED & COATED METAL MANUFACTURING

The market's move to galvanized steel, especially in the auto manufacturing industry, has created a whole new lease on life for this broad industry, which also manufactures a wide assortment of other metal products from beer cans to cooking utensils to license plates. The turnaround from decline back to long-term growth has yet to produce much in the way of job stability—in the final round of downsizing 57.9 percent of the people employed lost their jobs. Job security and job advancement, therefore, are presently very low. However, the much improved fortunes of the industry, in structural terms, should translate into a better future for people employed in the industry.

Salary levels in this low-knowledge business are moderate, and average salaries fell 4.8 percent in 1993. It is worth noting that the knowledge base is declining sharply and should be monitored quite carefully, since a decreasing Knowledge Ratio could throw this industry's future off course.

OVERALL SCORE

20

HOW THE INDUSTRY COMPARES:

Job Security: Very Low
Advancement: Very Poor
Average Salary: Moderate
Salary Change: Very Poor
Knowledge Base: Low
Industry Knowledge: Declining
Industry Stability: Low

VITAL STATISTICS

Average Lay-off Rate, 1989–93: 57.9%
Net Job Creation, 1989–93: −16,713
Average Salary Level, 1993: $576/week
Salary Increase, 1993: −4.8%
Knowledge Workers per 100 Employees: 15
Knowledge Base Change: −14.1%
Industry Volatility: 9.6
SIC Code: 304

WHERE THE JOBS ARE:	
TOTAL EMPLOYMENT	29,000
British Columbia	2,081
Alberta	2,120
Saskatchewan	255
Manitoba	941
Ontario	18,855
Quebec	4,406
New Brunswick	149
Nova Scotia	106
Prince Edward Island	n/a
Newfoundland	n/a
Northwest Territories	n/a
Yukon Territory	n/a

WATCH LIST INDUSTRIES

The following industries have not peaked structurally. However, they have either clearly peaked in the United States or are displaying many of the characteristics of industries that are about to peak, and they could go either way.

FEDERAL GOVERNMENT

Job security for federal employees used to be very high as shown by the zero lay-off rate at this level of government. Indeed, the federal government even hired an additional 6,235 net new employees over the 1989–93 period.

OVERALL
SCORE

Average salaries are very high and salary increases have been moderate, with average raises of 1.1 percent in 1993.

The knowledge base is high and rising, and for the most part the federal government provides stable and well-paying jobs in many different occupations or at the very least, it used to.

85

Of particular concern to both civil servants and job seekers is the serious crisis in federal finances, and the government's inability to sustain past levels of spending. With downsizing under way, the federal government is on the Watch List.

HOW THE INDUSTRY COMPARES:

Job Security: Very High
Advancement: Very Good
Average Salary: Very High
Salary Change: Moderate
Knowledge Base: High
Industry Knowledge: Rising
Industry Stability: Very High

WHERE THE JOBS ARE:

TOTAL EMPLOYMENT	260,910
British Columbia	27,552
Alberta	17,124
Saskatchewan	n/a
Manitoba	11,344
Ontario	110,065
Quebec	51,301
New Brunswick	8,589
Nova Scotia	n/a
Prince Edward Island	2,848
Newfoundland	6,960
Northwest Territories	1,470
Yukon Territory	808

VITAL STATISTICS

Average Lay-off Rate, 1989–93: Zero
Net Job Creation, 1989–93: +6,235
Average Salary Level, 1993: $828/week
Salary Increase, 1993: +1.1%
Knowledge Workers per 100 Employees: 42
Knowledge Base Change: +5.7%
Industry Volatility: 1.7 (empl.)
SIC Code: 810

MUNICIPAL & LOCAL GOVERNMENTS

Municipal and local governments in Canada employ over 200,000 Canadians, and are a big business by any yardstick. Communities that are leveraged to the New Economy and derive increasing percentages of their tax revenues from growing industries will fare better than those that are tied to industries in decline. With federal and provincial funding pressures rising, many communities will be caught short financially in the years ahead. Downsizing and mergers between municipalities, to cut back on duplication of services, will be the likely result.

Meanwhile, as the storm clouds gather, municipal and local governments have enjoyed excellent job security and a zero lay-off rate through the tough recession years of 1989–93. Advancement prospects—for the moment—remain very good.

High average salaries and very high average wage increases of 5.4 percent in 1993 make this high-knowledge sector attractive to people who also enjoy an environment where the knowledge base is rising. Municipal and local governments offer a broad range of opportunities in administration, finance, parks, recreation, support services and maintenance.

VITAL STATISTICS

Average Lay-off Rate, 1989–93: Zero
Net Job Creation, 1989–93: +13,877
Average Salary Level, 1993: $681/week
Salary Increase, 1993: +5.4%
Knowledge Workers per 100 Employees: 42
Knowledge Base Change: +5.7%
Industry Volatility: 1.7 (empl.)
SIC Code: 830

OVERALL SCORE

85

HOW THE INDUSTRY COMPARES:

Job Security: Very High
Advancement: Very Good
Average Salary: High
Salary Change: Very High
Knowledge Base: High
Industry Knowledge: Rising
Industry Stability: Very High

WHERE THE JOBS ARE:

TOTAL EMPLOYMENT	204,158
British Columbia	20,217
Alberta	21,075
Saskatchewan	n/a
Manitoba	6,254
Ontario	81,634
Quebec	53,923
New Brunswick	3,758
Nova Scotia	n/a
Prince Edward Island	351
Newfoundland	2,515
Northwest Territories	1,524
Yukon Territory	291

INSURANCE COMPANIES

Insurance companies offer a very high level of job security and very good prospects for advancement in a moderately knowledge-intensive industry.

OVERALL SCORE

75

The fact that banks and other financial institutions are moving into the traditional business of insurance poses a clear threat now and in the future. But the real challenge will be for insurance providers to adapt and meet the needs of this New Economy, where physical property is being replaced by intellectual property, and where knowledge workers demand different life and health insurance benefits.

Advancement prospects are very good in this industry, despite the challenges ahead. Between 1989 and 1993 11,998 new employees joined the ranks, filling a very wide range of professions and occupations from office services to building maintenance to actuaries to sales personnel. A high average salary was topped off with a high wage increase of 4.2 percent in 1993, making insurance a very attractive Watch List industry.

HOW THE INDUSTRY COMPARES:

Job Security: Very High
Advancement: Very Good
Average Salary: High
Salary Change: High
Knowledge Base: Moderate
Industry Knowledge: Rising
Industry Stability: High

VITAL STATISTICS

Average Lay-off Rate, 1989–93: Zero
Net Job Creation, 1989–93: +11,998
Average Salary Level, 1993: $712/week
Salary Increase, 1993: +4.2%
Knowledge Workers per 100 Employees: 22
Knowledge Base Change: +4.3%
Industry Volatility: 5.1
SIC Code: 730

WHERE THE JOBS ARE:

TOTAL EMPLOYMENT	102,057
British Columbia	10,086
Alberta	5,394
Saskatchewan	3,791
Manitoba	6,444
Ontario	49,143
Quebec	22,440
New Brunswick	1,192
Nova Scotia	2,611
Prince Edward Island	126
Newfoundland	788
Northwest Territories	n/a
Yukon Territory	n/a

PROVINCIAL GOVERNMENTS

★ ★ ★ ★ ★

Provincial government employees have enjoyed a very high degree of job security, but hiring freezes and layoffs in some provinces have become standard as many governments take steps to solve their financial problems and reduce or eliminate their deficits.

Average salaries are high, but salary changes have been very poor: the average salary declined by 8.7 percent in 1993.

The knowledge base is already high and rising in a sector that has provided excellent advancement opportunities.

OVERALL
SCORE

75

HOW THE INDUSTRY COMPARES:

Job Security: Very High
Advancement: Very Good
Average Salary: High
Salary Change: Very Poor
Knowledge Base: High
Industry Knowledge: Rising
Industry Stability: Very High

VITAL STATISTICS

Average Lay-off Rate, 1989–93: Zero
Net Job Creation, 1989–93: +977
Average Salary Level, 1993: $656/week
Salary Increase, 1993: –8.7%
Knowledge Workers per 100 Employees: 42
Knowledge Base Change: +5.7%
Industry Volatility: 1.7 (empl.)
SIC Code: 820

WHERE THE JOBS ARE:

TOTAL EMPLOYMENT	230,813
British Columbia	27,797
Alberta	30,132
Saskatchewan	n/a
Manitoba	10,067
Ontario	61,503
Quebec	62,915
New Brunswick	8,758
Nova Scotia	n/a
Prince Edward Island	2,119
Newfoundland	7,014
Northwest Territories	2,271
Yukon Territory	1,764

BANKS

The business of banking has evolved through the ages, and it continues to evolve as the New Economy raises new challenges for bankers, many of whom have little understanding of high-knowledge industries and how to lend to them. Fee-based services and a move into mutual funds, stock brokerage companies and insurance have been the major developments to date. But, sooner or later, banks will be required to lend to the New Economy.

OVERALL
SCORE

72.5

Job security in the banking business is very high and, on average, the industry has experienced a zero lay-off rate, despite redundancies in some specific departments. On a net basis, banks created 10,378 new jobs in Canada over the period 1989–93.

Average salaries are moderate and salary changes are equally moderate, although the recent surge in profits may pressure banks to open the purse strings a little more.

The knowledge base of this very stable industry is moderate, but rising sharply.

HOW THE INDUSTRY COMPARES:

Job Security: Very High
Advancement: Very Good
Average Salary: Moderate
Salary Change: Moderate
Knowledge Base: Moderate
Industry Knowledge: Rising Sharply
Industry Stability: Very High

VITAL STATISTICS

Average Lay-off Rate, 1989–93: Zero
Net Job Creation, 1989–93: +10,378
Average Salary Level, 1993: $589/week
Salary Increase, 1993: +1.3%
Knowledge Workers per 100 Employees: 39
Knowledge Base Change: +8.1%
Industry Volatility: 3.3 (empl.)
SIC Code: 700

WHERE THE JOBS ARE:

TOTAL EMPLOYMENT	194,646
British Columbia	22,370
Alberta	18,293
Saskatchewan	5,169
Manitoba	6,596
Ontario	93,044
Quebec	37,242
New Brunswick	n/a
Nova Scotia	5,728
Prince Edward Island	n/a
Newfoundland	2,009
Northwest Territories	n/a
Yukon Territory	165

MOTOR VEHICLE MANUFACTURING

★ ★ ★ ★

Manufacturers of cars, and chassis for trucks and buses, have provided their employees with a high level of job security, thanks both to Canada's favorable trade agreement with the United States and to the drive by Canadian manufacturers to become competitive and innovative. Between 1989 and 1993 only 0.3 percent of the people employed in the industry lost their jobs.

Advancement prospects are good, and average salary levels are very high. Average salary increases have been exceptional as well, with an increase of 8.9 percent in 1993.

The knowledge base is low, but has risen a sharp 22.6 percent in the last five years as more and more technology has made its way onto the shop floor. Most of the industry's jobs are centered in Ontario.

OVERALL SCORE

67.5

HOW THE INDUSTRY COMPARES:

Job Security: High
Advancement: Good
Average Salary: Very High
Salary Change: Very High
Knowledge Base: Low
Industry Knowledge: Rising Very Sharply
Industry Stability: Very Low

VITAL STATISTICS

Average Lay-off Rate, 1989–93: 0.3%
Net Job Creation, 1989–93: –154
Average Salary Level, 1993: $867/week
Salary Increase, 1993: +8.9%
Knowledge Workers per 100 Employees: 19
Knowledge Base Change: +22.6%
Industry Volatility: 14.9
SIC Code: 323

WHERE THE JOBS ARE:

TOTAL EMPLOYMENT	44,985
British Columbia	n/a
Alberta	n/a
Saskatchewan	n/a
Manitoba	n/a
Ontario	37,612
Quebec	5,340
New Brunswick	n/a
Nova Scotia	n/a
Prince Edward Island	n/a
Newfoundland	n/a
Northwest Territories	n/a
Yukon Territory	n/a

CAR DEALERSHIPS

★ ★ ★

Car dealerships employ 94,545 Canadians, and job security is very high. This industry enjoyed a zero lay-off rate through the tough recession years; indeed, it added 2,996 new employees net to the business between 1989 and 1993.

Advancement is also very good. However, average salaries are low and the wage increases have tended to be moderate only.

The knowledge base is rising in this industry where 8 out of every 100 employees are knowledge workers.

The major drawback is the high volatility of car dealerships, as they ride the ups and downs of the business cycle.

OVERALL
SCORE

52.5

HOW THE INDUSTRY COMPARES:

Job Security: Very High
Advancement: Very Good
Average Salary: Low
Salary Change: Moderate
Knowledge Base: Low
Industry Knowledge: Rising
Industry Stability: Low

VITAL STATISTICS

Average Lay-off Rate, 1989–93: Zero
Net Job Creation, 1989–93: +2,996
Average Salary Level, 1993: $537/week
Salary Increase, 1993: +0.5%
Knowledge Workers per 100 Employees: 8
Knowledge Base Change: +4.2%
Industry Volatility: 9.3 (empl.)
SIC Code: 631

WHERE THE JOBS ARE:

TOTAL EMPLOYMENT	94,545
British Columbia	11,083
Alberta	9,653
Saskatchewan	4,268
Manitoba	3,400
Ontario	31,900
Quebec	25,876
New Brunswick	2,740
Nova Scotia	3,130
Prince Edward Island	541
Newfoundland	1,803
Northwest Territories	n/a
Yukon Territory	n/a

RAILROADS

★ ★ ★

The railway industry has been a significant beneficiary of government support and subsidies, either directly or indirectly, to rail users in Canada. With current and future government spending seriously constrained, the industry will be forced to restructure and introduce new technologies and work processes in order to remain viable over the longer term.

OVERALL SCORE

52.5

The knowledge base is low, but it is encouraging to see that the Knowledge Ratio of railway transportation has increased 9.3 percent in the last five years.

Major layoffs—in the order of 22.4 percent for the industry as a whole—have already taken place, and advancement prospects are very poor at present. But the average salary level is very high, and salary increases have been significant: raises of 5.1 percent were the norm in 1993.

HOW THE INDUSTRY COMPARES:

Job Security: Low
Advancement: Very Poor
Average Salary: Very High
Salary Change: High
Knowledge Base: Low
Industry Knowledge: Rising Sharply
Industry Stability: High

VITAL STATISTICS

Average Lay-off Rate, 1989–93: 22.4%
Net Job Creation, 1989–93: −13,385
Average Salary Level, 1993: $893/week
Salary Increase, 1993: +5.1%
Knowledge Workers per 100 Employees: 15
Knowledge Base Change: +9.3%
Industry Volatility: 6.1
SIC Code: 453

WHERE THE JOBS ARE:

TOTAL EMPLOYMENT	57,312
British Columbia	7,994
Alberta	6,786
Saskatchewan	2,473
Manitoba	7,136
Ontario	15,475
Quebec	14,476
New Brunswick	2,108
Nova Scotia	849
Prince Edward Island	n/a
Newfoundland	n/a
Northwest Territories	n/a
Yukon Territory	n/a

CREDIT UNIONS

★ ★ ★

Credit unions, which experienced a zero lay-off rate between 1989 and 1993, offer excellent job security to current and prospective employees. New workers have been hired at a fairly rapid rate (3,450 during the recession years of 1989–93), providing very good advancement opportunities for those already employed and those entering the industry.

Average salaries, however, are low, and salary changes are poor: the average wage cut in 1993 was 1.2 percent.

Of great concern is the fact that the moderate knowledge base is declining. This trend threatens the competitive position of credit unions in a world where technology provides insititutions, large and small, with the all-important edge.

OVERALL
SCORE

50

HOW THE INDUSTRY COMPARES:

Job Security: Very High
Advancement: Very Good
Average Salary: Low
Salary Change: Poor
Knowledge Base: Moderate
Industry Knowledge: Declining
Industry Stability: Low

VITAL STATISTICS

Average Lay-off Rate, 1989–93: Zero
Net Job Creation, 1989–93: +3,450
Average Salary Level, 1993: $489/week
Salary Increase, 1993: −1.2%
Knowledge Workers per 100 Employees: 37
Knowledge Base Change: −4.0%
Industry Volatility: 10.1 (empl.)
SIC Code: 705

WHERE THE JOBS ARE:

TOTAL EMPLOYMENT	56,596
British Columbia	9,331
Alberta	n/a
Saskatchewan	n/a
Manitoba	2,573
Ontario	4,970
Quebec	32,727
New Brunswick	n/a
Nova Scotia	n/a
Prince Edward Island	140
Newfoundland	n/a
Northwest Territories	n/a
Yukon Territory	n/a

AUTO PARTS & ACCESSORIES STORES

★ ★

Auto parts and accessories retailers enjoyed a zero lay-off rate through the recession years of 1989–93, as consumers were drawn to less costly repair solutions for their aging cars. In fact, 1,198 new people were hired in the industry over that period. Job security is very high and advancement prospects are very good.

The main drawback in this business is the very low average salary level and very poor salary increases. Employees were more likely to receive a 2.7 percent wage cut than a raise in 1993.

The knowledge base of the industry is low, but rising very sharply, a promising trend for future salary levels in these stores.

OVERALL
SCORE

45

HOW THE INDUSTRY COMPARES:

Job Security: Very High
Advancement: Very Good
Average Salary: Very Low
Salary Change: Very Poor
Knowledge Base: Low
Industry Knowledge: Rising Very Sharply
Industry Stability: Very Low

VITAL STATISTICS

Average Lay-off Rate, 1989–93: Zero
Net Job Creation, 1989–93: +1,198
Average Salary Level, 1993: $339/week
Salary Increase, 1993: −2.7%
Knowledge Workers per 100 Employees: 5
Knowledge Base Change: +66.2%
Industry Volatility: 12.2 (empl.)
SIC Code: 634

WHERE THE JOBS ARE:

TOTAL EMPLOYMENT	44,404
British Columbia	3,816
Alberta	4,493
Saskatchewan	1,158
Manitoba	1,142
Ontario	22,642
Quebec	7,495
New Brunswick	1,081
Nova Scotia	1,232
Prince Edward Island	288
Newfoundland	969
Northwest Territories	n/a
Yukon Territory	n/a

AIRLINES

Airlines (both scheduled and charters), air cargo and freight-chartering face long-term uncertainties because of the ever-changing regulation of their industry. The airline business is on the Watch List, and could go either way. Stability is understandably low. Between 1989 and 1993, when lay-off rates rose to 15.4 percent, over 7,700 people left the industry. Job security is moderate at best and advancement is poor.

While average salaries are high, the average level dropped 4.9 percent in 1993 alone.

The knowledge base of airlines is moderate and stable—a cause for concern as we move increasingly into a higher-knowledge economy.

OVERALL SCORE

42.5

HOW THE INDUSTRY COMPARES:

Job Security: Moderate
Advancement: Poor
Average Salary: High
Salary Change: Very Poor
Knowledge Base: Moderate
Industry Knowledge: Reasonably Stable
Industry Stability: Low

VITAL STATISTICS

Average Lay-off Rate, 1989–93: 15.4%
Net Job Creation, 1989–93: −7,796
Average Salary Level, 1993: $729/week
Salary Increase, 1993: −4.9%
Knowledge Workers per 100 Employees: 23
Knowledge Base Change: +0.6%
Industry Volatility: 9.3
SIC Code: 451

WHERE THE JOBS ARE:

TOTAL EMPLOYMENT	48,284
British Columbia	11,639
Alberta	4,654
Saskatchewan	n/a
Manitoba	2,695
Ontario	14,682
Quebec	10,929
New Brunswick	203
Nova Scotia	1,753
Prince Edward Island	n/a
Newfoundland	532
Northwest Territories	n/a
Yukon Territory	n/a

AUTO PARTS MANUFACTURING

★ ★

The auto parts industry continues to undergo sweeping structural changes brought on by technological innovations, quality improvements and new product mandates. But job security in this Watch List industry is low, and the lay-off rate was high at 19.1 percent between 1989 and 1993, when 14,456 people lost their jobs. Understandably, job advancement is very poor.

However, average salaries are high and an increase of 4.1 percent in the average industry salary is exceedingly attractive.

The knowledge base in auto parts manufacturing is low: only 19 out of every 100 people employed in the field are knowledge workers. But it is important to note that the Knowledge Ratio is rising very sharply as manufacturers embrace new technologies and adapt to change.

OVERALL SCORE

42.5

HOW THE INDUSTRY COMPARES:

Job Security: Low
Advancement: Very Poor
Average Salary: High
Salary Change: High
Knowledge Base: Low
Industry Knowledge: Rising Very Sharply
Industry Stability: Very Low

VITAL STATISTICS

Average Lay-off Rate, 1989–93: 19.1%
Net Job Creation, 1989–93: −14,456
Average Salary Level, 1993: $663/week
Salary Increase, 1993: +4.1%
Knowledge Workers per 100 Employees: 19
Knowledge Base Change: +22.6%
Industry Volatility: 12.0
SIC Code: 325

WHERE THE JOBS ARE:

TOTAL EMPLOYMENT	75,366
British Columbia	774
Alberta	n/a
Saskatchewan	n/a
Manitoba	539
Ontario	69,909
Quebec	3,087
New Brunswick	n/a
Nova Scotia	n/a
Prince Edward Island	n/a
Newfoundland	n/a
Northwest Territories	n/a
Yukon Territory	n/a

INSURANCE & REAL ESTATE AGENCIES

★ ★

Both insurance and real estate agencies are on the Watch List and could go either way. Consequently, insurance agencies and real estate agencies face a rising degree of uncertainty as the industries that underpin them may undergo major structural changes in the years ahead.

Job security is moderate as shown by the 18.5 percent lay-off rate between 1989 and 1993. During that period, 18,502 people lost their jobs, and therefore advancement prospects in these flatter and leaner organizations are very poor at present.

Average salaries are moderate, but the statistics mask the fact that many people in the industry are paid on commission. Salary increases are very poor; the business suffered a 3.6 percent average decline in salaries in 1993.

The knowledge base in this moderately knowledge-intensive industry is rising as agents keep up with the challenge of a higher-knowledge-intensive customer base.

OVERALL SCORE

40

HOW THE INDUSTRY COMPARES:

Job Security: Moderate
Advancement: Very Poor
Average Salary: Moderate
Salary Change: Very Poor
Knowledge Base: Moderate
Industry Knowledge: Rising
Industry Stability: Moderate

VITAL STATISTICS

Average Lay-off Rate, 1989–93: 18.5%
Net Job Creation, 1989–93: −18,502
Average Salary Level, 1993: $607/week
Salary Increase, 1993: −3.6%
Knowledge Workers per 100 Employees: 30
Knowledge Base Change: +6.6%
Industry Volatility: 7.4 (empl.)
SIC Code: 761

WHERE THE JOBS ARE:

TOTAL EMPLOYMENT	89,477
British Columbia	15,969
Alberta	7,173
Saskatchewan	2,482
Manitoba	2,498
Ontario	36,949
Quebec	18,891
New Brunswick	1,908
Nova Scotia	2,366
Prince Edward Island	304
Newfoundland	778
Northwest Territories	n/a
Yukon Territory	n/a

REAL ESTATE OPERATORS

★

This industry includes landlords of almost every description, from apartment building owners to shopping center and stadium operators. The performance of these businesses is tied to the fortune of the communities where they are found: communities that are leveraged to the New Economy have fared better than those tied to high lay-off rate industries in the old economy, where property values and the tax base have been particularly hard hit.

OVERALL
SCORE

37.5

But average lay-off rates for real estate operators are reasonably low at 8.5 percent, and consequently, job security is high compared to most other industries. Advancement prospects are poor, however, because this Watch List industry could go either way.

Average salary levels in this moderate-knowledge business are very low, but have increased at a reasonable rate.

HOW THE INDUSTRY COMPARES:

Job Security: High
Advancement: Poor
Average Salary: Very Low
Salary Change: Moderate
Knowledge Base: Moderate
Industry Knowledge: Rising
Industry Stability: Moderate

WHERE THE JOBS ARE:

TOTAL EMPLOYMENT	88,245
British Columbia	12,134
Alberta	8,372
Saskatchewan	3,249
Manitoba	2,299
Ontario	33,042
Quebec	24,014
New Brunswick	1,141
Nova Scotia	2,190
Prince Edward Island	313
Newfoundland	727
Northwest Territories	680
Yukon Territory	n/a

VITAL STATISTICS

Average Lay-off Rate, 1989–93: 8.5%
Net Job Creation, 1989–93: −7,323
Average Salary Level, 1993: $439/week
Salary Increase, 1993: +0.6%
Knowledge Workers per 100 Employees: 30
Knowledge Base Change: +6.6%
Industry Volatility: 8.7 (empl.)
SIC Code: 750

MOTOR VEHICLE & PARTS WHOLESALERS

Wholesalers of cars, trucks, buses and parts continue to undergo major restructuring brought on by profit-margin pressures in the industry. While the auto industry has not peaked structurally, it could go either way, and accordingly places wholesalers at risk.

The lay-off rate in the wholesale end of the business rose to 12.7 percent between 1989 and 1993; not surprisingly, job security is moderate at best. The high level of job loss (7,320 employees were "de-hired" between 1989 and 1993) means that advancement prospects are poor—fewer managers, supervisors and people on work teams leave few opportunities for promotion.

Average salaries in the industry are low, and salary changes are poor, with the average wage 2.4 percent lower in 1993 than in the previous year.

While the knowledge base is low, it is rising sharply, which is a very positive development in the industry for the longer term.

OVERALL SCORE

35

HOW THE INDUSTRY COMPARES:

Job Security: Moderate
Advancement: Poor
Average Salary: Low
Salary Change: Poor
Knowledge Base: Low
Industry Knowledge: Rising Sharply
Industry Stability: Moderate

VITAL STATISTICS

Average Lay-off Rate, 1989–93: 12.7%
Net Job Creation, 1989–93: −7,320
Average Salary Level, 1993: $573/week
Salary Increase, 1993: −2.4%
Knowledge Workers per 100 Employees: 13
Knowledge Base Change: +13.5%
Industry Volatility: 8.5 (empl.)
SIC Code: 55

WHERE THE JOBS ARE:

TOTAL EMPLOYMENT	57,848
British Columbia	7,013
Alberta	7,153
Saskatchewan	3,102
Manitoba	2,537
Ontario	22,108
Quebec	12,875
New Brunswick	1,242
Nova Scotia	1,151
Prince Edward Island	n/a
Newfoundland	n/a
Northwest Territories	n/a
Yukon Territory	n/a

MOTOR VEHICLE REPAIR SHOPS

★

Repair garages, paint and body shops, muffler and auto glass replacement shops and transmission repair shops laid off 13.6 percent of their employees between 1989 and 1993. Compared to other industries, they provide moderate job security with very poor advancement prospects.

The average salary level is low, but salary increases averaged an attractive 5.6 percent in 1993.

The knowledge base is low, with the industry employing an average of 13 knowledge workers per 100 employees. However, the Knowledge Ratio is rising, and in the last five years has climbed 4.9 percent.

OVERALL SCORE

35

HOW THE INDUSTRY COMPARES:

Job Security: Moderate
Advancement: Very Poor
Average Salary: Low
Salary Change: Very High
Knowledge Base: Low
Industry Knowledge: Rising
Industry Stability: Very Low

VITAL STATISTICS

Average Lay-off Rate, 1989–93: 13.6%
Net Job Creation, 1989–93: −8,850
Average Salary Level, 1993: $463/week
Salary Increase, 1993: +5.6%
Knowledge Workers per 100 Employees: 13
Knowledge Base Change: +4.9%
Industry Volatility: 13.0 (empl.)
SIC Code: 635

WHERE THE JOBS ARE:

TOTAL EMPLOYMENT	67,156
British Columbia	7,929
Alberta	7,233
Saskatchewan	2,242
Manitoba	1,779
Ontario	27,614
Quebec	16,904
New Brunswick	1,003
Nova Scotia	1,433
Prince Edward Island	279
Newfoundland	693
Northwest Territories	n/a
Yukon Territory	n/a

TRUST COMPANIES

★

Trust companies are losing their strong separate identity in the financial services industry as the barriers that separate banks from trust companies and insurance and stock brokerages come tumbling down. And unlike banks, which enjoyed an average lay-off rate of zero through the recession of 1989–93, trust companies laid off 15.0 percent of their employees over that period. Uncertainty continues over how the industry will eventually shake itself out, and which firms will come to dominate which markets.

OVERALL
SCORE

35

Job security and advancement prospects are moderate. Although salary levels are low, the average wage increased by 2.9 percent in 1993.

Of concern to the industry's longer term health is the fact that the moderate knowledge base is declining at a time when technological and market changes are increasing rapidly.

HOW THE INDUSTRY COMPARES:

Job Security: Moderate
Advancement: Moderate
Average Salary: Low
Salary Change: High
Knowledge Base: Moderate
Industry Knowledge: Declining
Industry Stability: Low

VITAL STATISTICS

Average Lay-off Rate, 1989–93: 15.0%
Net Job Creation, 1989–93: −4,161
Average Salary Level, 1993: $549/week
Salary Increase, 1993: +2.9%
Knowledge Workers per 100 Employees: 37
Knowledge Base Change: −4.0%
Industry Volatility: 10.1 (empl.)
SIC Code: 703

WHERE THE JOBS ARE:

TOTAL EMPLOYMENT	25,686
British Columbia	n/a
Alberta	1,699
Saskatchewan	n/a
Manitoba	438
Ontario	16,593
Quebec	3,860
New Brunswick	n/a
Nova Scotia	n/a
Prince Edward Island	n/a
Newfoundland	n/a
Northwest Territories	n/a
Yukon Territory	n/a

AIRPORT & AIRCRAFT SERVICING

Public funding pressures, which have already resulted in some airport closings, make this industry very vulnerable to structural decline, especially if the government decides to reduce its expenditures more aggressively.

Job security in the business of airport operations, aircraft servicing and leasing is already low, as shown by the 29.7 percent lay-off rate between 1989 and 1993. Advancement prospects are moderate at best.

Average salaries in the industry are low, and salary changes are very poor: witness the 7.9 percent decline in the average wage in 1993 alone.

Of growing concern is the moderate and stable knowledge base of the industry, despite the urgent need to modernize and introduce new technologies.

OVERALL SCORE

30

HOW THE INDUSTRY COMPARES:

Job Security: Low
Advancement: Moderate
Average Salary: Low
Salary Change: Very Poor
Knowledge Base: Moderate
Industry Knowledge: Reasonably Stable
Industry Stability: Low

VITAL STATISTICS

Average Lay-off Rate, 1989–93: 29.7%
Net Job Creation, 1989–93: −1,735
Average Salary Level, 1993: $561/week
Salary Increase, 1993: −7.9%
Knowledge Workers per 100 Employees: 23
Knowledge Base Change: +0.6%
Industry Volatility: 9.3
SIC Code: 452

WHERE THE JOBS ARE:

TOTAL EMPLOYMENT	5,713
British Columbia	771
Alberta	703
Saskatchewan	n/a
Manitoba	n/a
Ontario	1,886
Quebec	1,531
New Brunswick	n/a
Nova Scotia	183
Prince Edward Island	n/a
Newfoundland	n/a
Northwest Territories	n/a
Yukon Territory	n/a

GAS STATIONS

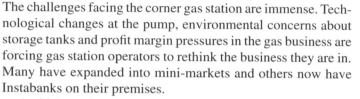

The challenges facing the corner gas station are immense. Technological changes at the pump, environmental concerns about storage tanks and profit margin pressures in the gas business are forcing gas station operators to rethink the business they are in. Many have expanded into mini-markets and others now have Instabanks on their premises.

Amid these changes, job security is low, lay-off rates are high at 27.1 percent between 1989 and 1993 and advancement prospects are very poor.

Very low average salaries and poor salary changes are the norm in this low-knowledge-intensive industry.

Fortunately, the knowledge base is rising very sharply: 3 out of every 100 employees in the industry are now knowledge workers.

OVERALL
SCORE

22.5

HOW THE INDUSTRY COMPARES:

Job Security: Low
Advancement: Very Poor
Average Salary: Very Low
Salary Change: Poor
Knowledge Base: Low
Industry Knowledge: Rising Very Sharply
Industry Stability: Very Low

VITAL STATISTICS

Average Lay-off Rate, 1989–93: 27.1%
Net Job Creation, 1989–93: −22,393
Average Salary Level, 1993: $263/week
Salary Increase, 1993: 0.2%
Knowledge Workers per 100 Employees: 3
Knowledge Base Change: +68.7%
Industry Volatility: 11.3 (empl.)
SIC Code: 633

WHERE THE JOBS ARE:

TOTAL EMPLOYMENT	71,911
British Columbia	10,114
Alberta	7,899
Saskatchewan	3,139
Manitoba	3,853
Ontario	22,710
Quebec	14,953
New Brunswick	2,619
Nova Scotia	4,105
Prince Edward Island	661
Newfoundland	1,587
Northwest Territories	n/a
Yukon Territory	215

HOMEBUILDERS

★

The residential construction industry is on the Watch List and could go either way. The aging population in Canada means that fewer new homes need to be built, but high levels of immigration into Canada have kept the demand for new houses rising, despite the poor demographics.

Meanwhile, technological changes are challenging homebuilders and are also creating opportunities for smart builders to meet new needs in energy efficiency and home design.

But job security is very low in this industry—lay-off rates topped 46.5 percent between 1989 and 1993. With 33,452 fewer people employed in 1993 than in 1989, it is little wonder that advancement prospects for those who remain are very poor.

Average wages in the homebuilding business are low, with the average salary level falling 3.6 percent in 1993.

The low knowledge base of the industry is declining—a cause for concern.

OVERALL SCORE

15

HOW THE INDUSTRY COMPARES:

Job Security: Very Low
Advancement: Very Poor
Average Salary: Low
Salary Change: Very Poor
Knowledge Base: Low
Industry Knowledge: Reasonably Stable
Industry Stability: Low

VITAL STATISTICS

Average Lay-off Rate, 1989–93: 46.5%
Net Job Creation, 1989–93: −33,452
Average Salary Level, 1993: $519/week
Salary Increase, 1993: −3.6%
Knowledge Workers per 100 Employees: 16
Knowledge Base Change: −1.5%
Industry Volatility: 10.5
SIC Code: 401

WHERE THE JOBS ARE:	
TOTAL EMPLOYMENT	59,939
British Columbia	11,999
Alberta	5,800
Saskatchewan	954
Manitoba	1,728
Ontario	22,436
Quebec	11,902
New Brunswick	1,524
Nova Scotia	1,598
Prince Edward Island	213
Newfoundland	1,333
Northwest Territories	289
Yukon Territory	162

OLD ECONOMY INDUSTRIES

The following industries are past their peak in terms of contributing to the gross domestic product. As industries peak, their free-fall is more severe than could reasonably be associated with a recession. Subsequent business cycle recoveries do not bring the industry back to its past glory.

However, old economy industries can become integrated into the growing New Economy by producing new goods, by using new technologies to revitalize the industry and by finding new markets, either domestically or abroad.

BROADCASTING

★ ★ ★ ★ ★

Quite surprisingly, the broadcasting industry has been in long-term structural decline since 1985. Despite the promise of information highways, regulations have kept the industry on a tight leash, and growth has been hard to come by. Broadcasting companies are now looking beyond their traditional mandates.

But job security in the industry is high, as the very low lay-off rate of only 0.5 percent between 1989 and 1993 demonstrates. And advancement prospects are good.

Other attractions are the very high average salaries and very high average salary changes: the average increase in salaries amounted to 11.8 percent in 1993.

Although the industry's knowledge base is high, its erosion is a great cause for concern. In the last five years, the Knowledge Ratio has declined by 17.8 percent—at a point when technological challenges have never been greater.

OVERALL
SCORE

70

HOW THE INDUSTRY COMPARES:

Job Security: High
Advancement: Good
Average Salary: Very High
Salary Change: Very High
Knowledge Base: High
Industry Knowledge: Declining
Industry Stability: Moderate

VITAL STATISTICS

Average Lay-off Rate, 1989–93: 0.5%
Net Job Creation, 1989–93: −204
Average Salary Level, 1993: $792/week
Salary Increase, 1993: +11.8%
Knowledge Workers per 100 Employees: 60
Knowledge Base Change: −17.8%
Industry Volatility: 6.7 (empl.)
SIC Code: 481

WHERE THE JOBS ARE:

TOTAL EMPLOYMENT	42,649
British Columbia	3,568
Alberta	2,989
Saskatchewan	n/a
Manitoba	1,227
Ontario	17,474
Quebec	11,676
New Brunswick	n/a
Nova Scotia	n/a
Prince Edward Island	n/a
Newfoundland	n/a
Northwest Territories	n/a
Yukon Territory	n/a

DAIRY PRODUCTS MANUFACTURING

★ ★ ★ ★ ★

Manufacturers of dairy products such as milk, ice cream, cheese and butter peaked structurally in 1979, but conditions have remained reasonably buoyant thanks to a myriad of marketing boards and regulations that have protected the industry's interests and kept revenues high.

OVERALL
SCORE

70

As long as the industry remains protected, job security will be high and advancement prospects moderate. But the great era of protectionism is drawing rapidly to a close. Governments can no longer afford the subsidy levels of the past, consumers are unable to pay the high prices that result from these distortions and our trading partners are waging war on agricultural subsidies (although they want to continue protecting their own industries).

Average salary levels are high and wage increases have been generous. An encouraging sign is that the industry's knowledge base is rising very sharply. This trend indicates that dairy product manufacturers are preparing to operate more competitively in a world where the subsidies of yesterday will be replaced more and more by the market forces of tomorrow.

HOW THE INDUSTRY COMPARES:

Job Security: High
Advancement: Moderate
Average Salary: High
Salary Change: High
Knowledge Base: Moderate
Industry Knowledge: Rising Very Sharply
Industry Stability: Very High

VITAL STATISTICS

Average Lay-off Rate, 1989–93: 9.8%
Net Job Creation, 1989–93: −1,977
Average Salary Level, 1993: $638/week
Salary Increase, 1993: +2.1%
Knowledge Workers per 100 Employees: 20
Knowledge Base Change: +20.7%
Industry Volatility: 3.3
SIC Code: 104

WHERE THE JOBS ARE:

TOTAL EMPLOYMENT	20,330
British Columbia	2,611
Alberta	1,371
Saskatchewan	n/a
Manitoba	618
Ontario	7,644
Quebec	5,160
New Brunswick	713
Nova Scotia	965
Prince Edward Island	254
Newfoundland	n/a
Northwest Territories	n/a
Yukon Territory	n/a

PUBLIC TRANSIT

The public transit industry peaked structurally in 1981, but government funding and mounting subsidies have kept growth strong in spite of the rapid reduction in the number of riders. The aging of Canada's population does not bode well for this industry's future. Despite the environmental imperatives to use public transit, older baby boomers are increasingly inclined to opt for the comfort and security of private cars. Government funding constraints are sure to be felt more and more by public transit providers.

Meanwhile, job security remains very high and will continue to be so as long as public funds meet revenue shortfalls. Average salary levels are moderate, and wage increases are very high.

The knowledge base is low but rising sharply, as the industry embraces new transportation technologies.

OVERALL SCORE

70

HOW THE INDUSTRY COMPARES:

Job Security: Very High
Advancement: Very Good
Average Salary: Moderate
Salary Change: Very High
Knowledge Base: Low
Industry Knowledge: Rising Sharply
Industry Stability: Very High

VITAL STATISTICS

Average Lay-off Rate, 1989–93: Zero
Net Job Creation, 1989–93: +10,060
Average Salary Level, 1993: $576/week
Salary Increase, 1993: +10.7%
Knowledge Workers per 100 Employees: 17
Knowledge Base Change: +7.4%
Industry Volatility: 2.6
SIC Code: 457

WHERE THE JOBS ARE:

TOTAL EMPLOYMENT	77,914
British Columbia	5,931
Alberta	6,744
Saskatchewan	1,975
Manitoba	1,983
Ontario	37,096
Quebec	21,996
New Brunswick	383
Nova Scotia	885
Prince Edward Island	n/a
Newfoundland	802
Northwest Territories	n/a
Yukon Territory	n/a

RAILCAR & LOCOMOTIVE MANUFACTURING

★ ★ ★ ★

Manufacturers of locomotives and railcars have been in long-term structural decline since 1974 when the industry peaked. But the involvement of government has meant a moderate level of job security for employees.

Although government support of this moderately knowledge-intensive industry may well lessen in the future, advancement prospects remain fairly good as long as the knowledge base continues to rise very sharply, as it has in the last five years.

Average salary levels are very high, and those working in the industry enjoyed average salary increases of 7.1 percent in 1993.

OVERALL SCORE

65

HOW THE INDUSTRY COMPARES:

Job Security: Moderate
Advancement: Good
Average Salary: Very High
Salary Change: Very High
Knowledge Base: Moderate
Industry Knowledge: Rising Very Sharply
Industry Stability: Very Low

VITAL STATISTICS

Average Lay-off Rate, 1989–93: 15.4%
Net Job Creation, 1989–93: –997
Average Salary Level, 1993: $768/week
Salary Increase, 1993: +7.1%
Knowledge Workers per 100 Employees: 27
Knowledge Base Change: 53.3%
Industry Volatility: 11.5
SIC Code: 326

WHERE THE JOBS ARE:

TOTAL EMPLOYMENT	6,593
British Columbia	n/a
Alberta	n/a
Saskatchewan	n/a
Manitoba	n/a
Ontario	4,086
Quebec	1,707
New Brunswick	n/a
Nova Scotia	n/a
Prince Edward Island	n/a
Newfoundland	n/a
Northwest Territories	n/a
Yukon Territory	n/a

MACHINERY & EQUIPMENT WHOLESALERS FOR CONSTRUCTION, FORESTRY & MINING

Wholesalers of new and used machinery, equipment and supplies for the construction, forestry and mining industries provide a high level of job security. The lay-off rate between 1989 and 1993 was 3.8 percent, which is quite low by Canadian standards. Advancement prospects are good, but the industry is in long-term structural decline.

An attraction, however, in this broadly based industry is the high average salary, and the sharply rising Knowledge Ratio.

OVERALL
SCORE

60

HOW THE INDUSTRY COMPARES:

Job Security: High
Advancement: Good
Average Salary: High
Salary Change: Moderate
Knowledge Base: Moderate
Industry Knowledge: Rising Very Sharply
Industry Stability: Very Low

VITAL STATISTICS

Average Lay-off Rate, 1989–93: 3.8%
Net Job Creation, 1989–93: −527
Average Salary Level, 1993: $692/week
Salary Increase, 1993: +0.3%
Knowledge Workers per 100 Employees: 28
Knowledge Base Change: +18.0%
Industry Volatility: 13.6 (empl.)
SIC Code: 572

WHERE THE JOBS ARE:

TOTAL EMPLOYMENT	16,273
British Columbia	2,741
Alberta	5,034
Saskatchewan	584
Manitoba	388
Ontario	3,473
Quebec	2,933
New Brunswick	285
Nova Scotia	332
Prince Edward Island	n/a
Newfoundland	434
Northwest Territories	n/a
Yukon Territory	n/a

TOBACCO PRODUCTS

★ ★ ★ ★

The tobacco industry may be in long-term structural decline (it peaked in 1977), but the folks who sort and grade tobacco and who manufacture cigarettes, cigars and chewing tobacco (presumably for baseball players) enjoy a high degree of job security and good advancement prospects.

Average salaries are very high and average salary increases in 1993 were an enviable 4.5 percent.

But the knowledge base is low and declining rapidly in this dying industry.

OVERALL
SCORE

60

HOW THE INDUSTRY COMPARES:

Job Security: High
Advancement: Good
Average Salary: Very High
Salary Change: High
Knowledge Base: Low
Industry Knowledge: Declining
Industry Stability: High

VITAL STATISTICS

Average Lay-off Rate, 1989–93: 8.2%
Net Job Creation, 1989–93: −387
Average Salary Level, 1993: $989/week
Salary Increase, 1993: +4.5%
Knowledge Workers per 100 Employees: 17
Knowledge Base Change: −12.1%
Industry Volatility: 5.8
SIC Code: 120

WHERE THE JOBS ARE:

TOTAL EMPLOYMENT	4,780
British Columbia	n/a
Alberta	n/a
Saskatchewan	n/a
Manitoba	n/a
Ontario	n/a
Quebec	2,922
New Brunswick	n/a
Nova Scotia	n/a
Prince Edward Island	n/a
Newfoundland	n/a
Northwest Territories	n/a
Yukon Territory	n/a

PETROLEUM & NATURAL GAS EXPLORATION

★ ★ ★

While the petroleum side of this industry has peaked structurally, natural gas has rapidly emerged as the New Economy's fuel of choice. A lay-off rate of 31.6 percent between 1989 and 1993 masks the underlying shifts that are taking place, as large oil companies downsize while natural gas producers expand.

As a whole, the industry provides low job security and very poor advancement prospects, but employees should look to a bright future in the natural gas side of the business.

Average salaries are very high. Very high average salary increases of 6.2 percent in 1993 also reflect the fact that the natural gas industry is highly profitable.

The growth in natural gas producers has moved the industry back into the high-knowledge category and has provided a real future for many of the best and the brightest. While many of the job opportunities require engineering and geological specialities, ample room exists for clerical, administrative and hourly paid workers as well.

OVERALL
SCORE

57.5

HOW THE INDUSTRY COMPARES:

Job Security: Low
Advancement: Very Poor
Average Salary: Very High
Salary Change: Very High
Knowledge Base: High
Industry Knowledge: Reasonably Stable
Industry Stability: High

VITAL STATISTICS

Average Lay-off Rate, 1989–93: 31.6%
Net Job Creation, 1989–93: −10,476
Average Salary Level, 1993: $1,114/week
Salary Increase, 1993: +6.2%
Knowledge Workers per 100 Employees: 43
Knowledge Base Change: +1.1%
Industry Volatility: 4.7 (empl.)
SIC Code: 071

WHERE THE JOBS ARE:

TOTAL EMPLOYMENT	34,254
British Columbia	508
Alberta	31,791
Saskatchewan	842
Manitoba	n/a
Ontario	542
Quebec	n/a
New Brunswick	n/a
Nova Scotia	n/a
Prince Edward Island	n/a
Newfoundland	n/a
Northwest Territories	n/a
Yukon Territory	n/a

PETROLEUM PRODUCTS WHOLESALERS

★ ★ ★

Wholesalers of petroleum products, including natural gas, created 2,577 net new jobs through the tough recession years of 1989–93, and produced a zero lay-off rate for the industry as a whole. With strong increases in the number of new employees, advancement prospects in the industry are very good.

OVERALL SCORE

57.5

While the average salary level is moderate, salary changes have been poor; the average wage dropped 1.7 percent in 1993.

The industry's knowledge base is moderate, but rising sharply as new processes and technologies are adopted.

HOW THE INDUSTRY COMPARES:

Job Security: Very High
Advancement: Very Good
Average Salary: Moderate
Salary Change: Poor
Knowledge Base: Moderate
Industry Knowledge: Rising Sharply
Industry Stability: Very Low

VITAL STATISTICS

Average Lay-off Rate, 1989–93: Zero
Net Job Creation, 1989–93: +2,577
Average Salary Level, 1993: $603/week
Salary Increase, 1993: −1.7%
Knowledge Workers per 100 Employees: 25
Knowledge Base Change: +9.1%
Industry Volatility: 12.5 (empl.)
SIC Code: 511

WHERE THE JOBS ARE:	
TOTAL EMPLOYMENT	27,271
British Columbia	3,095
Alberta	4,969
Saskatchewan	2,218
Manitoba	853
Ontario	7,559
Quebec	5,517
New Brunswick	1,262
Nova Scotia	1,009
Prince Edward Island	169
Newfoundland	462
Northwest Territories	121
Yukon Territory	n/a

PAPER BOX, CARTON & BAG MANUFACTURING

⭐ ⭐ ⭐

This industry peaked structurally in 1978 and has been affected by a series of structural changes: the trend toward product miniaturization has reduced the demand for large cartons; the growth of high-knowledge service industries has meant that manufacturers of paper containers are not full partners in economic growth, as they once were; and, more recently, sweeping environmental concerns have made consumers more intent on recycling and reusing their boxes and bags than ever before.

OVERALL
SCORE

55

Despite the challenges, the industry's lay-off rate of 7.3 percent has been low, and consequently employees enjoy a high degree of job security. Compared to most industries, advancement prospects are reasonably good.

Average salary levels are high and workers enjoyed an average salary gain of 4.9 percent in 1993.

Of concern, however, is that the industry's low-knowledge base is declining: in the last five years, the Knowledge Ratio has dropped 8.5 percent.

HOW THE INDUSTRY COMPARES:

Job Security: High
Advancement: Good
Average Salary: High
Salary Change: High
Knowledge Base: Low
Industry Knowledge: Declining
Industry Stability: High

VITAL STATISTICS

Average Lay-off Rate, 1989–93: 7.3%
Net Job Creation, 1989–93: −1,238
Average Salary Level, 1993: $667/week
Salary Increase, 1993: +4.9%
Knowledge Workers per 100 Employees: 12
Knowledge Base Change: −8.5%
Industry Volatility: 5.2
SIC Code: 273

WHERE THE JOBS ARE:

TOTAL EMPLOYMENT	16,781
British Columbia	1,252
Alberta	n/a
Saskatchewan	n/a
Manitoba	452
Ontario	9,027
Quebec	4,564
New Brunswick	280
Nova Scotia	n/a
Prince Edward Island	n/a
Newfoundland	n/a
Northwest Territories	n/a
Yukon Territory	n/a

PETROLEUM REFINING

★ ★ ★

The refining industry peaked structurally in 1977 after one oil shock too many. During the 1989–93 recession, lay-off rates of 52.5 percent reduced this once very large industry even further. Consequently, job security remains very low and advancement prospects are poor, despite the fact that production is reasonably stable.

However, average salaries are very high and increases averaged 10.4 percent in 1993. The knowledge base of this moderately knowledge-intensive industry is rising sharply. Sweeping restructuring has increased the number of higher-paid knowledge workers.

OVERALL
SCORE

55

HOW THE INDUSTRY COMPARES:

Job Security: Very Low
Advancement: Poor
Average Salary: Very High
Salary Change: Very High
Knowledge Base: Moderate
Industry Knowledge: Rising Sharply
Industry Stability: High

VITAL STATISTICS

Average Lay-off Rate, 1989–93: 52.5%
Net Job Creation, 1989–93: –7,319
Average Salary Level, 1993: $1,037/week
Salary Increase, 1993: +10.4%
Knowledge Workers per 100 Employees: 32
Knowledge Base Change: +7.4%
Industry Volatility: 5.5
SIC Code: 36

WHERE THE JOBS ARE:

TOTAL EMPLOYMENT	13,065
British Columbia	n/a
Alberta	2,985
Saskatchewan	n/a
Manitoba	n/a
Ontario	n/a
Quebec	n/a
New Brunswick	n/a
Nova Scotia	n/a
Prince Edward Island	n/a
Newfoundland	n/a
Northwest Territories	n/a
Yukon Territory	n/a

PLUMBING FIXTURES, VALVES, PIPES & OTHER FABRICATED METAL PRODUCTS

This broadly diversified industry manufactures a wide range of metal products from stainless steel kitchen sinks and bathroom faucets to rail spikes, firearms and radiator valves.

On average, job security is high and advancement is good. Only 1.6 percent of the people employed in this business found themselves out of work between 1989 and 1993.

Average salaries are moderate and increases have been high, averaging 3.5 percent in 1993.

The low knowledge base of the industry is changing rapidly as manufacturers introduce new technologies and processes.

OVERALL SCORE

52.5

HOW THE INDUSTRY COMPARES:

Job Security: High
Advancement: Good
Average Salary: Moderate
Salary Change: High
Knowledge Base: Low
Industry Knowledge: Rising Sharply
Industry Stability: Low

WHERE THE JOBS ARE:

TOTAL EMPLOYMENT	13,703
British Columbia	1,658
Alberta	1,708
Saskatchewan	110
Manitoba	n/a
Ontario	7,413
Quebec	2,619
New Brunswick	n/a
Nova Scotia	n/a
Prince Edward Island	n/a
Newfoundland	n/a
Northwest Territories	n/a
Yukon Territory	n/a

VITAL STATISTICS

Average Lay-off Rate, 1989–93: 1.6%
Net Job Creation, 1989–93: −212
Average Salary Level, 1993: $618/week
Salary Increase, 1993: +3.5%
Knowledge Workers per 100 Employees: 17
Knowledge Base Change: +12.9%
Industry Volatility: 10.2
SIC Code: 309

PRINTING INK, ADHESIVES & ADDITIVES MANUFACTURING

This branch of the chemical industry covers a wide range of products from printing inks to tile cement to chemicals for the textile and paper industries. Lay-off rates averaged 50.8 percent during the tough recession years; consequently, job security is very low and advancement prospects are poor.

However, salary levels are high, and a sharply rising knowledge base in this high-knowledge-intensive industry has produced a healthy increase in average wages.

OVERALL
SCORE

52.5

HOW THE INDUSTRY COMPARES:

Job Security: Very Low
Advancement: Poor
Average Salary: High
Salary Change: High
Knowledge Base: High
Industry Knowledge: Rising Sharply
Industry Stability: High

VITAL STATISTICS

Average Lay-off Rate, 1989–93: 50.8%
Net Job Creation, 1989–93: −7,321
Average Salary Level, 1993: $736/week
Salary Increase, 1993: +3.3%
Knowledge Workers per 100 Employees: 40
Knowledge Base Change: +7.9%
Industry Volatility: 6.3
SIC Code: 379

WHERE THE JOBS ARE:

TOTAL EMPLOYMENT	14,416
British Columbia	468
Alberta	1,063
Saskatchewan	n/a
Manitoba	148
Ontario	8,130
Quebec	4,232
New Brunswick	n/a
Nova Scotia	n/a
Prince Edward Island	n/a
Newfoundland	n/a
Northwest Territories	n/a
Yukon Territory	n/a

READY-MIX CONCRETE MANUFACTURING & DELIVERY

The business of manufacturing ready-mix concrete peaked structurally in 1973 and has been in long-term decline for over twenty years.

Job security is moderate; the industry experienced a lay-off rate of 17.9 percent over the 1989–93 period.

Average salaries are high, but increases are only moderate in this low-knowledge field.

The very sharp rise in the knowledge base indicates a strong undercurrent of technological change. In the last five years, the Knowledge Ratio of the ready-mix concrete industry rose an impressive 20.1 percent.

OVERALL SCORE

52.5

HOW THE INDUSTRY COMPARES:

Job Security: Moderate
Advancement: Moderate
Average Salary: High
Salary Change: Moderate
Knowledge Base: Low
Industry Knowledge: Rising Very Sharply
Industry Stability: Moderate

VITAL STATISTICS

Average Lay-off Rate, 1989–93: 17.9%
Net Job Creation, 1989–93: −1,611
Average Salary Level, 1993: $642/week
Salary Increase, 1993: +0.9%
Knowledge Workers per 100 Employees: 18
Knowledge Base Change: +20.1%
Industry Volatility: 8.3
SIC Code: 355

WHERE THE JOBS ARE:

TOTAL EMPLOYMENT	8,534
British Columbia	2,692
Alberta	1,182
Saskatchewan	170
Manitoba	162
Ontario	2,740
Quebec	1,148
New Brunswick	n/a
Nova Scotia	n/a
Prince Edward Island	n/a
Newfoundland	n/a
Northwest Territories	n/a
Yukon Territory	n/a

AGRICULTURAL IMPLEMENTS

★ ★ ★

Manufacturers of agricultural implements employ only 7,668 Canadians, but provide remarkable job security after undergoing serious restructuring in the past. With 856 net new employees coming onto payrolls, the industry provides very good advancement prospects.

Average salary levels, however, are low and wage increases have been very poor, with an average drop of 4.2 percent in 1993.

The knowledge base of the business is moderate, but rising sharply as manufacturers continue to embrace new technologies and processes.

Although its stability is very low, the industry has been successful in recent years at pursuing export markets. Business with these new clients has helped to minimize some of the volatility.

OVERALL
SCORE

50

HOW THE INDUSTRY COMPARES:

Job Security: Very High
Advancement: Very Good
Average Salary: Low
Salary Change: Very Poor
Knowledge Base: Moderate
Industry Knowledge: Rising Sharply
Industry Stability: Very Low

VITAL STATISTICS

Average Lay-off Rate, 1989–93: Zero
Net Job Creation, 1989–93: +856
Average Salary Level, 1993: $532/week
Salary Increase, 1993: −4.2%
Knowledge Workers per 100 Employees: 21
Knowledge Base Change: +8.7%
Industry Volatility: 23.5
SIC Code: 311

WHERE THE JOBS ARE:

TOTAL EMPLOYMENT	7,668
British Columbia	n/a
Alberta	497
Saskatchewan	2,422
Manitoba	n/a
Ontario	1,967
Quebec	935
New Brunswick	n/a
Nova Scotia	n/a
Prince Edward Island	n/a
Newfoundland	n/a
Northwest Territories	n/a
Yukon Territory	n/a

BEVERAGE MANUFACTURING

All beverages are not created equally: the industry includes soft drinks, breweries, wines and distillery products—everything from rye whiskey to tequila coolers. Despite great differences in the fortunes of each type of beverage, the industry as a whole peaked structurally in 1974. "If you drink, don't drive" campaigns and the baby-boomers love affair with mineral water and private label pop have had a significant impact on the consumption of alcoholic beverages; while generic soft drink manufacturers have benefited from the explosive growth of house-brand soft drinks.

Job security in the industry as a whole is low, as revealed by the 28.0 percent lay-off rate in the industry between 1989 and 1993. But average salary levels are high and rising: employees enjoyed a wage increase of 7.3 percent in 1993.

The knowledge base of this fairly stable industry is moderate but rising.

OVERALL SCORE

50

HOW THE INDUSTRY COMPARES:

Job Security: Low
Advancement: Poor
Average Salary: High
Salary Change: Very High
Knowledge Base: Moderate
Industry Knowledge: Rising
Industry Stability: Moderate

VITAL STATISTICS

Average Lay-off Rate, 1989–93: 28.0%
Net Job Creation, 1989–93: −6,905
Average Salary Level, 1993: $736/week
Salary Increase, 1993: +7.3%
Knowledge Workers per 100 Employees: 26
Knowledge Base Change: +4.9%
Industry Volatility: 7.5 (empl.)
SIC Code: 110

WHERE THE JOBS ARE:

TOTAL EMPLOYMENT	24,041
British Columbia	2,477
Alberta	1,370
Saskatchewan	411
Manitoba	615
Ontario	9,630
Quebec	7,556
New Brunswick	945
Nova Scotia	703
Prince Edward Island	n/a
Newfoundland	n/a
Northwest Territories	n/a
Yukon Territory	n/a

DRY CLEANERS & LAUNDRIES

⭐ ⭐ ⭐

This industry provides very high job security, and current employees enjoyed a zero lay-off rate between 1989 and 1993. Advancement prospects are also very good; 1,511 net new employees have created a basis for people to move up to supervisory positions. The industry also lends itself to franchise opportunities for those who are entrepreneurially inclined.

OVERALL SCORE

50

The major drawback in the business is the very low average salary. But wages have risen very sharply, with the average increase an attractive 9.4 percent in 1993.

The knowledge base in this otherwise very stable industry is low and declining.

Although the clothes cleaning industry has peaked structurally (environmental concerns have converted many consumers to natural fibers that require less care, and "casual Fridays" have reduced the dry cleaning toll on office wear), dry cleaners and laundries provide an impressive degree of job stability and security.

HOW THE INDUSTRY COMPARES:

Job Security: Very High
Advancement: Very Good
Average Salary: Very Low
Salary Change: Very High
Knowledge Base: Low
Industry Knowledge: Declining
Industry Stability: High

VITAL STATISTICS

Average Lay-off Rate, 1989–93: Zero
Net Job Creation, 1989–93: +1,511
Average Salary Level, 1993: $348/week
Salary Increase, 1993: +9.4%
Knowledge Workers per 100 Employees: 13
Knowledge Base Change: −19.3%
Industry Volatility: 5.0 (empl.)
SIC Code: 972

WHERE THE JOBS ARE:

TOTAL EMPLOYMENT	26,305
British Columbia	4,175
Alberta	2,514
Saskatchewan	n/a
Manitoba	1,274
Ontario	9,626
Quebec	6,183
New Brunswick	709
Nova Scotia	n/a
Prince Edward Island	155
Newfoundland	303
Northwest Territories	n/a
Yukon Territory	n/a

FEED, FLOUR & CEREAL MANUFACTURING

The feed, flour and cereal manufacturing industry, centered primarily in Ontario, Quebec and Alberta, is in long-term structural decline, having peaked in 1986. But the overall decline has been modest, leaving employees with a high level of job security and good advancement prospects.

While average salaries are moderate, salary changes have been poor, with an average decline of 1.2 percent in 1993. This moderately knowledge-intensive industry is very stable, but the knowledge base is declining, a trend that does not bode well as domestic and international trade barriers come tumbling down.

OVERALL SCORE

50

HOW THE INDUSTRY COMPARES:

Job Security: High
Advancement: Good
Average Salary: Moderate
Salary Change: Poor
Knowledge Base: Moderate
Industry Knowledge: Declining
Industry Stability: High

VITAL STATISTICS

Average Lay-off Rate, 1989–93: 5.8%
Net Job Creation, 1989–93: −934
Average Salary Level, 1993: $612/week
Salary Increase, 1993: −1.2%
Knowledge Workers per 100 Employees: 25
Knowledge Base Change: −7.9%
Industry Volatility: 4.5
SIC Code: 105

WHERE THE JOBS ARE:	
TOTAL EMPLOYMENT	16,346
British Columbia	n/a
Alberta	2,111
Saskatchewan	595
Manitoba	716
Ontario	7,321
Quebec	3,548
New Brunswick	n/a
Nova Scotia	534
Prince Edward Island	n/a
Newfoundland	n/a
Northwest Territories	n/a
Yukon Territory	n/a

DETERGENT & CLEANING PRODUCTS MANUFACTURING

The industry that keeps our clothes whiter than white and smelling fresher than fresh peaked structurally in 1984. Job security has declined in tandem with the industry's fortunes as businesses attempt to become competitive in the face of free trade. Between 1989 and 1993, 35.3 percent of employees lost their jobs.

However, average salaries are high and increases averaged 0.4 percent in 1993.

The knowledge base of this declining industry is moderate but rising, which is a vital development for the future of the industry.

OVERALL SCORE

47.5

HOW THE INDUSTRY COMPARES:

Job Security: Low
Advancement: Moderate
Average Salary: High
Salary Change: Moderate
Knowledge Base: Moderate
Industry Knowledge: Rising
Industry Stability: Moderate

WHERE THE JOBS ARE:

TOTAL EMPLOYMENT	6,349
British Columbia	213
Alberta	144
Saskatchewan	n/a
Manitoba	n/a
Ontario	4,648
Quebec	1,141
New Brunswick	n/a
Nova Scotia	n/a
Prince Edward Island	n/a
Newfoundland	n/a
Northwest Territories	n/a
Yukon Territory	n/a

VITAL STATISTICS

Average Lay-off Rate, 1989–93: 35.3%
Net Job Creation, 1989–93: –2,370
Average Salary Level, 1993: $705/week
Salary Increase, 1993: +0.4%
Knowledge Workers per 100 Employees: 32
Knowledge Base Change: +5.3%
Industry Volatility: 7.0
SIC Code: 376

PULP & PAPER MANUFACTURING

The industry that produces wood pulp, newsprint, toilet paper, paperboard and building board peaked structurally in 1974 and has been challenged repeatedly by technological and environmental change. Between 1989 and 1993, lay-off rates across the industry rose to 27.9 percent and translated into 18,211 jobs lost. Understandably, job security is low and advancement is very poor.

However, average salaries are very high in the industry, despite decreases.

The knowledge base in pulp and paper manufacturing is low, but has risen an impressive 24.7 percent in the last five years.

OVERALL SCORE

47.5

HOW THE INDUSTRY COMPARES:

Job Security: Low
Advancement: Very Poor
Average Salary: Very High
Salary Change: Poor
Knowledge Base: Low
Industry Knowledge: Rising Very Sharply
Industry Stability: High

VITAL STATISTICS

Average Lay-off Rate, 1989–93: 27.9%
Net Job Creation, 1989–93: –18,211
Average Salary Level, 1993: $877/week
Salary Increase, 1993: –0.5%
Knowledge Workers per 100 Employees: 18
Knowledge Base Change: +24.7%
Industry Volatility: 6.3
SIC Code: 271

WHERE THE JOBS ARE:

TOTAL EMPLOYMENT	65,331
British Columbia	16,824
Alberta	2,394
Saskatchewan	n/a
Manitoba	679
Ontario	14,399
Quebec	21,178
New Brunswick	4,528
Nova Scotia	2,374
Prince Edward Island	n/a
Newfoundland	n/a
Northwest Territories	n/a
Yukon Territory	n/a

BAKERY PRODUCTS MANUFACTURING

★ ★

The bread and cookie business peaked structurally in 1973, and production has crumbled 25 percent since then. Most of the downsizing has already taken place and, consequently, job security is high: the industry experienced a 10.4 percent lay-off rate between 1989 and 1993, which is low by old economy standards. Advancement is moderate compared to other industries in Canada.

OVERALL
SCORE

45

However, the salary level is low and increases have been modest; employees received a 0.1 percent average increase in 1993.

Of concern is that the low knowledge base of the industry has remained very stable while new manufacturing and production technologies have come rapidly onto the market.

HOW THE INDUSTRY COMPARES:

Job Security: High
Advancement: Moderate
Average Salary: Low
Salary Change: Moderate
Knowledge Base: Low
Industry Knowledge: Reasonably Stable
Industry Stability: Very High

VITAL STATISTICS

Average Lay-off Rate, 1989–93: 10.4%
Net Job Creation, 1989–93: −2,896
Average Salary Level, 1993: $492/week
Salary Increase, 1993: +0.1%
Knowledge Workers per 100 Employees: 10
Knowledge Base Change: +0.4%
Industry Volatility: 3.9
SIC Code: 107

WHERE THE JOBS ARE:

TOTAL EMPLOYMENT	28,223
British Columbia	2,224
Alberta	1,465
Saskatchewan	194
Manitoba	891
Ontario	12,948
Quebec	9,743
New Brunswick	214
Nova Scotia	334
Prince Edward Island	n/a
Newfoundland	n/a
Northwest Territories	n/a
Yukon Territory	n/a

CEMENT MANUFACTURING

⭐ ⭐

The cement industry peaked structurally in 1979, and production has fallen over 41 percent since that time. In the face of such widespread industry collapse, it is little wonder that job security is very low. Between 1989 and 1993 alone, the lay-off rate soared to 95.1 percent. Cement manufacturers provide modest room for advancement at best.

However, average salary levels are very high and a salary increase of 5.0 percent in 1993 is attractive compared to other industries. The sharply rising knowledge base allows for higher wage rates.

OVERALL
SCORE

45

HOW THE INDUSTRY COMPARES:

Job Security: Very Low
Advancement: Moderate
Average Salary: Very High
Salary Change: High
Knowledge Base: Low
Industry Knowledge: Rising Very Sharply
Industry Stability: Very Low

VITAL STATISTICS

Average Lay-off Rate, 1989–93: 95.1%
Net Job Creation, 1989–93: −2,346
Average Salary Level, 1993: $845/week
Salary Increase, 1993: +5.0%
Knowledge Workers per 100 Employees: 18
Knowledge Base Change: 20.1%
Industry Volatility: 12.9
SIC Code: 352

WHERE THE JOBS ARE:	
TOTAL EMPLOYMENT	2,272
British Columbia	322
Alberta	n/a
Saskatchewan	n/a
Manitoba	n/a
Ontario	896
Quebec	571
New Brunswick	n/a
Nova Scotia	n/a
Prince Edward Island	n/a
Newfoundland	n/a
Northwest Territories	n/a
Yukon Territory	n/a

HOUSEHOLD APPLIANCE & FURNITURE WHOLESALERS

Wholesalers of household appliances and furnishings provide moderate job security in an industry that experienced an 18.6 percent lay-off rate during the tough recession years of 1989–93. Advancement prospects are also moderate.

Salary levels are equally mid-range, but increases have been generous: an enviable 5.1 percent on average in 1993.

While the knowledge base is low, it is encouraging to see that the industry's Knowledge Ratio has climbed 9.5 percent in the last five years. This is a sharp rise compared to other industries in Canada.

OVERALL
SCORE

42.5

HOW THE INDUSTRY COMPARES:

Job Security: Moderate
Advancement: Moderate
Average Salary: Moderate
Salary Change: High
Knowledge Base: Low
Industry Knowledge: Rising Sharply
Industry Stability: Very Low

VITAL STATISTICS

Average Lay-off Rate, 1989–93: 18.6%
Net Job Creation, 1989–93: –3,524
Average Salary Level, 1993: $619/week
Salary Increase, 1993: +5.1%
Knowledge Workers per 100 Employees: 17
Knowledge Base Change: +9.5%
Industry Volatility: 19.9 (empl.)
SIC Code: 54

WHERE THE JOBS ARE:

TOTAL EMPLOYMENT	18,858
British Columbia	2,143
Alberta	857
Saskatchewan	119
Manitoba	441
Ontario	7,443
Quebec	7,231
New Brunswick	188
Nova Scotia	310
Prince Edward Island	n/a
Newfoundland	n/a
Northwest Territories	n/a
Yukon Territory	n/a

PRIMARY TEXTILE MANUFACTURING

⭐ ⭐

Cloth and fabric manufacturers have been in long-term structural decline, and provide low job security for their employees: witness the 33.1 percent lay-off rate between 1989 and 1993.

Average salary levels in the industry are moderate, but increases have been attractive, with the average wage rate rising 2.6 percent in 1993.

It is encouraging to see that the industry's low knowledge base has risen sharply; primary textile manufacturers now employ 12 knowledge workers per 100 employees. The future of the industry lies in becoming an increasingly high-knowledge producer—not in trying to compete with low wage–low knowledge countries abroad.

OVERALL SCORE

42.5

HOW THE INDUSTRY COMPARES:

Job Security: Low
Advancement: Poor
Average Salary: Moderate
Salary Change: High
Knowledge Base: Low
Industry Knowledge: Rising Sharply
Industry Stability: High

VITAL STATISTICS

Average Lay-off Rate, 1989–93: 33.1%
Net Job Creation, 1989–93: −5,682
Average Salary Level, 1993: $596/week
Salary Increase, 1993: +2.6%
Knowledge Workers per 100 Employees: 12
Knowledge Base Change: +10.8%
Industry Volatility: 4.8
SIC Code: 180

WHERE THE JOBS ARE:

TOTAL EMPLOYMENT	16,724
British Columbia	146
Alberta	n/a
Saskatchewan	n/a
Manitoba	n/a
Ontario	6,978
Quebec	9,146
New Brunswick	n/a
Nova Scotia	n/a
Prince Edward Island	n/a
Newfoundland	n/a
Northwest Territories	n/a
Yukon Territory	n/a

SHIPBUILDING & REPAIR

★ ★

The shipbuilding and repair industry is one of the most volatile in Canada, and has been in long-term structural decline despite the government's regional economic development initiatives. The lay-off rate soared to 29.2 percent between 1989 and 1993. Not surprisingly, job security is low.

Average salaries are high but fell 2.1 percent in 1993. A positive factor in this moderate knowledge industry is that the knowledge base is rising sharply.

OVERALL
SCORE

42.5

HOW THE INDUSTRY COMPARES:

Job Security: Low
Advancement: Moderate
Average Salary: High
Salary Change: Poor
Knowledge Base: Moderate
Industry Knowledge: Rising Sharply
Industry Stability: Very Low

VITAL STATISTICS

Average Lay-off Rate, 1989–93: 29.2%
Net Job Creation, 1989–93: –2,682
Average Salary Level, 1993: $683/week
Salary Increase, 1993: –2.1%
Knowledge Workers per 100 Employees: 21
Knowledge Base Change: +10.3%
Industry Volatility: 17.8
SIC Code: 327

WHERE THE JOBS ARE:	
TOTAL EMPLOYMENT	8,378
British Columbia	855
Alberta	n/a
Saskatchewan	n/a
Manitoba	n/a
Ontario	728
Quebec	n/a
New Brunswick	n/a
Nova Scotia	n/a
Prince Edward Island	n/a
Newfoundland	n/a
Northwest Territories	n/a
Yukon Territory	n/a

STEEL MANUFACTURING

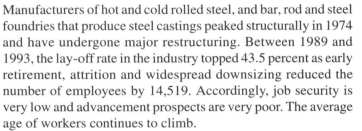

Manufacturers of hot and cold rolled steel, and bar, rod and steel foundries that produce steel castings peaked structurally in 1974 and have undergone major restructuring. Between 1989 and 1993, the lay-off rate in the industry topped 43.5 percent as early retirement, attrition and widespread downsizing reduced the number of employees by 14,519. Accordingly, job security is very low and advancement prospects are very poor. The average age of workers continues to climb.

However, the average salary is very high and climbed 4.5 percent in 1993 alone.

Although the knowledge base of the industry is low (only 14 out of every 100 employees are knowledge workers), it is rising very sharply and will help to underpin the steel industry in the longer term.

OVERALL SCORE

42.5

HOW THE INDUSTRY COMPARES:

Job Security: Very Low
Advancement: Very Poor
Average Salary: Very High
Salary Change: High
Knowledge Base: Low
Industry Knowledge: Rising Very Sharply
Industry Stability: Low

VITAL STATISTICS

Average Lay-off Rate, 1989–93: 43.5%
Net Job Creation, 1989–93: −14,519
Average Salary Level, 1993: $832/week
Salary Increase, 1993: +4.5%
Knowledge Workers per 100 Employees: 14
Knowledge Base Change: +34.8%
Industry Volatility: 9.2 (empl.)
SIC Code: 291

WHERE THE JOBS ARE:	
TOTAL EMPLOYMENT	32,314
British Columbia	n/a
Alberta	677
Saskatchewan	n/a
Manitoba	700
Ontario	24,857
Quebec	4,857
New Brunswick	n/a
Nova Scotia	n/a
Prince Edward Island	n/a
Newfoundland	n/a
Northwest Territories	n/a
Yukon Territory	n/a

GENERAL FOOD PRODUCTS MANUFACTURING

Although manufacturers in this group produce an amazingly broad range of food products—from tea and coffee to pasta, potato chips and diet food—the industry as a whole peaked structurally in 1985. During the recession years of 1989–93, 18.6 percent of employees lost their jobs; consequently, job security is moderate at best, while advancement is poor.

Average salary levels in the food products business are low and increases have been only moderate.

The low knowledge base of the industry (19 out of every 100 employees are knowledge workers) has been rising of late. The Knowledge Ratio is now 6.3 percent higher than it was five years ago.

OVERALL SCORE

40

HOW THE INDUSTRY COMPARES:

Job Security: Moderate
Advancement: Poor
Average Salary: Low
Salary Change: Moderate
Knowledge Base: Low
Industry Knowledge: Rising
Industry Stability: Very High

VITAL STATISTICS

Average Lay-off Rate, 1989–93: 18.6%
Net Job Creation, 1989–93: −4,623
Average Salary Level, 1993: $570/week
Salary Increase, 1993: +0.8%
Knowledge Workers per 100 Employees: 19
Knowledge Base Change: +6.3%
Industry Volatility: 2.7
SIC Code: 109

WHERE THE JOBS ARE:	
TOTAL EMPLOYMENT	25,686
British Columbia	1,476
Alberta	2,033
Saskatchewan	n/a
Manitoba	711
Ontario	13,378
Quebec	6,955
New Brunswick	388
Nova Scotia	n/a
Prince Edward Island	n/a
Newfoundland	n/a
Northwest Territories	n/a
Yukon Territory	n/a

MEAT & POULTRY PRODUCTS MANUFACTURING

Health and lifestyle changes have led to repeated downsizings in the meat and meat products industry, which peaked structurally in 1977.

Poultry production, however, has continued to grow in structural terms, and because of its strong growth, job security in the industry as a whole has remained comparatively high. Between 1989 and 1993, the lay-off rate was 7.4 percent.

While advancement is moderate, salary levels are low and averaged an unexciting zero increase in 1993.

In this low-knowledge industry, only 8 out of every 100 employees are knowledge workers.

OVERALL SCORE

40

HOW THE INDUSTRY COMPARES:

Job Security: High
Advancement: Moderate
Average Salary: Low
Salary Change: Poor
Knowledge Base: Low
Industry Knowledge: Reasonably Stable
Industry Stability: High

VITAL STATISTICS

Average Lay-off Rate, 1989–93: 7.4%
Net Job Creation, 1989–93: −3,283
Average Salary Level, 1993: $494/week
Salary Increase, 1993: Zero
Knowledge Workers per 100 Employees: 8
Knowledge Base Change: −0.6%
Industry Volatility: 5.6 (empl.)
SIC Code: 101

WHERE THE JOBS ARE:

TOTAL EMPLOYMENT	43,515
British Columbia	3,679
Alberta	6,125
Saskatchewan	2,038
Manitoba	2,744
Ontario	17,231
Quebec	9,359
New Brunswick	848
Nova Scotia	792
Prince Edward Island	n/a
Newfoundland	602
Northwest Territories	n/a
Yukon Territory	n/a

VENEER & PLYWOOD MANUFACTURING

The veneer and plywood manufacturing industry peaked structurally in 1978 and job security has worsened; the lay-off rate averaged 18.6 percent during the tough recession years of 1989–1993. But advancement prospects remain resonably good because because the structural decline has been moderate.

On average, salaries are moderate and increases are very high. People in this industry enjoyed an average wage increase of 8.0 percent in 1993.

Of great concern is that the low knowledge base is declining: in the last five years, the Knowledge Ratio has fallen 12.8 percent.

OVERALL
SCORE

40

HOW THE INDUSTRY COMPARES:

Job Security: Moderate
Advancement: Good
Average Salary: Moderate
Salary Change: Very High
Knowledge Base: Low
Industry Knowledge: Declining
Industry Stability: Very Low

VITAL STATISTICS

Average Lay-off Rate, 1989–93: 18.6%
Net Job Creation, 1989–93: −1,398
Average Salary Level, 1993: $611/week
Salary Increase, 1993: +8.0%
Knowledge Workers per 100 Employees: 12
Knowledge Base Change: −12.8%
Industry Volatility: 14.3
SIC Code: 252

WHERE THE JOBS ARE:

TOTAL EMPLOYMENT	7,408
British Columbia	3,800
Alberta	n/a
Saskatchewan	n/a
Manitoba	n/a
Ontario	1,981
Quebec	1,082
New Brunswick	n/a
Nova Scotia	n/a
Prince Edward Island	n/a
Newfoundland	n/a
Northwest Territories	n/a
Yukon Territory	n/a

METAL MINING

⭐

The mining industry in Canada covers a diverse range of metals, including nickel, copper and aluminium, which are the premier metals of the New Economy; gold, which is on the Watch List and could go either way; and uranium and iron, which are in the old economy. But the long-term future of mining in Canada is uncertain given the environmental pressures that have been brought to bear on the industry. Some mining companies have opted to expand abroad where ore deposits and cheaper costs create attractive incentives. Increasingly, the management of the mining business is becoming separate from the actual mining activity itself.

With layoffs topping 38.5 percent between 1989 and 1993, job security and advancement prospects are understandably low.

However, average salaries are very high, and the rising knowledge base in this essentially low-knowledge industry is well worth noting.

OVERALL
SCORE

37.5

HOW THE INDUSTRY COMPARES:

Job Security: Very Low
Advancement: Very Poor
Average Salary: Very High
Salary Change: High
Knowledge Base: Low
Industry Knowledge: Rising
Industry Stability: Low

VITAL STATISTICS

Average Lay-off Rate, 1989–93: 38.5%
Net Job Creation, 1989–93: −12,789
Average Salary Level, 1993: $987/week
Salary Increase, 1993: +4.7%
Knowledge Workers per 100 Employees: 18
Knowledge Base Change: +6.9%
Industry Volatility: 10.7
SIC Code: 061

WHERE THE JOBS ARE:

TOTAL EMPLOYMENT	31,993
British Columbia	3,336
Alberta	n/a
Saskatchewan	712
Manitoba	n/a
Ontario	13,021
Quebec	7,015
New Brunswick	n/a
Nova Scotia	n/a
Prince Edward Island	n/a
Newfoundland	2,195
Northwest Territories	n/a
Yukon Territory	n/a

MAJOR APPLIANCE MANUFACTURING

★

Manufacturers of washers, dryers, fridges, stoves and other major appliances have had a difficult transition from the old economy into the New Economy. The industry peaked structurally in 1979, about the time when the baby boomers had bought their first homes. The introduction of new products, such as microwaves, has slowed the decline, but not enough to save the industry from a 46 percent plunge in production from its peak.

Job security, therefore, has been minimal. Between 1989 and 1993, a further 39.8 percent of the people in the industry were laid off. However, average salaries remain high and rose an unexpectedly large 11.0 percent in 1993. A very worrying sign in this low-knowledge industry is that the knowledge base continues to decline, a trend that offers few prospects for the industry over the longer term.

OVERALL
SCORE

35

HOW THE INDUSTRY COMPARES:

Job Security: Very Low
Advancement: Moderate
Average Salary: High
Salary Change: Very High
Knowledge Base: Low
Industry Knowledge: Declining
Industry Stability: Low

VITAL STATISTICS

Average Lay-off Rate, 1989–93: 39.8%
Net Job Creation, 1989–93: −2,680
Average Salary Level, 1993: $638/week
Salary Increase, 1993: +11.0%
Knowledge Workers per 100 Employees: 16
Knowledge Base Change: −7.5%
Industry Volatility: 9.9
SIC Code: 332

WHERE THE JOBS ARE:

TOTAL EMPLOYMENT	6,443
British Columbia	n/a
Alberta	n/a
Saskatchewan	n/a
Manitoba	n/a
Ontario	3,628
Quebec	2,775
New Brunswick	n/a
Nova Scotia	n/a
Prince Edward Island	n/a
Newfoundland	n/a
Northwest Territories	n/a
Yukon Territory	n/a

OFFICE FURNITURE MANUFACTURING

The market for office furniture has changed dramatically as large old economy companies downsize, as small businesses (often on tight cash flows) emerge and as home-based businesses take off. The resale market for furniture has also caused a serious dent in new furniture manufacturing.

Companies in this industry have been under mounting pressure to cut their costs and address the lower-priced market niches that have emerged. Amid the turmoil and change, job security is very low; 48.2 percent of employees in the industry lost their jobs between 1989 and 1993.

Average salary levels are moderate and did not change in 1993.

Although the knowledge base is low, the number of knowledge workers in the industry is rising very sharply. In the last five years, the Knowledge Ratio rose 24.2 percent.

OVERALL SCORE

35

HOW THE INDUSTRY COMPARES:

Job Security: Very Low
Advancement: Moderate
Average Salary: Moderate
Salary Change: Poor
Knowledge Base: Low
Industry Knowledge: Rising Very Sharply
Industry Stability: Moderate

VITAL STATISTICS

Average Lay-off Rate, 1989–93: 48.2%
Net Job Creation, 1989–93: −3,796
Average Salary Level, 1993: $578/week
Salary Increase, 1993: Zero
Knowledge Workers per 100 Employees: 14
Knowledge Base Change: +24.2%
Industry Volatility: 7.3
SIC Code: 264

WHERE THE JOBS ARE:

TOTAL EMPLOYMENT	8,329
British Columbia	151
Alberta	1,092
Saskatchewan	n/a
Manitoba	n/a
Ontario	5,400
Quebec	1,589
New Brunswick	n/a
Nova Scotia	n/a
Prince Edward Island	n/a
Newfoundland	n/a
Northwest Territories	n/a
Yukon Territory	n/a

CONSTRUCTION, MINING, SAWMILL & MATERIALS HANDLING EQUIPMENT MANUFACTURING, POWER TRANSMISSION EQUIPMENT & COMPRESSORS

APPENDIX A

OLD ECONOMY
INDUSTRIES

Manufacturers of machinery for this broad range of industries peaked structurally in 1980 and provide very low job security, as shown by the 52.1 percent lay-off rate between 1989 and 1993. With job losses across the industry totalling 28,190 in that time period, it is little wonder that advancement prospects are very poor.

Salary levels are high but declining; average wages fell by 3.3 percent in 1993.

The knowledge base is moderate: 25 out of every 100 employees are knowledge workers. Fortunately, however, the Knowledge Ratio is rising very sharply—the industry's survival depends on it.

OVERALL
SCORE

32.5

HOW THE INDUSTRY COMPARES:

Job Security: Very Low
Advancement: Very Poor
Average Salary: High
Salary Change: Very Poor
Knowledge Base: Moderate
Industry Knowledge: Rising Very Sharply
Industry Stability: Very Low

VITAL STATISTICS

Average Lay-off Rate, 1989–93: 52.1%
Net Job Creation, 1989–93: −28,190
Average Salary Level, 1993: $658/week
Salary Increase, 1993: −3.3%
Knowledge Workers per 100 Employees: 25
Knowledge Base Change: +23.8%
Industry Volatility: 11.6
SIC Code: 319

WHERE THE JOBS ARE:

TOTAL EMPLOYMENT	57,399
British Columbia	6,440
Alberta	5,287
Saskatchewan	551
Manitoba	n/a
Ontario	30,909
Quebec	12,251
New Brunswick	264
Nova Scotia	n/a
Prince Edward Island	n/a
Newfoundland	n/a
Northwest Territories	n/a
Yukon Territory	n/a

INDUSTRIAL MACHINERY, EQUIPMENT & SUPPLY WHOLESALERS

Wholesalers of industrial machinery and equipment for the chemical, printing, pulp and paper and textile industries have been buffeted by change because many of their traditional buyers have peaked structurally. The saving grace for wholesalers is that, to survive, industries have had to modernize their plants and update their equipment. But wholesalers can only be as successful as the industries that they sell to.

Consequently, job security in this business is moderate; the lay-off rate averaged 13.7 percent between 1989 and 1993. Advancement is equally moderate.

But salaries are attractively high, despite the 2.6 percent average drop in 1993.

Of concern, however, is the low and declining knowledge base, a poor indication of the industry's ability to meet the needs of customers in a new and higher-knowledge economy.

OVERALL
SCORE

32.5

HOW THE INDUSTRY COMPARES:

Job Security: Moderate
Advancement: Moderate
Average Salary: High
Salary Change: Very Poor
Knowledge Base: Low
Industry Knowledge: Declining
Industry Stability: Very Low

VITAL STATISTICS

Average Lay-off Rate, 1989–93: 13.7%
Net Job Creation, 1989–93: –3,761
Average Salary Level, 1993: $665/week
Salary Increase, 1993: –2.6%
Knowledge Workers per 100 Employees: 14
Knowledge Base Change: –13.0%
Industry Volatility: 14.0 (empl.)
SIC Code: 573

WHERE THE JOBS ARE:

TOTAL EMPLOYMENT	27,291
British Columbia	5,034
Alberta	3,077
Saskatchewan	693
Manitoba	619
Ontario	11,298
Quebec	5,540
New Brunswick	145
Nova Scotia	487
Prince Edward Island	n/a
Newfoundland	n/a
Northwest Territories	n/a
Yukon Territory	n/a

LUMBER & BUILDING MATERIAL WHOLESALERS

Wholesalers of lumber and building materials provide a high level of job security, as demonstrated by the fact that only 9.6 percent of the people employed in the industry lost their jobs during the tough recession years of 1989–93.

Low average salary levels in the lumber business were boosted by a high salary increase of 4.0 percent in 1993.

The knowledge base of the industry is low and declining: the Knowledge Ratio has dropped 5.3 percent in the last five years.

OVERALL
SCORE

32.5

HOW THE INDUSTRY COMPARES:

Job Security: High
Advancement: Poor
Average Salary: Low
Salary Change: High
Knowledge Base: Low
Industry Knowledge: Declining
Industry Stability: Very Low

VITAL STATISTICS

Average Lay-off Rate, 1989–93: 9.6%
Net Job Creation, 1989–93: −5,904
Average Salary Level, 1993: $492/week
Salary Increase, 1993: +4.0%
Knowledge Workers per 100 Employees: 16
Knowledge Base Change: −5.3%
Industry Volatility: 11.3
SIC Code: 563

WHERE THE JOBS ARE:

TOTAL EMPLOYMENT	58,953
British Columbia	9,519
Alberta	6,760
Saskatchewan	1,594
Manitoba	1,657
Ontario	22,690
Quebec	12,963
New Brunswick	1,535
Nova Scotia	1,253
Prince Edward Island	n/a
Newfoundland	641
Northwest Territories	n/a
Yukon Territory	n/a

TEXTILE PRODUCTS MANUFACTURING

This sector of the textile industry manufactures products that range from baby blankets and ribbons to canvas awnings and carpets.

Job security is moderate compared to other industries. The 1993 lay-off rate of 15.2 percent is below average for old economy industries.

Average salary levels in the industry are low and salary changes are very poor: in 1993, the average wage declined by 5.5 percent.

Although the knowledge base of the industry is low, it is encouraging to see that the Knowledge Ratio is rising sharply.

OVERALL SCORE

32.5

HOW THE INDUSTRY COMPARES:

Job Security: Moderate
Advancement: Moderate
Average Salary: Low
Salary Change: Very Poor
Knowledge Base: Low
Industry Knowledge: Rising Sharply
Industry Stability: Low

WHERE THE JOBS ARE:

TOTAL EMPLOYMENT	27,522
British Columbia	1,182
Alberta	477
Saskatchewan	169
Manitoba	615
Ontario	9,809
Quebec	14,108
New Brunswick	110
Nova Scotia	954
Prince Edward Island	n/a
Newfoundland	n/a
Northwest Territories	n/a
Yukon Territory	n/a

VITAL STATISTICS

Average Lay-off Rate, 1989–93: 15.2%
Net Job Creation, 1989–93: −4,194
Average Salary Level, 1993: $447/week
Salary Increase, 1993: −5.5%
Knowledge Workers per 100 Employees: 12
Knowledge Base Change: +10.8%
Industry Volatility: 9.6 (empl.)
SIC Code: 190

WIRE & WIRE PRODUCTS MANUFACTURING

⭐

Manufacturers of wire, wire rope, upholstery and coil springs, and metal fasteners such as nuts and bolts peaked structurally in 1974. Job security in the industry remains low as the 29.2 percent lay-off rate between 1989 and 1993 clearly indicates.

Although average salary levels are moderate, increases have been dismal; the average wage dropped by 7.1 percent in 1993.

The low knowledge base of the industry—in which only 17 out of every 100 employees are knowledge workers—is rising sharply. In the last five years alone, the Knowledge Ratio has risen 12.9 percent.

OVERALL
SCORE

32.5

HOW THE INDUSTRY COMPARES:

Job Security: Low
Advancement: Moderate
Average Salary: Moderate
Salary Change: Very Poor
Knowledge Base: Low
Industry Knowledge: Rising Sharply
Industry Stability: Low

VITAL STATISTICS

Average Lay-off Rate, 1989–93: 29.2%
Net Job Creation, 1989–93: −3,871
Average Salary Level, 1993: $607/week
Salary Increase, 1993: −7.1%
Knowledge Workers per 100 Employees: 17
Knowledge Base Change: +12.9%
Industry Volatility: 11.1
SIC Code: 305

WHERE THE JOBS ARE:

TOTAL EMPLOYMENT	12,822
British Columbia	1,262
Alberta	211
Saskatchewan	n/a
Manitoba	125
Ontario	6,641
Quebec	4,461
New Brunswick	n/a
Nova Scotia	n/a
Prince Edward Island	n/a
Newfoundland	n/a
Northwest Territories	n/a
Yukon Territory	n/a

CONCRETE PRODUCTS MANUFACTURING

Manufacturers of concrete products, such as concrete pipes for sewers and precast and reinforced concrete products for construction, offer very low job security as the industry's 62.9 percent lay-off rate between 1989 and 1993 demonstrates.

Average salaries are moderate, but they declined by 3.5 percent in 1993 alone.

The knowledge base is low; only 18 of every 100 people employed in the industry are knowledge workers. However, the Knowledge Ratio has quickly increased by 20.1 percent in the last five years as businesses have been modernizing their production processes.

OVERALL SCORE

30

HOW THE INDUSTRY COMPARES:

Job Security: Very Low
Advancement: Moderate
Average Salary: Moderate
Salary Change: Very Poor
Knowledge Base: Low
Industry Knowledge: Rising Very Sharply
Industry Stability: Low

VITAL STATISTICS

Average Lay-off Rate, 1989–93: 62.9%
Net Job Creation, 1989–93: 4,046
Average Salary Level, 1993: $597/week
Salary Increase, 1993: −3.5%
Knowledge Workers per 100 Employees: 18
Knowledge Base Change: +20.1%
Industry Volatility: 10.1
SIC Code: 354

WHERE THE JOBS ARE:

TOTAL EMPLOYMENT	5,322
British Columbia	620
Alberta	502
Saskatchewan	n/a
Manitoba	136
Ontario	2,422
Quebec	1,382
New Brunswick	128
Nova Scotia	n/a
Prince Edward Island	n/a
Newfoundland	n/a
Northwest Territories	n/a
Yukon Territory	n/a

RETAIL FABRIC & YARN STORES

★

Retailers of fabrics and yarns offer moderate job security in an industry that has experienced a lay-off rate of 15.8 percent. On average, advancement prospects are reasonable compared to most other industries.

Although average salaries are very low, increases have been impressive: in 1993, average wages rose a startling 25.7 percent.

A discouraging sign, however, is the low knowledge base, which has declined precipitously in the last five years.

OVERALL SCORE

30

HOW THE INDUSTRY COMPARES:

Job Security: Moderate
Advancement: Good
Average Salary: Very Low
Salary Change: Very High
Knowledge Base: Low
Industry Knowledge: Declining
Industry Stability: Very Low

WHERE THE JOBS ARE:

TOTAL EMPLOYMENT	8,109
British Columbia	1,198
Alberta	687
Saskatchewan	317
Manitoba	107
Ontario	2,071
Quebec	3,119
New Brunswick	n/a
Nova Scotia	200
Prince Edward Island	n/a
Newfoundland	n/a
Northwest Territories	n/a
Yukon Territory	n/a

VITAL STATISTICS

Average Lay-off Rate, 1989–93: 15.8%
Net Job Creation, 1989–93: −1,051
Average Salary Level, 1993: $228/week
Salary Increase, 1993: +25.7%
Knowledge Workers per 100 Employees: 6
Knowledge Base Change: −23.7%
Industry Volatility: 18.7 (empl.)
SIC Code: 615

STEEL PLATE & FABRICATED METAL PRODUCTS MANUFACTURING

Manufacturers of steel plate, heavy gauge tanks, metal building parts and heavy steel parts used for bridges and transmission towers have been hard hit by structural change: between 1989 and 1993, almost six out of every ten people in the industry lost their jobs. Understandably, job security is very low and advancement prospects are very poor.

Average salaries are high, but this beleaguered industry can offer little in the way of salary increases.

While the knowledge base is low, it is worth noting that the number of knowledge workers in this manufacturing sector is rising sharply.

OVERALL SCORE

30

HOW THE INDUSTRY COMPARES:

Job Security: Very Low
Advancement: Very Poor
Average Salary: High
Salary Change: Poor
Knowledge Base: Low
Industry Knowledge: Rising Sharply
Industry Stability: Low

VITAL STATISTICS

Average Lay-off Rate, 1989–93: 58.1%
Net Job Creation, 1989–93: −8,717
Average Salary Level, 1993: $639/week
Salary Increase, 1993: −0.2%
Knowledge Workers per 100 Employees: 19
Knowledge Base Change: +8.0%
Industry Volatility: 10.8
SIC Code: 302

WHERE THE JOBS ARE:	
TOTAL EMPLOYMENT	14,172
British Columbia	950
Alberta	2,792
Saskatchewan	303
Manitoba	642
Ontario	4,735
Quebec	3,771
New Brunswick	385
Nova Scotia	439
Prince Edward Island	n/a
Newfoundland	n/a
Northwest Territories	n/a
Yukon Territory	n/a

IRON FOUNDRIES

⭐

Iron foundries are a declining knowledge industry offering only low job security. The lay-off rate exceeded 36 percent during the recession years of 1989–93. Advancement prospects are moderate at best, and industry stability is very low.

While the average salary is high in comparison to other industries, salary levels are being eroded: in 1993 alone, average wages declined by 4.7 percent.

The knowledge base has fallen 18.8 percent in the last five years, a statistic that does not bode well for the competitive position of the industry in the New Economy.

OVERALL
SCORE

27.5

HOW THE INDUSTRY COMPARES:

Job Security: Low
Advancement: Moderate
Average Salary: High
Salary Change: Very Poor
Knowledge Base: Low
Industry Knowledge: Declining
Industry Stability: Very Low

VITAL STATISTICS

Average Lay-off Rate, 1989–93: 36.1%
Net Job Creation, 1989–93: −1,960
Average Salary Level, 1993: $670/week
Salary Increase, 1993: −4.7%
Knowledge Workers per 100 Employees: 12
Knowledge Base Change: −18.8%
Industry Volatility: 11.7
SIC Code: 294

WHERE THE JOBS ARE:	
TOTAL EMPLOYMENT	5,486
British Columbia	n/a
Alberta	n/a
Saskatchewan	n/a
Manitoba	n/a
Ontario	3,621
Quebec	934
New Brunswick	n/a
Nova Scotia	n/a
Prince Edward Island	n/a
Newfoundland	n/a
Northwest Territories	n/a
Yukon Territory	n/a

SHOE STORES

★

Shoe stores are a big business in Canada, where the winter climate makes running barefoot an undesirable option. Despite long-term structural decline (baby boomers' feet stopped growing years ago), the industry enjoys high job security and a lay-off rate (10.1 percent in 1993) that is below average for industries that have peaked structurally.

Average salaries are very low and salary increases are poor at best.

The low knowledge base has dropped an enormous 47.8 percent as the industry consolidates around chain stores, at the expense of the independent, owner-operated store.

OVERALL SCORE

27.5

HOW THE INDUSTRY COMPARES:

Job Security: High
Advancement: Moderate
Average Salary: Very Low
Salary Change: Poor
Knowledge Base: Low
Industry Knowledge: Declining
Industry Stability: Low

VITAL STATISTICS

Average Lay-off Rate, 1989–93: 10.1%
Net Job Creation, 1989–93: −1,780
Average Salary Level, 1993: $286/week
Salary Increase, 1993: −0.2%
Knowledge Workers per 100 Employees: 3
Knowledge Base Change: −47.8%
Industry Volatility: 10.1 (empl.)
SIC Code: 611

WHERE THE JOBS ARE:	
TOTAL EMPLOYMENT	18,244
British Columbia	2,066
Alberta	1,019
Saskatchewan	303
Manitoba	541
Ontario	6,236
Quebec	7,085
New Brunswick	433
Nova Scotia	369
Prince Edward Island	n/a
Newfoundland	125
Northwest Territories	n/a
Yukon Territory	n/a

GLASS & GLASS PRODUCTS MANUFACTURING

The glass industry peaked structurally in 1987, and through the tough recession years of 1989–93, 43.0 percent of employees lost their jobs. As wave after wave of downsizing rocks glass manufacturers, job security is becoming very low.

OVERALL SCORE

The salary level is moderate, but increases of the past have given way to a gradual erosion: in 1993, average wages declined 1.3 percent.

22.5

The low knowledge base of the industry is a source of increasing concern because it is declining: in the last five years, the Knowledge Ratio has fallen 28.5 percent.

HOW THE INDUSTRY COMPARES:

Job Security: Very Low
Advancement: Moderate
Average Salary: Moderate
Salary Change: Poor
Knowledge Base: Low
Industry Knowledge: Declining
Industry Stability: Low

VITAL STATISTICS

Average Lay-off Rate, 1989–93: 43.0%
Net Job Creation, 1989–93: −3,817
Average Salary Level, 1993: $609/week
Salary Increase, 1993: −1.3%
Knowledge Workers per 100 Employees: 15
Knowledge Base Change: −28.5%
Industry Volatility: 8.9
SIC Code: 356

WHERE THE JOBS ARE:	
TOTAL EMPLOYMENT	8,747
British Columbia	1,183
Alberta	n/a
Saskatchewan	n/a
Manitoba	n/a
Ontario	5,270
Quebec	1,755
New Brunswick	n/a
Nova Scotia	n/a
Prince Edward Island	n/a
Newfoundland	n/a
Northwest Territories	n/a
Yukon Territory	n/a

HOUSEHOLD FURNITURE, APPLIANCE & FURNISHINGS STORES

Retailers of furniture, appliances, electronics and household furnishings, such as drapes and floor coverings, provide moderate
job security, but very few opportunities for advancement.
Through the recession years of 1989–93, lay-off rates reached
17.4 percent, which translated into job losses for 13,349 people
in this low-knowledge industry.

Average salary levels are very low, but are sometimes
supplemented by commissions on sales. Salary increases of
0.9 percent in 1993 are moderate com-
pared to increases in other industries.

OVERALL
SCORE

22.5

HOW THE INDUSTRY COMPARES:

Job Security: Moderate
Advancement: Very Poor
Average Salary: Very Low
Salary Change: Moderate
Knowledge Base: Low
Industry Knowledge: Reasonably Stable
Industry Stability: Low

VITAL STATISTICS

Average Lay-off Rate, 1989–93: 17.4%
Net Job Creation, 1989–93: −13,349
Average Salary Level, 1993: $398/week
Salary Increase, 1993: +0.9%
Knowledge Workers per 100 Employees: 9
Knowledge Base Change: 0.7%
Industry Volatility: 8.9 (empl.)
SIC Code: 62

WHERE THE JOBS ARE:	
TOTAL EMPLOYMENT	87,397
British Columbia	16,072
Alberta	6,706
Saskatchewan	1,651
Manitoba	2,578
Ontario	35,053
Quebec	21,368
New Brunswick	1,457
Nova Scotia	1,318
Prince Edward Island	190
Newfoundland	913
Northwest Territories	n/a
Yukon Territory	n/a

HOUSEHOLD FURNITURE MANUFACTURING

★

The household furniture industry peaked in 1973, and production has fallen by 40 percent since then. Successive waves of restructuring have produced little real growth. Between 1989 and 1993, the lay-off rate soared to a staggering 80.8 percent, which translated into job losses for 17,561 employees. Job security is virtually nonexistent and advancement is very poor.

Average salary levels in the industry are very low and falling: the average decrease in this low wage–low knowledge industry was 0.4 percent in 1993.

However, in the last five years the knowledge base has risen by 24.2 percent. The future of this once-thriving industry depends on its willingness and ability to modernize what remains.

OVERALL SCORE

17.5

HOW THE INDUSTRY COMPARES:

Job Security: Very Low
Advancement: Very Poor
Average Salary: Very Low
Salary Change: Poor
Knowledge Base: Low
Industry Knowledge: Rising Very Sharply
Industry Stability: Low

VITAL STATISTICS

Average Lay-off Rate, 1989–93: 80.8%
Net Job Creation, 1989–93: –17,561
Average Salary Level, 1993: $427/week
Salary Increase, 1993: –0.4%
Knowledge Workers per 100 Employees: 14
Knowledge Base Change: +24.2%
Industry Volatility: 10.8
SIC Code: 261

WHERE THE JOBS ARE:	
TOTAL EMPLOYMENT	23,949
British Columbia	2,603
Alberta	1,211
Saskatchewan	n/a
Manitoba	1,992
Ontario	6,314
Quebec	11,358
New Brunswick	236
Nova Scotia	122
Prince Edward Island	n/a
Newfoundland	n/a
Northwest Territories	n/a
Yukon Territory	n/a

LEATHER PRODUCTS MANUFACTURING

Leather tanning and finishing businesses, and manufacturers of leather products, such as footwear, wallets, luggage and belts, peaked structurally in 1984, and the industry has been through wave after wave of restructuring. Between 1989 and 1993, the lay-off rate reached a staggering 62.1 percent. Needless to say, job security is very low and advancement is poor in this very low-paying industry.

To top off the tales of woe, average salaries dropped 3.3 percent in 1993.

But this low-knowledge industry is adapting to technological change, and the very large increase in the knowledge base is a cause for some optimism.

OVERALL SCORE

17.5

HOW THE INDUSTRY COMPARES:

Job Security: Very Low
Advancement: Poor
Average Salary: Very Low
Salary Change: Very Poor
Knowledge Base: Low
Industry Knowledge: Rising Very Sharply
Industry Stability: Low

VITAL STATISTICS

Average Lay-off Rate, 1989–93: 62.1%
Net Job Creation, 1989–93: −7,940
Average Salary Level, 1993: $396/week
Salary Increase, 1993: −3.3%
Knowledge Workers per 100 Employees: 16
Knowledge Base Change: +45.4%
Industry Volatility: 10.8
SIC Code: 171

WHERE THE JOBS ARE:

TOTAL EMPLOYMENT	11,442
British Columbia	174
Alberta	164
Saskatchewan	n/a
Manitoba	373
Ontario	5,437
Quebec	4,964
New Brunswick	n/a
Nova Scotia	n/a
Prince Edward Island	n/a
Newfoundland	n/a
Northwest Territories	n/a
Yukon Territory	n/a

BARS, NIGHTCLUBS & TAVERNS

Evening jobs at bars, nightclubs and taverns offer very low average salary levels (often supplemented by tips) and very low job security. The lay-off rate in the industry topped 86 percent between 1989 and 1993 as customers opted to stay at home and cocoon. The crackdown on drinking and driving in Canada has also persuaded many night owls to watch more late-night television.

Average salary levels, low to begin with, were cut a further 15.9 percent in 1993.

The aging of Canada's population will continue to take a harsh toll on bars, nightclubs and taverns: the older we get, the less we party.

OVERALL
SCORE

10

HOW THE INDUSTRY COMPARES:

Job Security: Very Low
Advancement: Very Poor
Average Salary: Very Low
Salary Change: Very Poor
Knowledge Base: Low
Industry Knowledge: Reasonably Stable
Industry Stability: Moderate

VITAL STATISTICS

Average Lay-off Rate, 1989–93: 86.1%
Net Job Creation, 1989–93: −31,344
Average Salary Level, 1993: $181/week
Salary Increase, 1993: −15.9%
Knowledge Workers per 100 Employees: 17
Knowledge Base Change: +2.4%
Industry Volatility: 6.4
SIC Code: 922

WHERE THE JOBS ARE:

TOTAL EMPLOYMENT	34,016
British Columbia	5,953
Alberta	1,853
Saskatchewan	n/a
Manitoba	330
Ontario	7,596
Quebec	14,704
New Brunswick	1,229
Nova Scotia	n/a
Prince Edward Island	112
Newfoundland	715
Northwest Territories	n/a
Yukon Territory	n/a

COATED & TREATED PAPER PRODUCTS MANUFACTURING

This manufacturing industry covers a wide assortment of products from wallpaper and diapers to envelopes and Kleenex. Job security is very low; 42.7 percent of the people in the industry were laid off between 1989 and 1993. Environmental concerns have created a major challenge for any paper manufacturer that has not moved rapidly into the recycled paper products business.

Average salary statistics are not available, but industry knowledge figures show that the Knowledge Ratio is rising very sharply as companies make major efforts to modernize their production processes by introducing New Economy technologies.

OVERALL
SCORE

HOW THE INDUSTRY COMPARES:

Job Security: Very Low
Advancement: Poor
Average Salary: N/A
Salary Change: N/A
Knowledge Base: Moderate
Industry Knowledge: Rising Very Sharply
Industry Stability: Low

WHERE THE JOBS ARE:

TOTAL EMPLOYMENT	15,558
British Columbia	n/a
Alberta	262
Saskatchewan	n/a
Manitoba	n/a
Ontario	8,035
Quebec	6,042
New Brunswick	111
Nova Scotia	n/a
Prince Edward Island	n/a
Newfoundland	n/a
Northwest Territories	n/a
Yukon Territory	n/a

VITAL STATISTICS

Average Lay-off Rate, 1989–93: 42.7%
Net Job Creation, 1989–93: −6,918
Average Salary Level, 1993: N/A
Salary Increase, 1993: N/A
Knowledge Workers per 100 Employees: 20
Knowledge Base Change: +47.3%
Industry Volatility: 9.2 (empl.)
SIC Code: 279

COMMERCIAL REFRIGERATION & AIR CONDITIONING MANUFACTURING

The commercial refrigeration and air conditioning business peaked structurally in 1984 and has been in a virtual free-fall since then. Lay-off rates of 74.8 percent between 1989 and 1993 attest to the massive downsizing as the industry tumbles into the old economy.

Average salary levels in the industry are low and salary cuts of 9.8 percent prevailed in 1993.

OVERALL SCORE

N/A

HOW THE INDUSTRY COMPARES:

Job Security: Very Low
Advancement: Moderate
Average Salary: Low
Salary Change: Very Poor
Knowledge Base: N/A
Industry Knowledge: N/A
Industry Stability: Low

VITAL STATISTICS

Average Lay-off Rate, 1989–93: 74.8%
Net Job Creation, 1989–93: −2,534
Average Salary Level, 1993: $540/week
Salary Increase, 1993: −9.8%
Knowledge Workers per 100 Employees: N/A
Knowledge Base Change: N/A
Industry Volatility: 10.1
SIC Code: 312

WHERE THE JOBS ARE:

TOTAL EMPLOYMENT	3,421
British Columbia	n/a
Alberta	158
Saskatchewan	n/a
Manitoba	n/a
Ontario	2,272
Quebec	457
New Brunswick	n/a
Nova Scotia	n/a
Prince Edward Island	n/a
Newfoundland	n/a
Northwest Territories	n/a
Yukon Territory	n/a

The industry that provides contract drilling services for the oil, gas and mining industries experiences a great deal of volatility and provides little in the way of job security for employees. Over the recession years of 1989–93, the industry's lay-off rate of 29.9 percent translated into 8,441 employees losing their jobs.

Average salaries in the industry are high. However, the average wage in 1993 fell by 2.5 percent.

OVERALL
SCORE

N/A

HOW THE INDUSTRY COMPARES:

Job Security: Low
Advancement: Very Poor
Average Salary: High
Salary Change: Poor
Knowledge Base: N/A
Industry Knowledge: N/A
Industry Stability: Very Low

VITAL STATISTICS

Average Lay-off Rate, 1989–93: 29.9%
Net Job Creation, 1989–93: –8,441
Average Salary Level, 1993: $670/week
Salary Increase, 1993: –2.5%
Knowledge Workers per 100 Employees: N/A
Knowledge Base Change: N/A
Industry Volatility: 28.5
SIC Code: 09

WHERE THE JOBS ARE:

TOTAL EMPLOYMENT	30,677
British Columbia	1,031
Alberta	21,939
Saskatchewan	2,712
Manitoba	n/a
Ontario	2,825
Quebec	1,307
New Brunswick	n/a
Nova Scotia	n/a
Prince Edward Island	n/a
Newfoundland	n/a
Northwest Territories	n/a
Yukon Territory	n/a

FARM MACHINERY, EQUIPMENT & SUPPLY WHOLESALERS

Despite pressures in the industry, job security has remained quite high, as shown by the 7.1 percent lay-off rate during 1989–93. Advancement prospects are reasonable, but average salaries are low. Indeed, salary levels in 1993 fell 0.3 percent from their already low levels.

The knowledge base of the industry is low, but of even greater concern is that it is declining: in the last five years, the Knowledge Ratio has fallen 13.0 percent.

Wholesalers (and retailers as well) will eventually recognize that marketing successfully in this New Economy requires them to be as smart as the customers that they're selling to. Wholesalers should be raising their knowledge base, rather than allowing it to erode.

OVERALL SCORE

N/A

HOW THE INDUSTRY COMPARES:

Job Security: High
Advancement: Good
Average Salary: Low
Salary Change: Poor
Knowledge Base: Low
Industry Knowledge: Declining
Industry Stability: N/A

VITAL STATISTICS

Average Lay-off Rate, 1989–93: 7.1%
Net Job Creation, 1989–93: –1,370
Average Salary Level, 1993: $518/week
Salary Increase, 1993: –0.3%
Knowledge Workers per 100 Employees: 14
Knowledge Base Change: –13.0%
Industry Volatility: N/A
SIC Code: 571

WHERE THE JOBS ARE:

TOTAL EMPLOYMENT	20,080
British Columbia	621
Alberta	2,382
Saskatchewan	2,415
Manitoba	1,209
Ontario	9,769
Quebec	3,141
New Brunswick	192
Nova Scotia	213
Prince Edward Island	n/a
Newfoundland	n/a
Northwest Territories	n/a
Yukon Territory	n/a

The fish products industry has been especially hard hit by the closure of the East Coast fisheries, and, on average, 37.8 percent of employees lost their jobs between 1989 and 1993. Advancement is understandably poor.

The average salary level is very low and increases are poor: the average wage in the industry fell 1.9 percent in 1993.

OVERALL
SCORE

N/A

HOW THE INDUSTRY COMPARES:

Job Security: Very Low
Advancement: Poor
Average Salary: Very Low
Salary Change: Poor
Knowledge Base: N/A
Industry Knowledge: N/A
Industry Stability: Very Low

VITAL STATISTICS

Average Lay-off Rate, 1989–93: 37.8%
Net Job Creation, 1989–93: −7,238
Average Salary Level, 1993: $382/week
Salary Increase, 1993: −1.9%
Knowledge Workers per 100 Employees: N/A
Knowledge Base Change: N/A
Industry Volatility: 12.3
SIC Code: 102

WHERE THE JOBS ARE:

TOTAL EMPLOYMENT	11,836
British Columbia	2,844
Alberta	n/a
Saskatchewan	n/a
Manitoba	n/a
Ontario	n/a
Quebec	n/a
New Brunswick	2,605
Nova Scotia	3,235
Prince Edward Island	n/a
Newfoundland	1,955
Northwest Territories	n/a
Yukon Territory	n/a

OFFICE & STORE EQUIPMENT & SUPPLIES WHOLESALERS

Wholesalers of cash registers, office and store furnishings, shoe repair equipment and morticians' supplies have enjoyed moderate job security as the 12.8 percent lay-off rate between 1989 and 1993 demonstrates. Average salaries across this broadly diversified industry are moderate, but average increases are poor: on average, wages decreased by 1.2 percent in 1993.

Most sectors employ only 14 knowledge workers per 100 employees, and the Knowledge Ratio is declining. In the last five years, the knowledge base in this wholesale industry has fallen 13.0 percent.

OVERALL
SCORE

N/A

HOW THE INDUSTRY COMPARES:

Job Security: Moderate
Advancement: Poor
Average Salary: Moderate
Salary Change: Poor
Knowledge Base: Low
Industry Knowledge: Declining
Industry Stability: N/A

VITAL STATISTICS

Average Lay-off Rate, 1989–93: 12.8%
Net Job Creation, 1989–93: −7,133
Average Salary Level, 1993: $617/week
Salary Increase, 1993: −1.2%
Knowledge Workers per 100 Employees: 14
Knowledge Base Change: −13.0%
Industry Volatility: N/A
SIC Code: 579

WHERE THE JOBS ARE:	
TOTAL EMPLOYMENT	56,494
British Columbia	5,769
Alberta	5,312
Saskatchewan	1,320
Manitoba	865
Ontario	24,244
Quebec	16,094
New Brunswick	792
Nova Scotia	1,530
Prince Edward Island	n/a
Newfoundland	399
Northwest Territories	n/a
Yukon Territory	n/a

SNOWMOBILE & ALL-TERRAIN VEHICLE MANUFACTURING

Manufacturers of snowmobiles, all-terrain vehicles and amphibious vehicles provide very high job security: witness the zero lay-off rate through the 1989–93 recession. Export markets and diversification have been the key for many of the leading firms in this industry. As a consequence of sound business planning, advancement prospects are good.

Although detailed salary data is not available, the knowledge base figures show that the industry's move to embrace new technologies and manufacturing processes, as well as its commitment to innovation, has produced a sharply rising Knowledge Ratio.

While the underlying stability of the business is very low and given to seasonal and cyclical swings, this volatility has not had a harsh impact on the job security or advancement opportunities of employees. Although this is a fairly small manufacturing industry, production, distribution, design, marketing and support staff jobs are available.

OVERALL SCORE

N/A

HOW THE INDUSTRY COMPARES:

Job Security: Very High
Advancement: Good
Average Salary: N/A
Salary Change: N/A
Knowledge Base: Moderate
Industry Knowledge: Rising Sharply
Industry Stability: Very Low

VITAL STATISTICS

Average Lay-off Rate, 1989–93: Zero
Net Job Creation, 1989–93: +78
Average Salary Level, 1993: N/A
Salary Increase, 1993: N/A
Knowledge Workers per 100 Employees: 24
Knowledge Base Change: +12.7%
Industry Volatility: 18.3 (empl.)
SIC Code: 329

WHERE THE JOBS ARE:

TOTAL EMPLOYMENT	2,132
British Columbia	n/a
Alberta	n/a
Saskatchewan	n/a
Manitoba	n/a
Ontario	106
Quebec	n/a
New Brunswick	n/a
Nova Scotia	n/a
Prince Edward Island	n/a
Newfoundland	n/a
Northwest Territories	n/a
Yukon Territory	n/a

STORAGE & WAREHOUSING

Employees in the storage and warehousing industry enjoy a high level of job security—a 0.1 percent lay-off rate was the norm through the recession of 1989–93. A large increase in the number of small businesses, the manufacture of higher value-added goods in Canada and the free trade agreement between Canada and the United States have all played a part in creating opportunity for the many companies involved in the storage and warehousing industry. A particularly high growth end of the market has been the self-storage business, which has proliferated across Canada. Advancement prospects are consequently quite good, and very few people have lost their jobs in this industry.

The low knowledge base is a cause for concern because it has continued to decline: in the last five years, it has dropped 9.1 percent. Information technologies have already moved rapidly into the transportation industry (witness the brilliant success of FedEx in the courier business, which used to be a very low-knowledge field), and it is only a matter of time before these technologies find their way into the warehousing and storage business as well.

OVERALL SCORE

N/A

HOW THE INDUSTRY COMPARES:

Job Security: High
Advancement: Good
Average Salary: N/A
Salary Change: N/A
Knowledge Base: Low
Industry Knowledge: Declining
Industry Stability: Very Low

VITAL STATISTICS

Average Lay-off Rate, 1989–93: 0.1%
Net Job Creation, 1989–93: −19
Average Salary Level, 1993: N/A
Salary Increase, 1993: N/A
Knowledge Workers per 100 Employees: 19
Knowledge Base Change: −9.1%
Industry Volatility: 15.4 (empl.)
SIC Code: 47

WHERE THE JOBS ARE:

TOTAL EMPLOYMENT	15,894
British Columbia	2,909
Alberta	2,036
Saskatchewan	n/a
Manitoba	n/a
Ontario	4,605
Quebec	n/a
New Brunswick	357
Nova Scotia	n/a
Prince Edward Island	n/a
Newfoundland	n/a
Northwest Territories	n/a
Yukon Territory	n/a

Sugar and candy manufacturers provide an enviable degree of job security and excellent advancement prospects. Between 1989 and 1993, employees in the industry enjoyed a zero lay-off rate, and companies hired an additional 1,057 net new employees.

One of the most attractive aspects of sugar and candy manufacturing is the sharply rising knowledge base, albeit from a low level. This large increase of 30.6 percent in the industry's Knowledge Ratio in the last five years reflects the introduction of new technologies, new processes and tasty new products.

OVERALL SCORE

N/A

HOW THE INDUSTRY COMPARES:

Job Security: Very High
Advancement: Very Good
Average Salary: N/A
Salary Change: N/A
Knowledge Base: Low
Industry Knowledge: Rising Very Sharply
Industry Stability: Low

VITAL STATISTICS

Average Lay-off Rate, 1989–93: Zero
Net Job Creation, 1989–93: +1,057
Average Salary Level, 1993: N/A
Salary Increase, 1993: N/A
Knowledge Workers per 100 Employees: 17
Knowledge Base Change: +30.6%
Industry Volatility: 9.2 (empl.)
SIC Code: 108

WHERE THE JOBS ARE:

TOTAL EMPLOYMENT	9,763
British Columbia	508
Alberta	n/a
Saskatchewan	n/a
Manitoba	n/a
Ontario	5,809
Quebec	2,184
New Brunswick	n/a
Nova Scotia	n/a
Prince Edward Island	n/a
Newfoundland	n/a
Northwest Territories	n/a
Yukon Territory	n/a

APPENDIX B

CANADIAN KNOWLEDGE INTENSITY

CANADIAN KNOWLEDGE INTENSITY
[BASED ON U.S. INDUSTRY BENCHMARKS]

CANADA	M	30.42	30.65
INDUSTRY	KNOWLEDGE RATIO RANK–1994	1993 KNOWLEDGE RATIO	1994 KNOWLEDGE RATIO
AGRICULTURE & RELATED SERVICES	L	7.29	6.54
FISHING & TRAPPING	L	10.84	10.77
LOGGING & FORESTRY	M	36.00	33.93
TOTAL MINING, QUARRYING & OIL WELLS INDUSTRY	M	30.04	31.09
TOTAL MINING	M	30.04	31.09
Gold Mining	n/a	n/a	n/a
Metal Mining	L	18.37	18.03
Iron Mining	n/a	n/a	n/a
Asbestos Mining	n/a	n/a	n/a
Non-Metal Mines (excl. Coal & Asbestos)	L	14.81	14.15
Salt Mining	n/a	n/a	n/a
Coal Mining	L	10.53	11.21
CRUDE PETROLEUM & NATURAL GAS	H	43.13	43.67
MINERAL EXTRACTION SERVICES	n/a	n/a	n/a
TOTAL MANUFACTURING	M	24.71	24.87
Food Industry	L	15.71	15.27
Meat & Meat Products, excl. Poultry	L	7.78	6.11
Poultry Products	L	7.78	6.11

INDUSTRY	KNOWLEDGE RATIO RANK–1994	1993 KNOWLEDGE RATIO	1994 KNOWLEDGE RATIO
Fish Products	n/a	n/a	n/a
Fruit & Vegetable Processing	L	14.16	15.91
Dairy Products	L	20.00	19.88
Feed, Flour & Cereal Manufacturing	M	24.82	23.40
Bakery Products	L	9.65	12.08
Sugar & Candy Manufacturing	L	16.98	12.50
Misc. Food Products	L	19.20	18.63
Beverage Industry	M	26.48	26.11
Soft Drinks	n/a	n/a	n/a
Distillery Products	n/a	n/a	n/a
Brewery Products	n/a	n/a	n/a
Tobacco Products	L	16.67	16.00
Rubber Products	M	17.24	21.52
Plastic Products	L	17.24	16.85
Leather & Allied Industries	L	15.57	14.07
Footwear Industry	L	15.38	11.27
Primary Textile & Textile Products	L	12.26	9.49
Synthetic Fiber, Yarn & Woven Fabric	L	12.60	10.67
Wool Yarn & Woven Fabric	L	12.60	10.67
Misc. Textile Products	L	13.16	9.09
Carpet, Mats & Rugs	L	19.23	7.46
Clothing Industries	L	11.35	11.50
Hosiery Industries	n/a	n/a	n/a
Wood Industries	L	10.21	12.98
Sawmills, Planing & Shingle Mills	L	10.89	12.95
Veneer & Plywood Industries	L	11.97	17.02
Sash, Door & Other Millwork	L	10.89	12.95
Other Wood Industries	L	11.97	17.02
Furniture & Fixtures	L	13.78	14.50
Household Furniture	L	13.78	14.50
Office Furniture	L	13.78	14.50

INDUSTRY	KNOWLEDGE RATIO RANK–1994	1993 KNOWLEDGE RATIO	1994 KNOWLEDGE RATIO
Paper & Allied Industries	L	17.06	16.79
Pulp & Paper Industries	L	18.15	19.11
Paper Box & Bag Industries	L	12.16	12.44
Other Converted Paper Products	L	20.29	19.07
Printing, Publishing & Allied Industries	M	33.02	33.60
Commercial Printing Industry	M	31.55	31.62
Printing & Publishing Industries	M	33.02	33.60
Platemaking, Typesetting & Bindery	M	33.02	33.60
Primary Metals Industry	L	15.96	16.84
Primary Steel	L	14.20	17.51
Steel Pipe & Tube	n/a	n/a	n/a
Iron Foundries	L	11.70	10.81
Non-Ferrous Smelting & Refining	L	15.96	16.84
Aluminum Rolling, Casting & Extruding Industry	L	17.29	14.69
Copper Rolling, Casting & Extruding Industry	n/a	n/a	n/a
Fabricated Metal Products Industry	L	17.99	17.90
Power Boiler and Structural Metal	L	19.38	18.42
Ornamental & Architectural Metal Products	L	19.38	18.42
Stamped, Pressed and Coated Metal	L	15.27	13.01
Wire & Wire Products	L	16.58	16.35
Hardware, Tools & Cutlery	L	12.12	18.18
Heating Equipment Industry	M	25.32	24.27
Machine Shops	L	22.45	14.55
Other Metal Fabricating	L	16.58	16.35
Machinery Industries	M	32.82	31.24
Agricultural Implements	M	21.00	21.05
Commercial Refrigeration Equipment	n/a	n/a	n/a
Other Machinery & Equipment	M	25.32	24.27

INDUSTRY	KNOWLEDGE RATIO RANK–1994	1993 KNOWLEDGE RATIO	1994 KNOWLEDGE RATIO
Transportation Equipment Industry	M	29.53	29.88
Aircraft & Aircraft Parts	M	38.97	39.82
Motor Vehicles	L	18.53	18.56
Trucks, Bus Body & Trailer	L	18.53	18.56
Motor Vehicle Parts & Accessories	L	18.53	18.56
Railroad Rolling Stock	L	26.67	15.63
Shipbuilding & Repair	M	21.27	29.44
Boatbuilding & Repair	M	21.27	29.44
Misc. Transport Equipment	L	23.64	15.79
Electrical & Electronics Industry	M	35.17	35.10
Small Electrical Appliances	n/a	n/a	n/a
Major Appliances (Electrical & Non-Electrical)	L	15.97	18.40
Communications & Other Electronic Equipment	H	45.64	46.60
Consumer Electronics	H	45.64	46.60
Electronic Computing Equipment	H	57.72	55.51
Office Store & Business Machines	H	41.67	42.50
Battery Industry	n/a	n/a	n/a
Other Electric & Electronics	M	33.99	33.02
Non-Metallic Mineral Products	L	16.79	17.24
Cement	L	17.82	17.84
Concrete Products	L	17.82	17.84
Ready-Mix Concrete	L	17.82	17.84
Glass & Glass Products	L	14.97	16.40
Misc. Non-Metallic Mineral Products	L	19.61	17.00
Refined Petroleum & Coal Products	M	32.39	32.57
Chemical & Chemical Products	M	37.93	36.93
Industrial Chemical Products	M	40.19	34.87
Agricultural Chemicals	M	41.03	33.33
Plastic & Synthetic Resin Industry	M	24.09	25.32
Pharmaceutical & Medicine Industry	H	42.58	48.82

INDUSTRY	KNOWLEDGE RATIO RANK–1994	1993 KNOWLEDGE RATIO	1994 KNOWLEDGE RATIO
Paint & Varnish	M	38.10	38.57
Soap & Cleaning Compounds	M	31.90	32.11
Toilet Preparations	M	31.90	32.11
Misc. Chemical Products	M	40.19	34.87
Other Manufacturing	n/a	n/a	n/a
Jewellery & Precious Metals	n/a	n/a	n/a
Sporting Goods & Toys	M	19.73	22.49
Sign & Display Industry	n/a	n/a	n/a
Floor Tile, Linoleum & Coated Fabrics	n/a	n/a	n/a
Misc. Manufacturing	n/a	n/a	n/a
CONSTRUCTION INDUSTRY	L	15.48	16.72
Residential Construction	L	15.48	16.72
Non-Residential Construction	L	15.48	16.72
Industrial Construction (other than buildings)	H	84.45	85.28
Highway & Heavy Construction	L	15.48	16.72
Trade Contracting	n/a	n/a	n/a
Construction Services	n/a	n/a	n/a
TRANSPORTATION & STORAGE INDUSTRY	n/a	n/a	n/a
Transportation Industries	L	13.75	14.50
Air Transport & Services	M	23.26	23.35
Railway Transport & Services	L	14.95	13.19
Water Transport & Services	M	21.88	24.60
Truck Transport Industries	L	8.54	9.66
Urban Transit Systems	M	16.51	20.00
Interurban & Rural Transit Systems	M	16.51	20.00
Pipeline Transport Industries	M	20.00	31.25
Storage & Warehousing	L	18.59	18.67
Grain Elevators	n/a	n/a	n/a

INDUSTRY	KNOWLEDGE RATIO RANK–1994	1993 KNOWLEDGE RATIO	1994 KNOWLEDGE RATIO
COMMUNICATIONS INDUSTRIES	H	40.63	41.79
Telecommunication Broadcasting	H	59.90	62.22
Telecommunication Carriers & Other	M	34.18	34.83
Postal & Courier Services	L	8.47	8.27
UTILITIES	M	27.18	26.99
Electric Power Systems	M	29.40	29.92
Gas Distribution Systems	M	21.61	26.23
Water Systems	M	30.43	31.33
Waste Management & Other Utilities	M	37.50	20.00
WHOLESALE TRADE INDUSTRIES	L	14.50	13.94
Wholesale Farm Products	L	18.07	17.98
Wholesale Petroleum Products	M	25.33	23.88
Wholesale Food, Beverage, Drug & Tobacco	n/a	n/a	n/a
Wholesale Apparel & Dry Goods	L	14.06	17.74
Wholesale Household Goods	L	17.14	11.32
Wholesale Motor Vehicle, Parts & Accessories	L	13.00	14.60
Wholesale Metals, Hardware, Heating & Building Materials	L	9.96	9.70
Wholesale Machinery, Equipment & Supplies	L	13.52	15.96
RETAIL TRADE INDUSTRIES	L	10.50	10.60
Retail Food Stores	L	3.85	4.37
Retail Liquor, Wine & Beer Stores	L	1.65	3.05
Retail Drug Stores	M	29.35	30.41
Retail Shoe Stores	L	2.56	1.95
Retail Clothing Stores	L	5.29	5.90
Retail Fabric & Yarn Stores	L	6.15	5.00
Retail Household Furniture & Appliances	L	8.78	8.81

INDUSTRY	KNOWLEDGE RATIO RANK–1994	1993 KNOWLEDGE RATIO	1994 KNOWLEDGE RATIO
Automotive Vehicles, Parts & Accessories, Sales & Services	L	7.73	5.71
Gasoline Service Stations	L	2.66	1.87
General Retail Merchandising	L	6.87	2.17
FINANCE, INSURANCE & REAL ESTATE	M	31.40	32.31
Finance & Real Estate	n/a	n/a	n/a
Banks, Credit Unions & Other Deposit Institutions	H	38.51	40.12
Trust, Other Finance & Real Estate	n/a	n/a	n/a
Banks	H	38.51	40.12
Trust Companies	H	37.11	48.44
Deposit-Accepting Mortgage Co.	n/a	n/a	n/a
Credit Unions	H	37.11	48.44
Consumer & Business Finance Intermediaries	M	34.15	31.61
Investment Intermediaries	M	34.15	31.61
Real Estate Operators (excl. Developers)	M	30.08	30.46
Insurance Industries	M	21.99	23.50
Government Royalties on Natural Resources	n/a	n/a	n/a
Owner-Occupied Dwellings	n/a	n/a	n/a
COMMUNITY BUSINESS & PERSONAL SERVICES	H	48.81	49.42
Business Services	H	59.24	59.99
Professional Business Services	H	69.60	71.02
Employment Agencies	M	31.66	26.99
Computer Services	H	73.15	75.22
Accounting & Bookkeeping Services	H	66.88	67.50
Advertising Services	H	50.70	56.25
Architectural & Engineering Services	H	84.45	85.28
Legal Services	H	63.29	65.86

INDUSTRY	KNOWLEDGE RATIO RANK–1994	1993 KNOWLEDGE RATIO	1994 KNOWLEDGE RATIO
Management Consultants	H	79.32	81.49
Educational & Related Services	H	64.26	63.90
Elementary & Secondary Education	H	65.33	64.26
Community Colleges	H	68.29	68.63
University Education	H	61.07	62.27
Library Services	H	45.45	46.43
Museums & Archives	M	51.49	38.38
Health & Social Services	H	47.09	48.54
Non-Institutional Health Services	n/a	n/a	n/a
Community-Based Social Services	H	37.44	44.34
Offices of Physicians, Surgeons & Dentists	H	59.31	61.32
Offices of Optometrists, Physiotherapists, Chiropractors & Others	H	56.72	59.15
Offices of Social Services Practitioners	H	41.41	44.16
Labs	H	72.09	76.06
Health & Social Services Associations	n/a	n/a	n/a
Private Hospitals	H	61.63	62.25
Accommodation & Food Services	n/a	n/a	n/a
Hotels, Motels & Tourist Courts	L	17.99	17.92
Restaurants & Catering Services	L	16.84	16.55
Amusement & Recreational Services	H	42.91	40.91
Motion Picture, Audio & Video Production & Distribution	H	68.86	64.19
Motion Picture Exhibition	L	18.64	16.31
Theatrical & Entertainment Services	H	68.86	64.19
Sports, Gambling & Recreational Facilities	H	42.91	40.91
Personal & Household Services	L	1.26	1.33
Barber & Beauty Shops	L	0.81	0.93
Funeral Services	H	61.11	57.73
Laundries & Cleaners	L	13.36	14.17
Membership Organizations	H	50.53	50.69
Other Service Industries	n/a	n/a	n/a

INDUSTRY	KNOWLEDGE RATIO RANK–1994	1993 KNOWLEDGE RATIO	1994 KNOWLEDGE RATIO
Auto & Truck Leasing	L	21.47	18.18
Photographers	n/a	n/a	n/a
Services to Buildings & Dwellings	L	10.81	11.54
Travel Services	n/a	n/a	n/a
GOVERNMENT SERVICES	H	42.04	41.09
Defence	H	42.04	41.09
Other Federal Government Services	H	42.04	41.09
Provincial Government Services	H	42.04	41.09
Local Government Services	H	42.04	41.09

Excelerate

With Nuala Beck & Associates Inc.

INDUSTRIES WITH A FUTURE: CANADIAN NEW ECONOMY YEARBOOK™

The definitive guide to Canada's New Economy. Find out which industries are in the New Economy, which industries are in the old economy—and which industries are on the Watch List and could go either way. *Industries with a Future* will show you what's growing and what's not in Canada: Over 200 industries with ratings, growth trends, Knowledge Ratios and charts for each industry. For more information please call: Tel. (416) 364-8517 or Fax: (416) 364-7695.

INDUSTRIES WITH A FUTURE : THE U.S. NEW ECONOMY YEARBOOK™

Find out which industries are in the New Economy, which industries are in the old economy—and which industries are on the Watch List and could go either way. This definitive guide to America's New Economy covers 200 industries with ratings, growth trends, Knowledge Ratios and charts for each industry. *Industries with a Future* will show you what's growing and what's not. For more information please call: Tel. (416) 364-8517 or Fax: (416) 364-7695.

PROVINCES WITH A FUTURE: NEW ECONOMY YEARBOOKS™

Find out which provinces are leveraged to the New Economy, which provinces are exposed to the old economy, and which provinces are most vulnerable to the Watch List and could go either way. *Provinces with a Future* will show you what's growing and what's not and includes Provincial Knowledge Ratios, Regional Trends, Employment Trends in the last ten years, Lay-off Rates by industry, and much more. Available for the following provinces: • Newfoundland • New Brunswick • Nova Scotia • Prince Edward Island • Quebec • Ontario • Manitoba • Saskatchewan • Alberta • British Columbia. For more information please call: Tel. (416) 364-8517 or Fax: (416) 364-7695.

MANAGEMENT CONSULTING FOR THE NEW ECONOMY™

• Financial Institutions & Pension Funds • Lending to the New Economy • Corporate Advisory Practice • Corporate Benchmarking: Knowledge Ratios and New Economy Ratios • Financing the New Economy • Government Policy • Economic Development. For further information please call Anne-Marie Richter, Partner, Tel. (416) 364-8519 or fax request for proposal to (416) 364-7695.

TRACKING THE NEW ECONOMY™
You can't measure new growth with old tools

Track the New Economy and the four engines that are driving growth in the 1990s: Computers & Semiconductors; Health & Medical; Communications & Telecommunications; Instrumentation. This monthly monitor will provide you with a clear road map to the New Economy. It includes monthly New Economy indicators on Growth • Inflation • Employment • Trade • Capital Spending, and more. Composite Leading Indicators for Growth and Inflation let you track the New Economy's business cycle. This twenty-page monthly monitor is easy to read, easy to follow and the ideal New Economy tool kit for business and government. For more information please call: Tel. (416) 364-8517 or Fax: (416) 364-7695.

INVESTOR'S GUIDE TO THE NEW ECONOMY™
North American Economic & Capital Market Outlook

Find out: Which TSE 300 sectors are leveraged to the New Economy, old economy and Watch List • How the business cycle is changing and what the changes mean for stock and bond markets • Which New Economy sectors of the TSE are positioned to outperform • Where inflation and interest rates are heading in the New Economy • Composite Leading Indicators for growth and inflation and more. This forty-page quarterly report is the ideal Investor's Guide to the New Economy. Available in hard copy and on diskette. For more information please call: Tel. (416) 364-8517 or Fax: (416) 364-7695.

SPEAKING ENGAGEMENTS • CORPORATE SEMINARS • INDUSTRY & GOVERNMENT PRESENTATIONS • CONSULTING PACKAGES

Please address all inquiries to Nuala Beck & Associates Inc. Tel. (416) 364-8517 or Fax (416) 364-7695.

NEWSLETTERS

• **Shifting Gears . . . Thriving in The New Economy** published monthly (ten issues a year)

• **Investing in The New Economy** published monthly (ten issues a year)

For more information please call: Tel. (416) 364-8517 or Fax: (416) 364-7695.

SHIFTING GEARS VIDEO

Available in three customized versions: Business/Industry • Government • Education. For information call Enterprise Media Inc.: Tel. (800) 423-6021 or Fax (617) 354-1637.